ORTHODOX SAINTS

Orthodox Saints

Spiritual Profiles for Modern Man
January 1 to March 31

by

George Poulos

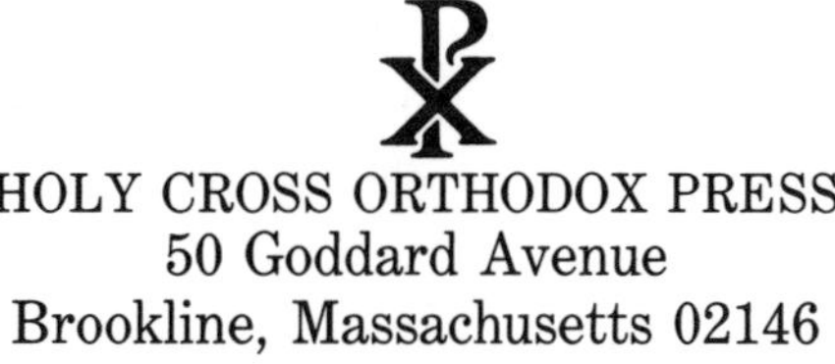

HOLY CROSS ORTHODOX PRESS
50 Goddard Avenue
Brookline, Massachusetts 02146

The icon drawings and cross designs are in the main the work of
JOHN CYRIL VAPORIS
with contributions from
Demetrios Dukas
and
Emmanuel Mantzouris

Cover and book design by
MARY C. VAPORIS

Published by Holy Cross Orthodox Press
50 Goddard Avenue
Brookline, MA 02146

Library of Congress Cataloging-in Publication Data

Poulos, George
Orthodox saints: spiritual profiles for modern man/
George Poulos. -- 2nd rev. and augm. ed.
p. cm.
Includes index.
Contents: v. 1. January 1 - March 31.
ISBN 0-917651-64-2 (v. 1)
1. Christian saints -- Biography.
2. Orthodox Eastern Church -- Biography.
3. Orthodox Eastern Church -- Liturgy -- Calendar.
4. Devotional calendars -- Orthodox Eastern Church.
I. Title. BX393.P67 1990
281.9'092'2--dc20
:B] 90-19768
CIP

For
Dr. Thomas and Anna Leontis
Benefactors of Religious Learning
In appreciation

FOREWORD

History is little more than a study of those who made it; in this sense, there can be no complete knowledge of Christianity without at least an acquaintance with the lives of the men and women who shaped the Church through a complete dedication to the service of Jesus Christ. These men and women from the early Disciples down through the ages to the Neo-martyrs, who have been canonized in recognition of their total dedication to the Messiah, are more than a mass of names that appear on religious calendars. They are flesh and blood human beings who acted above and beyond the call of Christian duty° some of their lives have been commonplace and some have been excitingly adventurous, in direct contrast to the concept of a saint kneeling in constant prayer. There are many saints who do not appear on icons, but whose spirited lives offer anything but dull reading; some have been among the greatest minds and hearts in all mankind. In fact, many Christians suffer from ignorance of these good folk, which is tantamount to being ignorant of Jesus Christ himself, since they were living examples of his faith.

To know and to understand the saints of the Church is to know and to understand the Savior better. Who among us does not feel the presence of the Messiah through the reading of Saints Peter and Paul, his greatest Apostles? It is regrettable that the average Christian can often call out the names in the lineup of his favorite baseball team, but cannot call to mind the twelve who were on the Savior's varsity, but for whom it might be a different ball game, as the saying goes.

It is hoped that these sketches of the lives of the saints will be read from time to time and that they will bring us all closer to a clearer understanding of our existence and prove to be inspirational and a help to knowing Jesus Christ better.

Fr. George Poulos

CONTENTS

January 1

Saint Basil the Great

The Christian community of the fourth century, struggling for survival against vast odds, found renewed hope and inspiration in the noble efforts of a family of six children, all of whom became saints of the Church. From this remarkable Christian family came St. Basil the Great, a spiritual giant. Many men in history have had the superlative "Great" added to their names primarily because they were monarchs such as Alexander the Great whose exploits spanned large land masses. St. Basil, however, earned this title for reaching the masses with the word of Christ. He was not a king, but he won the hearts of his fellowmen for service to the King of Kings. The title "Great" was no more richly deserved by any man in history, for he possessed the humility of Moses, the zeal of Elijah, the faith of Peter, the eloquence of John the Theologian, and the dedication of Paul. St. Basil's brothers and sisters, priests, bishops, and nuns served under his leadership as true workers in the vineyard of Christ.

Born in Caesarea, Asia Minor, in A.D. 330, Basil was reared by parents of unusal devotion: they imparted their love of God to their children with such success that each came to be canonized. These six branches of the family tree were bountifully blessed, and brought forth much spiritual fruit. St. Basil's spiritual heritage was bequeathed to the Christian community by his life of immeasurable religious expression. He was educated in such cultural centers of the empire as Constantinople and Athens. Under the guidance of his friend Gregory (Nazianzos) the Theologian, Basil became one of Christianity's most eloquent spokesmen, earning world renown for both his oratory and his writings. Although he could have had any high governmental position he wished, St. Basil had no desire for high office. Instead he was granted his wish to return to his native city, where he was ordained bishop of Caesarea on 14 June 370.

A man of considerable talent, Basil applied himself to establishing and setting down the rules of monasticism. With this accomplished, he turned to the formalizaton of the Divine Liturgy which bears his name. The Liturgy of St. Basil became the standard of Orthodox worship. In fact, the Liturgy of St. John Chrysostom, which is celebrated forty-two Sundays of the year, is a modified version of it. The Liturgy of St. Basil is celebrated on more solemn church observances, including Christmas and the feast day of Saint Basil, January 1, as well as during Sundays of the Lenten period. St. Basil's Liturgy is thus used a total of ten times during the church year.

An innovator as well as a creator and planner, Basil was the first to fulfill the desperate need for charitable institutions; he directed the creation and development of orphanages, hospitals, and homes for the aged. His concept of mutual love and respect and his practical application of brotherly love later led to the formation of the Christian philanthropic societies.

Aside from St. Paul, and despite the fact equality in the sight of God does not necessarily mean equality in human recognition of dedication, St. Basil quite possibly ranks at the head of all of the saints of the Greek Orthodox Church. Recognized as one of the three greatest hierarchs in Orthodox history, and so recognized on another day of the year known as the feast day of the Three Hierarchs, he is unexcelled as a protagonist for the Greek Orthodox faith.

Just as the flower which bears his name, Basil stands for the beauty and love in Christianity that assure his lofty place in ecclesiastical history for all eternity. A definitive biography of this beloved Saint, outlining in detail his glorious service to Jesus Christ could consume volumes, but it is no disservice to this magnificent cleric for him to be included in a rough sketch alongside his lesser known peers. As with great men, in or out of the Church, he counts among his attributes genuine humility that only adds to his considerable stature.

The Church celebrates the feast day of St. Basil on January 1, the date on which he fell asleep in the Lord in A.D. 379. Since this date coincides with the first day of the New Year, this holiday is especially meaningful for Orthodox Christians.

January 1

Gregory the Elder (Bishop of Nazianzos)

A noted philosopher had a grandson whose renown as a composer was greater than that of the grandparent, causing the composer's father to remark that at first he was known as his father's son and then known for being his son's father. There is a family in which all members are revered equally as saints, but of whose number, one was so outstanding that the others have dwelled in his shadows for 1500 years, something like the composer's parent.

This remarkable family had as its patriarch and sire the man who has come down to us as St. Gregory the Elder, referred to as such because he was the father of that masterful Christian, St. Gregory the Theologian, who outshone his famous father to such an extent that he is recognized as one of the three great hierarchs of Orthodoxy. At a time when celibacy was not a requirement for advancement in the ranks of churchmen, there were many married prelates who made a name for themselves as vicars of Christ, but nowhere in ecclesiastical history can there be found a single family of such prominence in God's work that each and every one of them has been honored with sainthood.

In addition to the mighty St. Gregory the Theologian, honored by a feast day on January 25, the elder's wife, Nonna, became a saint honored on August 5. The children of this outstanding couple were also to become saints, making for a family whose incredible feats in the name of Christianity stamp them as the greatest family in all Orthodoxy. Joining St. Gregory the Theologian in hallowed memory were his brother, St. Kaisarios, whose feast day is observed March 9, and his sister, St. Gorgonia, whose memory we honor on February 23.

St. Gregory the Elder got a somewhat late start in the service of Jesus Christ. A magistrate of the city and a man of considerable property, he was a stranger to Christianity until prevailed upon by his wife to seek the truth of the Savior, a task to which he applied himself with such vigor that he more than made up for his late start.

At the age of forty-five, St. Gregory the Elder abandoned the cult of "Hypsisarians," a strange name for a strange and now obscure belief which had little, if anything, to do with the elevation of the spirit and which has long since passed into oblivion. Although they were monotheists with combined Jewish and non-Jewish leanings, the Hypsisarians on the one hand observed the Jewish sabbath and Levitical prohibition of certain foods but on the other hand rejected sacrifice and circumcision, preferring to direct themselves to the symbols of light and fire, all of which was anything but a proper background for a man who was to become a saint.

The rise of St. Gregory the Elder to prominence in the affairs of fourth-century Cappadocia was meteoric and culminated in his being elevated by popular acclaim as bishop of the city of Nazianzos near the end of the year 325. In this office he gained recognition as a shepherd of the poor and the oppressed, and served with the Christian zeal that he was to pass on not only to his immediate family but to his family of friends as well, friends he had in great numbers who looked up to him with a reverence accorded to the saintly few.

Together with his wife, Nonna, who was his associate in the cause of Christianity, St. Gregory the Elder advanced the truth and light of the Savior in Cappadocia without ever running afoul of the laws, contrived or otherwise, which had doomed so many earlier saints to an untimely and agonizing death. As remarkable as his work, was the fact that he served as bishop of Nazianzos for fifty years and lived to the ripe old age of 100.

St. Gregory the Elder had the pleasure of witnessing the glorious services for the Savior of his eminent son, the Theologian. He knew the tragedy of losing a child since both Kaisarios and Gorgonia died young, but he himself was spared the agony of the fourth-century martyrs. He died peacefully in A.D. 380.

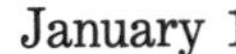

January 1

Basil of Ankyra (Ankara)

The commemoration of saints on given days of the year contradicts Shakespeare's classic remark that the evil that men do lives after them and that the good is oft interred with their bones. This may have applied to the Bard's Caesar and to other heroes featured in his tragedies, but had he written a eulogy for a man of God, it might have been the other way around, for the good of pious men lives after them, particularly those who sacrificed their lives for Jesus Christ. Thus it is that on the first day of the New Year of a calendar reckoned from the birth of the Savior, the memory of two holy men adds solemnity to our celebration.

The two saints who help us usher in the New Year were both named Basil, each of whom was born in the fourth century and each of whom died for Christ, but who were unknown to each other. Basil of Ankyra was destined to live in ecclesiastical history in the shadow of St. Basil the Great, whose magnificence is outlined elsewhere, but a closer look at the man from Ankyra reveals a purity of character equal to that of his namesake. They trod on different paths in life but found a common path to the gates of Heaven.

Unlike so many other saints who achieved immortality through a service to Christ as a disciple, apostle, prelate, or any other man of the cloth, Basil of Ankyra was an obscure layman whose service to the Lord was an unobstrusive enlistment in the common ranks of the army of devout Christians, who put their trust in God and their offering in the collection basket on Sunday. Until he stepped forth from the ranks for a moment of glory, he was unknown, and no amount of research can determine the background of this resolute man of God. But no matter what his place in society, it is enough to know he has a place in the company of saints for his crowned hour of glorious life.

It was in this fourth century of the two Basils that there came to power an emperor whose name was anathema to every Christian on earth and who lives in greater infamy than the cruel Nero. He was Julian the Apostate, so branded for his disavowal of Christ, after having been born and baptized into the Christian faith. Heaven has no rage like love to hatred turned, and the love of the Lord, which Julian spurned, became a bloody vendetta that for sheer savagery marks him as the most monstrous villian of all time. Basil of Ankyra was caught up in the web of this venomous spider, along with countless thousands of hapless Christians, who were subjected to unspeakable tortures and agonizing deaths for their belief.

The Roman governor of Ankyra, one Santorius, was one of Julian's favorite hatchet men, known for his ruthless cunning and pitiless cruelty in the persecution of Christians. No doubt, there were those who submitted and, at least outwardly, disavowed Christ rather than endure the suffering, and it was this conquest that Santorius relished more than the punishment he meted out. Among those hardy souls who bore the full wrath of his tormentors rather than submit was Basil of Ankyra.

Because of his reputation for Christian zeal, Basil represented a prized challenge to Santorius, before whom this pious man was summoned. Every form of guile was applied to win over to paganism a man whose being was pledged to the Savior, and when cajolery failed to serve its purpose, the hapless Basil was brought to public trial, where it was hoped the sight of a hostile mob might bring a change of heart. When this mock trial brought forth from Basil a public pledge of faith, the embarrassed and humiliated accusers spirited the doughty Christian to a dungeon, where they commenced a series of tortures calculated to bring the sturdiest man to his knees.

The dreaded rack wrenched endless hours of intense pain from the body of Basil, and when that failed he was virtually skinned alive. Strips of skin were cut from his brutally broken frame. Then his flesh was seared by the flames of torches to the point of death. Gasping out the praises of the Lord, he was tossed to the lions. He died for Christ on the first day of the year.

Saint Seraphim of Sarov

A lifelong intimacy with God, and an abiding Christian love for his fellow man, were two of the many attributes of a man of Sarov, Russia, known as Seraphim, who attained sainthood in the eighteenth century, a century in which far fewer saints were selected than in the early centuries when being a Christian meant risking one's life. A visionary of near divinity and a clergyman of rare compassion, Seraphim's piety was such that he has been linked with Sts. Theodosios and Sergios as the three greatest saints born of Mother Russia.

A native of Kursk, Seraphim, who was baptized with the name of Prokhor in 1759, was the son of a devout Christian woman named Agatha and a hard-driving man named Isidore, a successful building contractor. Seraphim's father met an untimely death while in the process of erecting the Cathedral of Our Lady of Kursk, leaving the widow and her ten-year-old son to see to the completion of the church. The boy fell from a scaffolding and recovered from what appeared to be fatal injuries, after which he revealed that in a vision while he lay stricken the Virgin Mary appeared to him with the message that he would survive. This vision, the first of many intimacies with God he was to experience thereafter, was the inspiration which set him on his lifetime course of service to the Lord.

While yet a boy, Seraphim turned to the Holy Scriptures, impressed particularly by the writings of Sts. Anthony and Pachomios of Egypt, whose monasticism fascinated him, and, after absorbing the teachings in the works of St. Basil, St. Makarios, and St. John the Ladder, he entered monastic life at the age of eighteen. Tonsured a monk in 1786 and given the name of Seraphim, he was ordained a priest in 1793 but chose not to preach until he had acquired a greater proximity to God, which he thought could come only through prayer and meditation in the complete solitude of the wilderness. The forbidding forest was to be his home for the next several years.

At one point, he broke off his sporadic contact with the monastery and took up residence on a stone slab, on which he is said to have remained for a thousand days and nights in emulation of St. Symeon, removing himself from his uncomfortable roost only for the bare essentials of life. After this test of spiritual and physical endurance, he sought the comparative comfort of a hut, from which he would emerge from time to time to tell of his visions, in which he had the company of the apostles Peter and John and occasionally the Virgin Mary.

Returning to the monastery, Seraphim had grown to such spiritual stature that he was visited by countless pilgrims seeking the way of the Lord, and was ultimately designated as the spiritual father of the nuns of the Diveyev Convent, an order which attested to his power of healing through Jesus Christ and offered its prayers to him when he was recognized as a prophet of the Lord and named a holy Staretz (Elder of the Faith). It was his firm belief that the Kingdom of God was within us all and that only through the Holy Spirit could come the joy of complete tranquility and the inner peace which comes with faith. His sermons on this particular theme brought the true meaning of God's love to all those privileged to hear him.

Even the animals of the forest came to know the friendship of the gentle Seraphim, and he would on frequent occasions seek out the solitude of the wilderness, returning to the monastery always with renewed faith and closeness to nature that refreshed the spirit. Whenever he became ill, he relied on his "joy," the Virgin Mary, to restore his health. This association with the Divine was to manifest itself many times over.

One of the most notable expressions of the power of healing through Jesus and Mary came about when Seraphim was called upon to help his friend, Nicholas Motovilov, a wealthy benefactor who had been paralyzed by a stroke. The prayers of Seraphim were answered and his friend was healed. The true compassion of Seraphim was shown when he obtained the release of three men who had looted his hut, which they mistakenly thought to contain treasure.

He died kneeling in prayer in 1833, and seventy years later was made a saint.

January 2

Saint Sylvester, Pope of Rome

Before Christianity was to become the official religion of the civilized world, over three hundred years were to pass after the resurrection of Jesus Christ. The instrument of God who helped to bring about the recognition of the Christian religion was Sylvester, bishop of Rome.

To understand the concept of papal authority, we must consider the ranks of the priestly orders. There are three spiritual stages or ranks of clergy: the diaconate, in which a candidate is ordained a deacon; the presbytery, in which he is ordained a priest; and the episcopacy, in which a priest is ordained a bishop. The third and highest order embraces celibates worthy to become bishops, then archbishops, metropolitans, and finally patriarchs or popes. Taken from the Greek word *papas,* or spiritual father, the title "pope" is given to those bishops whose service covered large metropolitan centers such as Alexandria, Constantinople, and Rome.

When we consider that the great majority of the saints of the Christian Church were of humble station and were nearly always martyred in agony, Pope Sylvester's high stature was perhaps an obstacle to his elevation to the company of the saints. Thus, he became a saint in spite of being a pope, and not because of it.

Ordained as bishop at the age of thirty, Sylvester became pope after the death of Pope Miltiades in A.D. 314. This was during the reign of Constantine the Great, who founded the Byzantine Empire in A.D. 324, whose capital Byzantium on the Bosporos became Constantinople.

When Constantine came to power, however, he was not a Christian, but a pagan. Unlike many of his predecessors, he did not condone the persecution of Christians, a practice so fierce and so intense that Christians were often forced to take to the hills and dwell in caves.

As champion of the Christian cause, Sylvester took to the hills himself, rallying his people to a renewed faith in Jesus Christ. His fame as a tireless man of God spread throughout the land, and through his pious work the ranks of Christians greatly increased. Such was his fervor in the name of Christ that he was revered and respected by pagans and Christians alike.

It was his fame that was responsible for the creation of a beautiful legend regarding his encounter with Constantine. According to this story, Emperor Constantine had fallen seriously ill. The high priests of the Temple of Zeus vainly ministered to the ailing monarch; his malady baffled the court physicians. Finally, when all seemed hopeless, the great Christian leader was summoned to the side of the emperor. In what must have been one of the most dramatic moments in history, the bishop of Rome stood before the stricken ruler as he lay helpless. He prayed to God for the sick man's recovery and God answered his prayer.

History, however, tells us that Constantine's interest in the Christian faith increased as time went on. He saw Christ in a vision holding a banner on which was a cross and an inscription reading, "In this sign conquer." Constantine was baptized before he died.

Linked in church history with the conversion of Constantine the Great, Pope Sylvester did not have to seek out a martyr's grave, having given his life over to the Savior to such an extent that after his death there was little choice for the Church Fathers but to make him a saint. At a time when Christianity needed a man of his spiritual strength the most, he stood between the darkness of paganism and the forces of evil with the light of Christ held aloft. Pope Sylvester used his power of office with a single purpose in mind and that was to bring the truth of Jesus Christ to all. In this he was eminently successful.

Meanwhile, Pope Sylvester continued to preach faith in Jesus Christ and to witness the decline of paganism in the civilized world. Just eleven years after the founding of the Byzantine Empire, unlike other saints whose end came violently, Sylvester died peacefully on 2 January 335.

Saint Zorzis (George) of Mytilene the Neomartyr

The feast day of St. Zorzis falls upon the same day as that of Pope Sylvester, even though the two were separated not only by a time span of more than 1400 years, but also by a wide gap in social standing. While Sylvester gloried in the exalted role of pope, Zorzis lived in the ignominy of slavery. That the Church honors on the same day one who lived in reverence while the other lived in wretchedness is further evidence that all men are equal in the sight of God.

During the 400 years under Turkish conquest, Orthodox Christians in general and Greeks in particular suffered untold hardships and persecution at the hands of the unrelenting Ottoman foe, whose Muslim fanaticism defiled the churches of Christ and wreaked every form of misery that could be devised. The survival of Orthodoxy is a tribute to the Christian courage of the Greek and other Orthodox people. Among the courageous was Zorzis, whose little-known life story epitomized the invincible Christian.

Born and baptized in the Orthodox faith, Zorzis was a mere lad of twelve and already a devout Christian when his captors sold him into slavery in 1710. His master's Muslim faith was intense; his hatred for Christians was equally so. Exactly what transpired between Zorzis and his master is not known, but it is speculated that they came to respect each other's devotion to their respective faiths, while at the same time not openly admitting it. The strange circumstances under which the boy appeared to have adopted the Muslim faith and language remain a mystery.

The widening social gap between Saints Sylvester, an exalted Pope, and Zorzis, a humble peasant, was bridged by the love of Jesus Christ. Because he had no lofty perch from which to serve the Savior, the lowly Zorzis, a virtual slave all his earthly years, in giving up his life for Christ, elevated himself into the company of saints much more famous than he but none more dedicated to the cause of Christianity. The span of fourteen centuries that separated these two saints while they were on earth is dissolved in the timelessness of God, as a result of which the devout Zorzis could have followed the illustrious pope in death by but a few moments and be no less a servant of Jesus Christ. Time does not have to encrust this eighteen-century martyr to be respected on the shelves of history. Meanwhile, a faithful Greek Orthodox communicant need put no strain on his imagination to piece together for himself the life and time of St. Zorzis. If anything, the vast majority can more easily identify with the peasant saint since only the select few step forward in their day to completely serve Christ officially as cleric or pope. It is rewarding to think that for three score years a man served outwardly another human being, all the while serving inwardly the King of Kings. It could happen to any Christian. It did happen to St. Zorzis.

During the sixty years of his slavery, the relationship between master and servant was such that Zorzis never sought to embarrass his master. That he continued to serve Christ is unquestionable and how he reconciled his true Christian faith and his apparent adoption of Islam became manifest upon the death of his master. Now that his obligation to his master was ended after sixty long years of enslaved service, his true service to God and Christ was his only obligation. He came forth to openly declare his faith in Christ, stating simply: "I was born an Orthodox Christian and now am prepared to die as an Orthodox Christian—not as a Muslim."

The enraged Turks brought him before the magistrate, declaring that he had made a mockery of the Muslims for sixty years by secretly worshiping Christ while feigning Muslim observances. His accusers railed at Zorzis, but he did not flinch. The Greek, who for sixty years had endured as a Christian in quiet acquiescence, now stood in staunch defiance of his captors.

Unable to accept this defiance as anything but false bravado in the light of sixty years of obeisance, the Turks unleashed their fury by casting Zorzis into a dungeon and thereafter torturing him for days. The will of this Christian was never broken; Zorzis never wavered. To the end denouncing the Muslim religion and refusing to deny his Christian faith, Zorzis was put to death on 2 January 1770.

January 3

Gordios the Martyr

In a Who's Who of our saints, the name of Gordios the Martyr takes up considerably less space than that devoted to St. Basil the Great, yet it was St. Basil who was a biographer of the lesser light of Christianity who preceded him by several score of years. Admired greatly by St. Basil, Gordios earned a niche in ecclesiastical history that time might have seriously eroded had his name not been indelibly recorded in the ecclesiastical writings of Basil, who together with St. Gregory of Nyssa and St. Gregory the Theologian, formed a triumvirate marking an era unsurpassed in Christian history. All three, like Gordios, came from Cappadocia, a city which they were instrumental in establishing as the spiritual center of the New Faith in early times.

Gordios aspired to the glory and honor of the military and rose to a position of leadership in the Roman army after distinguishing himself in the field. In the campaigns against the enemies of the state that were a constant menace, he showed an ingenuity as strategist that reduced casualties and effectively eliminated the threat to the security of the civilized world. Admired by those under him and respected by his superiors, he soon realized that what would have been the fulfillment of his ambition, as he had anticipated, became a tedium in which he grew restless in the realization that there was within him that which called for a greater kind of glory.

Gordios was disenchanted by the army's disregard for morality and human values and was drawn to the Christian faith. The qualities that had carried him up through the ranks of the army were now reasserted in the service of the Lord, complemented by virtues which had been dormant but now shone through in a commitment to Christ, which gave real meaning to his life. Turning his back to the military and its attendant evils, he chose to find God by going into the wilderness for eremitic meditation and prayer.

Gordios the hermit was not alone in the bleak hills outside of Cappadocia, and instead of soldiers he found himself in the company of the animals, most of which shied away but some of which, particularly the lions, posed a threat to his life. After a period of time he no longer felt himself a stranger among the animals, and in a remarkable return to nature became a companion to every creature, even the fearsome lion. The incredible sight of this holy man walking among beasts as tame as sheep in his presence was observed by an occasional nomad, and soon hundreds were drawn that they might witness this spectacle. They came out of curiosity, perhaps, but went away convinced that here was a man of God, articulate in his sermons about the Lord and impressive in his closeness to nature and to all of God's creatures.

Gordios was urged to go back to the city by many of his converts, all of whom stressed the greater need for his spiritual enlightenment for the multitudes mired in paganism who might not otherwise come to know the love of the Savior. He would have preferred to remain in the hills but felt it his duty to return to the society on which he had turned his back several years before. In his seclusion he was unaware that paganism was rampant and that Christians were pitifully few in number. Persecution and harassment had thinned the ranks of the Christian community, and idolatry was the order of the day.

The first place that Gordios sought out was the theater, in which the Greeks had just seated themselves in anticipation of the usual meaningless amusement. What they got instead was the imposing figure of Gordios, who strode onto the stage with arms upraised and, as Moses had done centuries before, denounced idolatry, and called upon the crowd for a return to sanity and the light of Christianity. In a torrent of impassioned pleas for Christ, he sought out all he could and brought into the fold thousands of converts.

Gordios' spectacular success, however, brought swift retribution from the Roman state which ordered his execution. He was beheaded on 3 January A.D. 421.

January 3

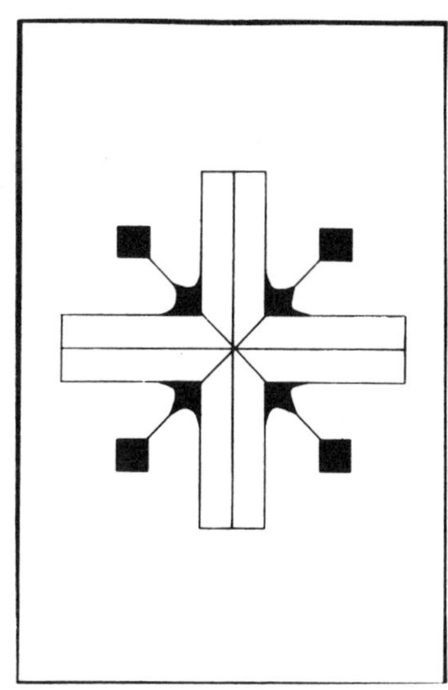

The Prophet Malachi

If one were to read the Holy Bible from cover to cover, something that is rarely done, as in the case of a novel, one would be ushered to the New Testament from the Old Testament by a man called Malachi, to whom the last book of the Old Testament is devoted and who appropriately enough was a prophet of God. He was the last of the prophets of the Old Testament who, though less in number than twenty centuries of saints, nevertheless belong in the same book if for no other reason than they are between the covers of the greatest book in the world—the Holy Bible.

It would be a disservice to the Savior to ignore mention of those who predicted his coming and are held therefore in the same high regard as the apostles of Christianity. The four major prophets were followed by a succession of twelve minor prophets, a number equal to the twelve disciples, and because they were all men of God, it is refreshing to call out their names which were: Hosea, Amos, Micah, Joel, Obadiah, Jonah, Nahum, Habakuk, Zephaniah, Haggai, Zechariah, and, of course, Malachi. These are added to the four major prophets, Isaiah, Jeremiah, Ezekiel and Daniel.

The name Malachi translates to mean "messenger," one sent by the Lord to speak for him, and therefore, as a spokesman of the Almighty, belongs in everyone's "who's who," with the thought expressed elsewhere that "the first shall be last, and the last shall be first." Malachi appeared in the year 450 B.C., when the land of Israel was under the domination of the Persians and needed a spiritual revival, not so much because it was oppressed but because it was far afield of the Ten Commandments received by Moses from God.

The nation of Malachi had sunk to the depths of immorality when he came forward to deplore the sins in which the people were wallowing. He was of necessity a fire and brimstone preacher whose duty it was to threaten with the wrath of God those who had lost complete sight of religious teaching. It is incredible to comprehend to what degradation the people had descended, seemingly forsaking the ways of God altogether and committing acts which even in those days of permissiveness would result in imprisonment for an entire population. When Malachi raised his voice in protest, he did so with ample reason and worked tirelessly to eliminate the insensitivity to moral law that ravaged an entire land. A list of sins being committed would comprise a list of everything punishable by any civilized nation, let alone a nation which was descended from those claiming to be chosen by God.

The reading of the last book of the Old Testament is like the preface of the New, because it concerns itself not only with the decline of a once proud nation but also with anticipation of the coming of one that must provide for salvation of the human soul in preparation for the everlasting life. In closing out the glorious chapters that precede it, the book of Malachi is like a New Year's Eve celebration, if it can be called that, for it is the "New Year" that will bring the Messiah.

Malachi stood aghast in the midst of orgiastic revelry, mixed marriages, adultery, deception, usury and a whole host of misdeeds, all of which were committed with the excuse that God had forsaken them. As proof of this, they complained of the oppression, the plagues, famine, pestilence, drought, and other natural disasters which had befallen them and which they construed to mean that God did not care about them anymore, in light of which they were not obliged to his law anymore.

With the dedication of a true man of God, the prophet Malachi first denounced the spiritual leaders who had abandoned their duty in the face of the raging river of sin, leaving the people to drown in a maelstrom of their own making, while priests offered token services to keep themselves above the torrent. He then went about the country, exhorting his people to abandon their sinful ways and to return to their religious heritage.

Malachi writes of the coming of the Messiah in the first verse of Chapter three, saying, "Behold I will send my messenger, and he shall prepare the way before me." The reference is to St. John the Baptist, the forerunner and prefiguration of the Savior, Jesus Christ.

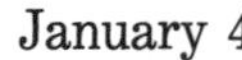

January 4

Onuphrios

The scion of a prosperous Greek family of the eighteenth century was in his early youth so far removed from Christianity that he very nearly fell off its edge into the abyss of spiritual darkness. A step further and he would have fallen from grace, but as he tottered on the brink, he summoned forth the nearly spent Christian spirit within him, not only to return to the community of God-fearing people but to acquire a piety which brought him a martyred sainthood.

Onuphrios was born and baptized with the name of Matthew into the family of Dezios and Anna in the village of Gabrova in Tirnovo, in the year 1786. He was denied nothing by his indulgent and doting parents, and as a result he grew from the proverbial spoiled brat into a selfish and headstrong youth whose parents belatedly applied discipline to no avail and watched helplessly as their son went from willful misbehavior to outright debauchery. He added insult to injury in his riotous living by deliberately mingling with the Turkish oppressors that dominated the village, currying their favor in a shameful manner that brought disgrace on the family name and the contempt of his fellow Greeks.

The parents of Onuphrios knew in their hearts that their son was essentially a decent boy whom they had unintentionally harmed by giving him free rein at a time when he needed guidance. Their unceasing exhortations, applied with Christian patience and parental love, finally brought the young man to his senses and he abruptly halted his dissipation. Looking back at the reckless abandon with which he had flirted with Islam, the avowed enemy of Christianity, Onuphrios grew more and more penitent until at last he resolved to atone for his lurid past by giving himself over entirely to the service of Jesus Christ.

Following a briefing by the local priest, Onuphrios went to the famous monastic community of Mount Athos with as his only credentials an eagerness not only to cleanse his soul but also to serve God and man. Welcomed under these circumstances, he was a willing student of the ancient lore, and after years of study, meditation and prayer, the one time profligate was ordained a deacon and thereafter won the respect of the venerable monks of the Holy Mountain with the solemn sincerity of his purpose.

Convinced that he was now qualified for complete service to the Savior, he asked for and was granted permission to be transferred to the Serbian monastery, which was another of the many sanctuaries of Mount Athos, known as Hilandari. He achieved there a pre-eminence among some quite eminent monks who were not only scholars, deep thinkers and spiritual leaders but were men who enjoyed a proximity to God. It was while serving in this hallowed place that he learned of the suffering of the people who lived in the beautiful island of Chios and felt that it was on this island that he could shore up the Christian spirit sagging under the oppressive Turks and hereby make a true atonement for his one-time intimacy with the loathsome oppressors.

The island of Chios was happy to see such a venerable man of God among them and the people were even more reassured when they learned from Onuphrios himself that his efforts would be strengthened on their behalf in his anxiousness not only to serve Jesus Christ but to show a meaningful repentance of his sins of long ago. To this end, he applied himself with a vigor that restored the confidence of the islanders who saw a ray of hope for their ultimate deliverance from their enemy. The mood of the once hapless populace was changed drastically and where there had been despair there was now nothing but the joy in the full realization of the love of Jesus Christ.

The Turkish authorities could not fail to notice the change since the arrival of the holy man from Mount Athos and began investigating his background, never suspecting that a potential uprising could be led by a man who posed as a priest. When it was discovered that he had once been in close association with Turks elsewhere, he was immediately brought up on charges falsified to suit their purpose and he was asked to once again embrace them or die. When he scoffed at this ludicrous proposal, he was put to death and his remains disposed of so that he might not live on in veneration. The earth on which his blood had spilled was even dug and removed, but there was nothing they could do to remove the memory of Onuphrios, who gave his life for Christ at the age of thirty-two.

January 4

Saint Appolinaria

Only in the fifth century can there be found an astounding chain of circumstances in the life of a woman, whose spark of divine grace was achieved in spite of her birthright, and of a covenant she made with God in a lifelong masquerade with mankind. As some of the amazing details of her life unfold, there is revealed a most extraordinary servant of God who is now known to us as St. Appolinaria, whose bright light was a beacon in a dark age when there was no limit to the measures taken by some to serve Jesus Christ.

Appolinaria was born in Rome, the daughter of Anthemios who had been appointed magistrate of Rome by the Byzantine Emperor Leo. She grew up in the best of circumstances, enjoying the luxuries of her station, enjoying the gatherings of the high and mighty at state functions and rubbing elbows with the elite of Rome.

From early childhood, Appolinaria evinced an unusual Christian devotion to the degree that by the time she had reached adulthood it was clearly evident that she was much more interested in serving the Savior than being the wife of any man, no matter how noble. She prevailed upon her father for permission to visit the Holy City of Jerusalem. Having denied her nothing up until then, her father saw her earnestness and not only gave her permission but for her safety and comfort provided an entourage fit for an empress, complete with body guards and enough money to buy anything that struck her fancy.

The well financed group found suitable quarters, and Appolinaria roamed at will. In due course she was so consumed by the spirit of the Savior and a desire to serve him that she dismissed her entourage and gave all her wealth to the poor. The servants that returned to Rome reported to her father but no word was heard from her. She seemed to have vanished.

Meanwhile, Appolinaria had become a monk under unorthodox but not original circumstances, since it had been done before. Shorn of her long locks, she donned a monk's habit and posed as a man, accounting for her delicate features and high voice by pretending she was an eunuch monk. Monks had private cells and gathered only at liturgies and at meals. Since solitude was the choice of many, it was an easy task for her to go undetected, yet still fulfill the spiritual obligations of the monastery.

A number of years passed at the monastery, but the seemingly frail monk who had taken the name Dorotheos, but who was actually Appolinaria, prayed and meditated with such fervor that she took on an aspect of holiness. Eventually her intense love of the Savior transformed her loving kindness into a miraculous power of healing. But it was only a select few who were permitted to know of this power. Word however, leaked out and spread everywhere, even to Rome.

There, Anthemios who had been saddened by the loss of one daughter, had another daughter attended by the greatest physicians of the realm, but none could cure her of a nervous disorder from which she suffered. At last when he heard of the mysterious Dorotheos, he arranged to have his daughter sent to this miraculous monk. Dorotheos received the ailing girl, spending much time with her and healed her, knowing all the while it was her own sister who was being healed. The sister returned to Rome healthier than she had ever been.

Soon after her return to Rome, the girl shocked her father Anthemios telling him that she was going to have a child out of wedlock. However, she refused to tell who was responsible. The distraught father remembered that she had been entrusted to the healing monk and concluded that his daughter had been cured at the cost of being deflowered. As magistrate of Rome, he had no trouble in having the alleged villain Dorotheos brought before him.

Later, when Dorotheos went to a room with her mother, she revealed her true identity and, dressed in one of her gowns, walked back to her father with a tearful mother. A planned prosecution turned into a joyous family reunion. Appolinaria remained with her loved ones until at last she felt compelled to return to the monastery. Sworn to secrecy, the family bade farewell to Appolinaria whom they never saw or heard from again.

It was not until her death on 4 January 502 that her true sex became known.

January 5

Romanos of Karpenesi

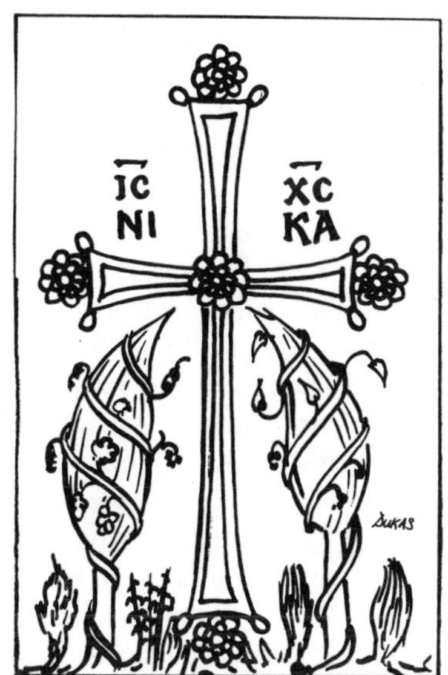

The flame of Christianity burns brightly in all corners of the globe: in churches and cathedrals, chapels and shrines. Nowhere does the flame of truth shine more brightly than in the ancient monasteries of Orthodoxy, which for centuries have been spiritual lighthouses beaming the approach to the gates of heaven. Manned by the ranks of holy men—the monks—monasteries have served as bastions of Christianity for hundreds of years. Their mightiest citadel remains Mount Athos, whose rugged terrain symbolizes the strength of Christianity.

It is said that this holy place was founded through a miracle of the Blessed Virgin Mary. Be that as it may, the lofty promontory of Mount Athos, which is comprised of 140 square miles of awesome Macedonian coastline, is the site of twenty monasteries of such grandeur and impressiveness that they form a miracle in themselves. This massive array of fortresses is occupied by Christian soldiers from whose ranks have come philosophers, bishops, archbishops, and patriarchs. Mount Athos has also produced saints, one of whom was Romanos of Karpenesi.

Romanos toiled unceasingly in the works of the Lord during his apprenticeship on Mount Athos. Because he did not have the benefit of high intellect, scholarly brilliance, or depth of philosophic perception which many other monks possessed, he had to work especially hard. Nevertheless, what he lacked in erudition he more than compensated for in intensity of purpose and complete dedication. He was later led to the Holy Land. When he returned to Mount Athos, he had become a learned and erudite servant of God. He then completed his spiritual training under the abbot of Kafsokalyvia, Monk Akakios. It was not long before Romanos, consumed by the spirit of Christianity, commanded the respect of those with whom he walked and worked in the vineyard of the Lord. When alone, he walked with God.

It is not exactly known which of the many sketes—small caves or huts where the monks prayed in solitude—he chose to make his home. There he meditated and prayed to God in a solitude which lent proximity to God. If his skete were known, it would surely be a shrine. However, the saintliness of Romanos and so many of his spiritual brothers of Mount Athos has been such that the entire peninsula can be considered a special holy place. No visitor has ever gone to Mount Athos without having enriched his soul and without leaving with an indelible impression and inspiration which would be remembered throughtout his lifetime. It is truly an oasis of Christianity without equal in all the world.

Romanos lived in the seventeenth century, a time in which the Turkish conquest of Greece had almost annihilated ancient Greek civilization and had defiled Christianity in every manner. The arrogant and ruthless conqueror preyed upon the Christian faithful, especially persecuting the more outstanding followers of Christ such as Romanos of Karpenesi.

The life of St. Romanos goes along the classic lines of utter devotion to Jesus Christ, the reward for which can end in sainthood since he was willing to die for Christianity. A scant six years before the turn of the eighteenth century, he made the supreme sacrifice not as a fanatic who crashes a suicide plane into an enemy warship, but as a deliberately betrayed man who calmly stood before the enemies of the Savior and died rather than disavow the King of Kings. The years of training and self denial have their part in preparing a man to meet his Maker, but there are no courses or lectures or meditations which provide the strength to face the executioner without flinching. It requires Christian courage and St. Romanos had this in abundance.

Romanos left the comparative safety of Mount Athos to lend his presence in Constantinople, where he encouraged the Christian people and gave them hope in Christ during the Turkish oppression. In 1694, while engaged in God's work in the ancient Byzantine capital, Romanos was apprehended by Turks. After a number of ceremonious gestures, they declared him to be a traitor, a crime for which this innocent and holy man was beheaded. Romanos lives on in the spiritual splendor of Mount Athos, and he is remembered by the Church on January 5.

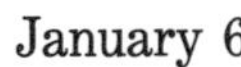

January 6

Epiphany

When the twelfth day of the Christmas season concludes on January 5, the joy of the celebration of the Savior's birth assumes another dimension with the celebration on January 6 of the day known as Epiphany to all Christendom but more properly referred to in the Greek Orthodox Church as Theophany. Epiphany means "manifestation" or "appearance" in Greek, but Theophany is more specific because it is the Greek word for the appearance of God. It declares in one word not only the appearance of the Savior but his divinity as well.

It was on January 6 that Jesus Christ stepped out of thirty years of obscurity to reveal himself as the Son of God and embark on a sacred mission which was to end three years later on a cross. The twenty centuries that have elapsed since then bear witness to the rise and fall of empires and emperors and to the eternity of the King of Kings who stepped into the Jordan River to be baptized by a man named John, a man sometimes considered the prefiguration of the Messiah but known to all the world as Saint John the Baptist, the man who baptized Jesus Christ.

In the Greek Orthodox Church the day of Epiphany ranks with Easter and Pentecost as the highest of the sacred celebrations of Christianity, all three of which seem to command in Orthodoxy greater attention than Christmas Day without detracting from the degree of reverence evidenced on the anniversary of the Savior's birth. This is so in part because although the birth of Jesus Christ was heralded and chronicled, it was on the day that he was baptized that a voice from Heaven was heard to say: "This is my beloved Son, in whom I am well pleased" (Matthew 3.17). As a symbol of the Holy Spirit, a heaven-sent white dove alit on the shoulder of the Messiah, revealing the true nature of God which is Father, Son and the Holy Spirit, the only salvation for mankind.

The Trinity, so often expressed throughout the year, often too casually, becomes a vibrant and inspiring reality on Theophany.

The twelve days of the calendar that separate Christmas and Theophany tend to obscure the fact that from the date of the birth of the Savior until the day he was baptized there was a gap of thirty years of the life of Jesus Christ that were spent in virtual anonymity, a prolonged period ten times greater than the duration of his ministry. Coronations of kings and other official ceremonies down through the ages have been held in the midst of clamorous throngs hailing as well as witnessing the event, but on the day Jesus Christ stepped out of the waters of the Jordan to save the world, the presence of witnesses in any number would have been superfluous because the highest Witness of all was there.

Nevertheless, the baptism of Jesus Christ would have been a challenge for the brush and canvas of an artist had God seen fit to have placed it in the midst of multitudes rather than whatever scattered few happened to be in the neighborhood. That is not the way of the Lord, however, and so, almost unnoticed, the greatest single event in the history of man took place on January 6, a day that lives in glory. Such was the impact of the humble Carpenter that in three short years of public presence he did what all the kings and heroes of history together could not do. He split history in two, and all the civilized world marks its days from before and after he was born.

The acknowledgement of the baby Jesus as the King is well chronicled in the New Testament, with particular emphasis placed on the veneration of the three kings of the Orient, or the three wise men as the case may be. These kings have varied in number all the way up to twelve, the number of days of Christmas, although it is generally accepted as three. It was not until the Trinity was revealed at the baptism of the Savior that God introduced the Son to mankind. The traditional blessing of the homes which commences on January 6 stems from the blessing of the Savior in the sanctified waters of the River Jordan.

January 7

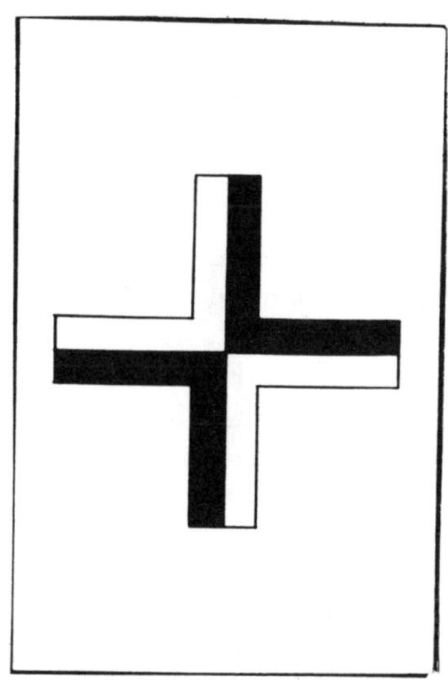

Saint John the Baptist

About two years before Jesus Christ began his mission, John the Baptist, known as the "Forerunner" of the Messiah, appeared publicly in a personal appeal for morality which undoubtedly was instrumental in setting the mood for a reception of the Lord in a world which otherwise might have been less responsive. It was about the year A.D. 27, in the reign of Tiberius, that John chose the rather hostile region of Judea, not far from the Dead Sea, as the scene of his campaign in which he employed a compelling oratory and the symbolic baptism in preparation for the next world. Orthodoxy considers him to be an angel of the Lord, one who prepared the way for Jesus Christ, acknowledging him as the Son of God, and one who died for the Savior.

According to Saint Luke, "the Glorious Physician," Saint John the Baptist was a native of the city of Judah, the son of Zacharias and Elizabeth, both of whom were of deeply religious lineage. The generation of Saint John, the first generation to know the grace and truth of Jesus Christ, comprised a humanity that ranged from wild paganism to holy asceticism. It was the aim of the Baptist to bring all classes to know the nearness of the Kingdom and the need for repentance as a preparation for admission. The drama of Saint Paul's meeting with Christ is equalled in solemnity with the meeting of Saint John the Baptist with Jesus, but it was the high honor of Saint John to baptize the Son of God.

Saint John is adequately referred to in the Bible, and there is no Christian that does not know of his service and that he ultimately was imprisoned in the dungeons of Machaerus and brutally murdered at the order of Herod Antipas. After his death there ensued a veneration that commenced with the recovery of part of his remains in the early Byzantine era and endures in Orthodoxy. According to Luke, the body of the Baptist was buried in Sebasteia in Samaria and cherished as a shrine by the Samaritans, who allowed Saint Luke to take with him the right hand of the great Baptist.

This holy relic was brought to Antioch by Saint Luke, a native of Syria, who caused to be erected a chapel dedicated to the memory of Saint John; a not too pretentious edifice which attracted thousands of Christian pilgrims, many of whom received miraculous cures at the site. For more than 800 years this site beckoned Christians from all corners of the Empire, including those from the great capital of Constantinople, the seat of the Emperor Constantine of the house of the so-called Porphyrogenitoi. It was the emperor's fondest wish that all the holy relics of Saint John be brought to the capital city, there to be accessible to many more thousands than in Antioch.

A young deacon by the name of Job was assigned the duty of carrying back to the center of the Byzantine Empire the sacred relics of Saint John the Baptist. With an observance of the most solemn ceremony, a procession headed by the emperor and the patriarch brought the holy remains to the magnificent Cathedral of Hagia Sophia, appropriately enough on September 14, the day of the Elevation of the Holy Cross of Jesus Christ. The celebration lasted for several days, for at least the time it took for countless thousands who streamed to the cathedral to pay their respects and to pray at the site of the sacred relic of one of Christendom's mightiest saints.

It was evident after many years that the most appropriate site for the holy remains of Saint John the Baptist was not in a public place where the sanctity was diminished in the babble of the crowds, however pious, but that these relics should abide in the aura of completely ascetic surroundings. The relics were, therefore, transferred to the great monastery of Mount Athos, a cloister of hallowed monastic edifices among which is one called Dionysiou, chosen as the final resting place for the relics of Saint John the Baptist, over which pious monks stand vigil.

The monastic community of Mount Athos, virtually inaccessible on a precipitous promontory extending twenty miles into the sea, is now open to all who would care to pray at the Chapel of Dionysiou, where reposes the right hand of Saint John the Baptist, whose memory is commemorated on January 7, the day following that of the Lord's baptism.

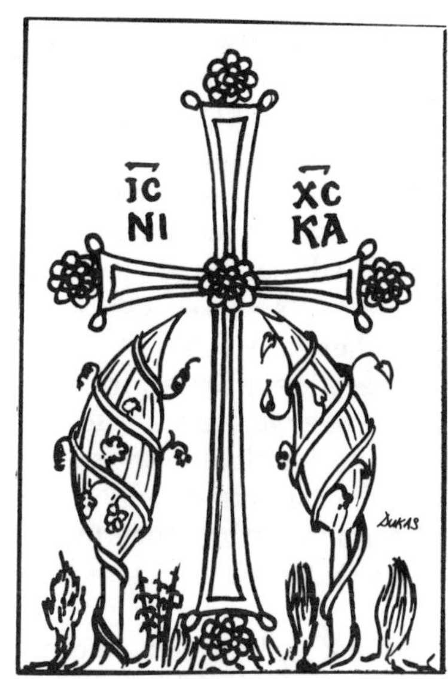

January 8

Saint Dominica the Righteous

The life expectancy of a late fourth-century Carthaginian was something less than half of what it is today, but one of the African city's most illustrious daughters lived for a full century, most of which was spent in the service of Jesus Christ. St. Dominica was born in Carthage in A.D. 384, the daughter of middle class parents who afforded her the finest in education but not in religion. The pagan household, for all its comfort and enlightenment, lacked the shining truth of the love of Jesus Christ, a spiritual deprivation that the bright girl might not have known for her one hundred years had she remained in Carthage, clinging to her ancestors' false beliefs.

St. Dominica was twenty-one years old when the magnificent capital city of Constantinople marked fifty years beyond completion by Emperor Constantine the Great as his center of the Byzantine Empire. The city's glorious heritage and culture, not its religion, fired the imagination of this polished young lady, and she prevailed on her parents to allow her to visit the capital. Together with four other young ladies of her social circle she went to the Byzantine metropolis, where she delighted in the cultural advancements of Hellenism and the grandeur of the sprawling city.

What impressed Dominica most, however, were the high ideals of the Christian community, and she felt compelled to explore the new religion of Jesus Christ. So great was her desire to become a part of Christianity that she was granted an audience with the Patriarch Nektarios, who was so taken in by the girl from Carthage that he personally officiated at her baptism. She was by then twenty-three years old and had received religious instruction from the fathers of the Patriarchate. A willing student, she ingratiated herself to all whom she came to know and felt in her heart that the service of Jesus Christ was what she desired more than anything she had discovered since coming to Constantinople.

Before she embarked on this career in religious service, she dutifully reported to her parents who, up to this point, were completely unaware of her conversion and were reluctant to grant her permission to seek what she protested was the single important thing in her life, but which her parents viewed as a waste of the talents they had encouraged in her early years. It was inconceivable to them that a life of asceticism for a girl of intelligence and spirit could be the result of anything but madness, and she was urged to once again assume her place in the society into which she had been born, a life that promised comfort and pleasure. She thanked her parents for all they had done for her and finally was able to convince them that what she chose to do was the highest order.

Back in Constantinople, Dominica entered the service of the Lord at the age of twenty-five, what she considered to be an advanced age for a novitiate, little knowing that she had been allotted a span of one hundred years of life, more than time enough to make up for her late start. Meanwhile, her four companions had followed with more than a passing interest the heartwarming activity of their dedicated friend, and all five entered the same convent in a joint service to the Savior.

Unlike many pious Christians whose road to glory was strewn with the obstacles of ignorance and ended with agonizing death, the next seventy-five years in the long life of Dominica were spent in comparative serenity and uninterrupted service to the Christian community and to God. She made full use of a life span of biblical proportion, and if she suffered any great tragedy or misfortune, it was never recorded.

The passing years were kind to Dominica, and as she aged her reputation as a tireless worker in the vineyard of Christ spread throughout the empire. Those privileged to visit with her saw in Dominica a spark of divine grace, and in the course of her ministrations she wrought miracles of healing. Alert to the end, she was granted the title of "Righteous" in recognition of her long and distinguished service of God.

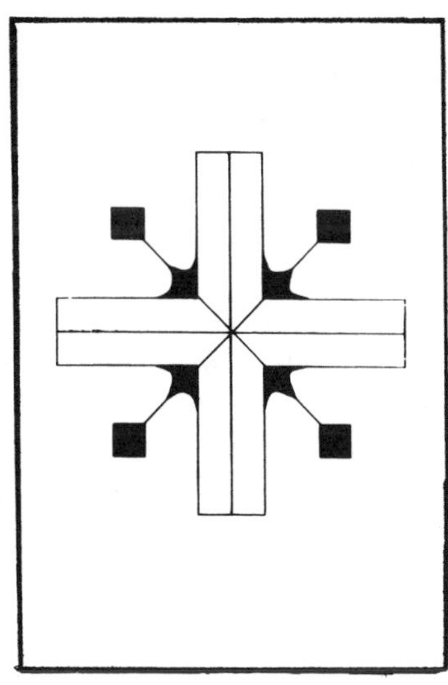

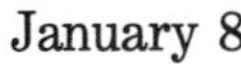

January 8

Saint Karterios the Martyr

At the close of the third century, it was evident that in spite of official discouragement, Christianity was not to be denied. St. Karterios emerged in the reign of the pagan Emperor Diocletian as a powerful protagonist for the ever increasing faith in Jesus Christ, attaining the prominence that would have placed him among the greatest of hierarchs had he lived in another century. On the other hand, it was because of men such as he whose presence in earlier and more dangerous times assured the permanence of Christianity.

St. Karterios pursued his course with a missionary zeal reminiscent of the Apostles. Little is known of his early life except that he was born in Caesaria in Cappadocia and that his brilliance shone through as a student, enhanced by an eagerness to serve the Lord. He applied his talents to every aspect of Church life, exhibiting a piety and wisdom far beyond his years.

St Karterios not only practiced what he preached but engaged in the teaching of theology and showed great resourcefulness in assuming the responsibility for the erection of a mighty cathedral, overseeing every detail of the project while still pursuing his many other duties with unrelenting vigor. His enthusiasm was infectious, stirring the passive members of his Christian community into an activist group whom he led in an astonishing wave of conversions to Christianity.

St. Karterios managed to escape the sporadic forays made on the Church by persecuting religious leaders and, either through intimidation or outright persecution, discouraged the hesitant from joining forces with the increasing number of Christians. One evening at Vespers, Karterios experienced a vision in which an angel of the Lord appeared to warn him that the magistrate Urbanus had planned an assault on the Church. Karterios was made aware of this because the new wave of persecution was to be carried on to the fullest until it had reached Karterios himself.

Realizing that he could save countless lives in blunting the thrust by appearing himself before Urbanus, he bade his followers to seek safety while he boldly presented himself to the authorities. He knew he was walking into a lion's den but he hoped to declaw the lion and, failing that, was willing to grapple with the beast regardless of the odds against him.

Presenting himself before Urbanus, Karterios lost no time in defending the faith. But Urbanus could only admire him for his oratory, but at no time acknowledging the truth of his words. After resting his case for Christ, the magistrate ordered Karterios to pay homage to the pagan god Serapis, a colossal statue which stood in the courtyard. He was led before the stone idol and commanded to pray but instead of praying to the idol, Karterios lifted his eyes towards the heavens and prayed to Almighty God.

Karterios had prayed for only a moment when, to the shock and surprise of all but the courageous Christian, the statue of Serapis disintegrated before their eyes and was reduced to rubble. Taken aback by this turn of events, the magistrate's amazement turned to rage and he ordered Karterios to be taken to the dungeon, there to be systematically tortured day by day until he died a slow and agonizing death.

According to plan, Karterios was mercilessly tortured and cast back into prison, only to be found the next morning healed of his wounds. Inflicting further punishment daily that would have killed an ordinary man, the healing process continued, a procedure that continued for days on end, and always with the same results. As the days wore on and the news leaked out about the healing power of the Lord, the magistrate pondered his next course as converts were won instead of lost.

One day a bolt of lightning struck the gate of the prison in which Karterios was held, whereupon he strode from the cell past awe-stricken guards but, rather than walk out to freedom, he walked directly to the magistrate. He hoped that this latest demonstration of the power of the Lord would help him to convince Urbanus that paganism was as false as the idol that had crumbled at a glance of the Lord. Not known for his erudition, but more widely known for his stupidity and flint-hearted intransigence, Urbanus ordered the immediate execution of his Christian opposite by the certain method of beheading. Karterios gave his life for Christ on 8 January 295.

January 9

Philip of Moscow

Like the Savior for whom he gave his life, Philip of Moscow was thirty years old when he appeared on the Christian scene, unlike most men of God who are by then several years down the road, but he nevertheless rose to the pinnacle of the Church in spite of a late start. An heroic figure in every respect, this bold Russian was endowed with all the attributes that marked him for greatness, but the single strand of his fiber that made him stand out was his absolute courage. He would have ascended to the top of any vocation he chose, and, fortunately for Russia in particular and the world in general, he chose to follow Jesus Christ.

Born in the early sixteenth century and baptized Theodore, Philip of Moscow was of aristocratic lineage in the house of the boyar Kolytchov. His father was guardian and tutor to the Grand Duke Yuri, brother of Ivan the Terrible, and his mother was heiress to vast estates. In accordance with the family tradition, he entered the military service and served honorably as an officer in campaigns against the Lithuanians and the Tartars of the Crimea.

In the course of a church service, he heard the priest cite a passage from the Scriptures that read, "No man can serve two masters," and it was that statement that led him to resign his commission at the age of thirty and to enlist in the service of the Savior. He exchanged his ornate uniform for the garb of a peasant and the luxury of his family's estates for the bleakness of a monastery, in this instance a remote monastery on the island of Solovky in the White Sea, a cloister which had been founded by two monks named Sabbatios and Germanos in 1429. Making no reference to his aristocratic and military background, he accepted an assignment as gardener and woodcutter for the period of his novitiate.

By the time he had fulfilled the requirements for monkhood, he had earned the great respect of the Abbot Alexis, who took pride in tonsuring the very bright and very noble novice, who then assumed the name of Philip. When the abbot left office he was succeeded by Philip, who was ordained priest by the archbishop of Novgorod, after which the new abbot donated his share of the family estates to the monastery, which he proceeded to direct to a position of prominence in the religious affairs of Russia. Under his astute administration, the cloister grew into a complex of monasteries that was the pride of the land and one of the greatest spiritual forces in Russian ecclesiastical history.

Philip drew the attention and respect of the Tzar Ivan IV, who prevailed upon him to assume the duties of metropolitan of Moscow, the most prestigious post of the realm. For a time peace reigned as Ivan heeded Philip's peace-seeking advice.

Soon, however, Ivan began to live up to the reputation that gave him his name and in vengeance filled the jails with those whom he feared would dethrone him, many of whom were executed unjustly. It became evident that Ivan's fears stemmed from a deranged mind. His secret police, known as the "Opritchniki," roamed the streets in search of real and imagined enemies of the tzar.

The demented Ivan attended church as usual, satisfied that his punishments, harsh though they were, were in the interest of justice. No one dared to suggest otherwise–no one but Philip, that is, who in the course of a service pointed an accusing finger at the royal pew and called for an end to the senseless killings. The infuriated Tzar stormed out of the church, humiliated before his subjects by the courageous prelate, and immediately called for a hearing during which Philip was forbidden to sermonize further on the subject.

The gallant Philip, remembering he served only one Master, refused to comply and denounced the ruthless Tzar for his barbaric acts. For this he was banished to a monastery, where he was smothered to death. To this day no one has accepted Ivan's plea that he had nothing to do with it. Twenty-one years after Philip's death, his body was disinterred and found intact. His relics remain in the Cathedral of the Assumption in Moscow, a reminder to one and all that Christianity still lives in Russia. He was canonized in 1652.

January 10

Saint Gregory of Nyssa

Christianity has faced serious crises which menaced its very existence. The most critical threats to our faith arose during the first few centuries of ecclesiastical history. One such crisis developed in the fourth century when the doctrine of Arianism undermined the unity of Orthodoxy as no other doctrine had before or has since. Among the voices that were raised against the heresy of Arius, none was more eloquent or more convincing than that of Gregory of Nyssa. Although Christendom has since splintered, the true faith of the Orthodox Church has been preserved intact thanks largely to men such as St. Gregory.

Gregory was a member of the family that boasted of such heroic figures as his brother St. Basil the Great, another brother Peter, archbishop of Sebastia, and his sister Macrina, the nun whose feast day is July 19. Born in Cappadocia, Asia Minor, Gregory traveled to all the corners of the empire on triumphant lecturing tours, accompanied by his lovely wife, Theosebia. It was not until his wife's untimely death, however, that Gregory devoted his energies exclusively as a standard bearer of the Orthodox Christian faith. He was ordained bishop of Nyssa and in that capacity he served with a distinction that was to bring him prominence as an intellectual and religious leader.

The heretical movement of Arius, a theologian and priest of Alexandria, shook the foundations of the Christian faith by claiming that Christ was not the true God, but that he was a man, created by God the Father. Since he was created by the Father, according to Arius, Christ was not equal to the Father, but was lower, subordinate to him. In this way, the followers of Arius undermined the doctrines of the Holy Trinity and of salvation through Jesus Christ, the God-man. Gregory of Nyssa was instrumental in combatting the false doctrine of Arius.

When the Emperor Valens, an Arian, came to power in A.D. 374, he forthwith banished Gregory who had gone to Constantinople to speak out against the heretical movement. His exile was not long, however. The Emperor Valens, in an ill-considered campaign against invaders streaming in from the Balkans, ordered an attack in which he and his entire army were slaughtered.

After the death of Valens, Gregory returned to his post at Nyssa and became part of the noble triumvirate with Basil the Great and Gregory the Theologian, which was greatly responsible for the defeat of Arianism and other heresies. The Second Ecumenical Synod (Constantinople, A.D. 381) completed the Nicene Creed as we know it today. The most eloquent voice of the Second Synod has generally been accepted to be that of Gregory, bishop of Nyssa.

Thus, Orthodoxy has withstood the ravages of dissension over a period of nearly two thousand years—a tribute to Christianity itself, to the Orthodox faithful, and to men such as St. Gregory of Nyssa who have come forward in time of crisis to meet the challenge.

The profusion of Gregories in ecclesiastical annals is such that one can scarcely be faulted for not immediately calling to mind that the voice of St. Gregory of Nyssa was the most stentorian of all his namesakes, and that it is to him that the Greek Orthodox faith owes so very much in Christian service, equalled by some but surpassed by none, with the possible exception of his brother, the great St. Basil. At a time when his family's posture assured him of laurels which he could share in with little or no effort, he independently hurled back challenge after challenge being thrust at the heart of the Church. In and out of favor to the point of exile and recall, all because of his bold defense of the sacred traditions of the Church, he achieved prominence on his own in spite of and not because of his illustrious family. In the light of history, he did nothing in his lifetime but add laurels to a family already revered for its service to Jesus Christ. Like his brother Basil, his attributes included humility so that his name can be linked with the great and near great who have assured the permanence of Greek Orthodoxy.

St. Gregory died most probably in the year 394 and his memory is commemorated on January 10.

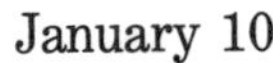

January 10

Saint Marcian

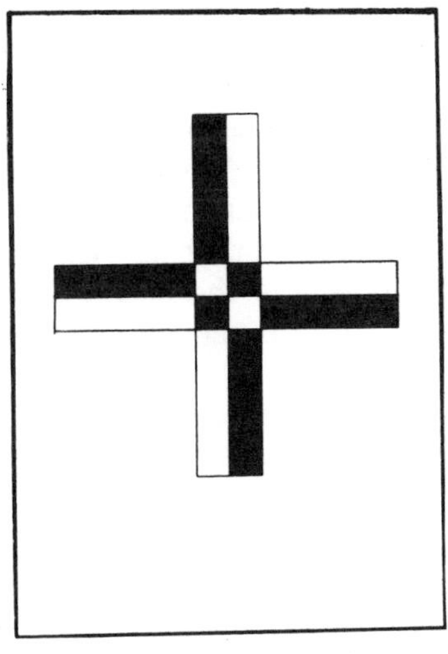

After more than a century since Constantine the Great had favored Christianity and set the course of an empire that was to last more than a thousand years, the influence of the Greek Orthodox Church had become manifest through the genius and dedication of men such as St. Marcian. Because of this man's talents, among others, the city of Byzantium became the most glorious cultural and religious city in the world under the name of Constantinople, to remain so until its decline under the present name of Istanbul.

The architectural style of churches had been set prior to his birth, but it remained for the genius of Marcian to establish a pattern of grandeur that was to be followed by the great architects that followed. What set this man's work apart from others was the divine inspiration that suggested the hand of God was to be seen in his work, true to the proverb that says: "Except the Lord build the house, they labor in vain that build it." None of the labor that went into the houses of God as envisioned by this master builder could ever have been said to have been in vain. His works reflect the Holy Spirit because he was first and foremost a devout Christian and cleric whose talents were applied in many ways but always for the sole purpose of glorifying Jesus Christ.

Born into wealth in the city of Rome, he was raised in the shadows of the majestic architecture of the eternal city that was to influence him in making architecture a part of his life's work, second only to his dedication to the Savior. He received the finest education money could buy. Throughtout his lifetime he had a genuine humility that went hand in hand with his piety, exhibiting nothing but Christian love to everyone. About the only thing he disliked was mediocrity, striving for excellence in all things.

Born into the leisure class, Marcian grew ill at ease in Rome where his talents were stifled and he was therefore drawn to Constantinople. In that city he was more at home with religious leaders who saw in him great promise. He was not long in establishing himself not only as an architectural genius but as a deeply religious figure as well. His work drew the attention of Patriarach Anatolios who prevailed upon him to enter church service. It was not until he was thirty years old that he was ordained a priest and was appointed to the patriarchal church. He was soon thereafter placed in charge of all projects of the Patriarchate, distinguishing himself as an administrator through his creativity and enormous skills in architecture.

While in this capacity, he came into an inheritance, all of which he poured into his ambitious projects which were of great benefit to the poor and the underprivileged. The homeless and dispossessed were provided shelter and those who wished to worship Jesus Christ were provided with churches. The name of Marcian was on the lips of every sincere Christian. His boundless benevolence was equalled by his humble genius which the beauty of Constantinople reflected in the works of art that he erected: churches, hospitals, and other buildings.

It was during a prayerful session at one of the older and smaller churches dedicated to St. Irene that Maracian had a vision in which an angel of the Lord instructed him to build a new and larger church of St. Irene. Selecting a site by the sea, Marcian set into motion plans for erecting a magnificent cathedral which took years to complete. When completed it stood as a mighty citadel of God, attracting worshipers who stood in awe as they felt the very presence of God in this divinely inspired creation.

The devout genius of Marcian drew support from the more affluent of the city, with whom he laid plans to build the mightiest cathedral of the Empire—the renowned Church of the Anastasis (Resurrection). The design which Marcian drew up in detail called for marble, precious stones, and metals that had to be imported, mostly from Greece and Italy. With infinite patience and consummate skill, he directed every phase of the cathedral until, after many years, it was completed. In the course of those years, he seemd to have acquired an aura of the divine about him so that at the dedication of the church he was observed to be not only a master builder but so favored of God that the power of the divine was within him.

With the passing years the power of healing through the grace of God was made evident by Marcian who continued his most impressive work until he was laid to rest on 10 January 471.

Theodosios the Cenobite

The province of Cappadocia, Asia Minor, has given to Christianity some of its most illustrious sons, the best remembered of whom are such greats as Saint Basil, Saint Gregory of Nyssa, and Saint Gregory the Theologian. Into this select company there came from this ancient cradle of Christendom a man named Theodosios, who may not have attained the prominence of his fellow Cappadocians but who nevertheless stands abreast of all of them in their glorious march for Jesus Christ. In his pursuit of Christian ideals he never shortened his stride in a lifetime devoted to God's service.

Theodosios, was born in A.D. 423 with all the attributes for leadership in a century of Christianity that cried out for firm resolve and quiet courage, needed not only for the forces of evil that assailed the Church from without but for the heresy from within as well. At the outset he evinced a purposeful dedication as an official reader in the family church but soon outgrew this slight service and set out for the Holy Land to seek the shrines that were to inspire him to his true greatness. If he sought a living inspiration, he found it in the person of Saint Symeon the Stylite, whose heroic figure beckoned him from faraway Antioch, Syria.

The awesome sight of Saint Symeon, perched atop a pillar that extended skyward forty feet above ground, was enough to bring the visiting faithful to their knees, but when his voice boomed out from above, it appeared to many as a near divine spectre calling them closer to God. Theodosios caught the eye of this renowned ascetic and was advised by him to return to Jerusalem to perpetuate the faith through the formation of cenobite monasteries. He returned to the Holy City forthwith and went to the renowned Longinus, who tonsured him as a monk in anticipation of the harsh service in the years of preparation that lay ahead to qualify himself in the eyes of God and man for the responsibility of directing the establishment of a monastery and its many projects in the name of the Savior.

The life of asceticism which Theodosios assumed for many years went beyond the accepted standards of austerity, but in his strong desire to cleanse his spirit by depriving himself of anything resembling comfort, he evinced a strength of character through self-denial which captured the hearts of those who knew him and which commanded the respect of those who only knew of him. When he was satisfied that he had more than met the requirements to enter the service of God, he set up the first of what was to become a chain of monasteries which in a few years attracted hundreds of pious men dedicating their lives for the cause of Jesus Christ.

In the course of this monastic development, Theodosios also sought to promote the welfare of all the people through a philanthropy which set up hospitals, orphanages and homes for the aged, all of which were administered by the monks with the assistance of many lay volunteers. In tribute to his benevolence, the patriarch of Jerusalem, Salloustios (486-494), appointed him chief abbot of all the monasteries of Palestine, which at that time were great in number and even greater in service to the needs of mankind.

Theodosios saw a menace within the framework of the Church which was outside his sphere of responsibility, but he could not stand by in a passive resistance, even if it spelled danger for him personally. The menance was Monophysitism, a heretical doctrine which held that Christ had only one nature—the divine—a doctrine which challenged the declaration of holy Scripture and holy Tradition that Christ is of dual nature—human and divine, or God and man. His stand in defense of Tradition brought many of the faithful back to the accepted fold, but it did not convince the Emperor Anastasios, who had swallowed the heretical potion and disdained the antidote of Truth. For daring to publicly oppose him, the Emperor banished Theodosios from Palestine.

Theodosios remained in exile until the death of the unrelenting Emperor at which time he was welcomed back by the multitudes whom he had so nobly served. According to his biographer and pupil, Bishop Theodore of Arabia, he resumed his charitable work with renewed vigor, working for God and man until he died on 11 January 529, at the age of 105.

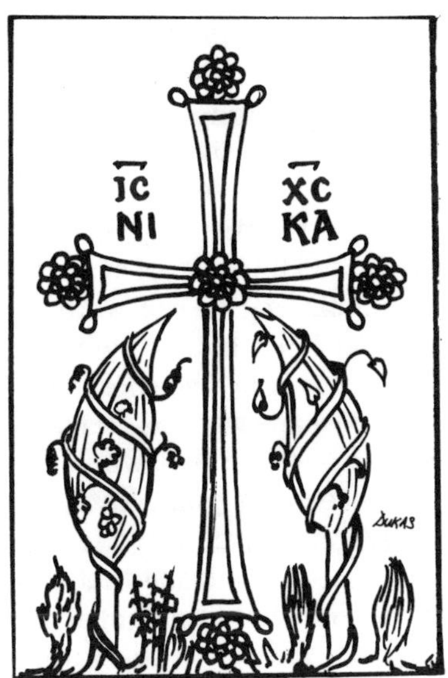

January 12

Saint Tatiani

Although biographical sketches tend to follow a certain pattern, particularly in the case of young women who died for Jesus Christ, there are no two whose lives have been exactly alike, just as the billions of people on earth no two look exactly alike, with the possible exception of identical twins. The similarites among saints have been in their common purpose of serving the Savior, but to say that they are all alike is to say that they have all looked alike, which is hardly the case. The brief life span of St. Tatiani follows the time honored pattern of living and dying for the Savior, but she had an identity all her own and an individuality both humble and noble, a rare combination.

Tatiani was born during the reign of the Roman Emperor, Alexander Severus (223-235 A.D.), an emperor whose cruelty to Christians also follow the pattern of the early rulers of the Roman Empire, the worst of whom was Julian the Apostate. Tatiani's father was a man of means who was the overseer to a sizable estate, but he was also a Christian who saw to the spiritual needs of the circle by serving as a deacon. He was one of many of the landed aristocracy who embraced Jesus Christ but were forced to keep their religion a secret, lest they be betrayed by some covetous pagan ever anxious to win the favor of the state by exposing a Christian in high station.

Tatiani and her father looked to the need of those less fortunate than themselves, giving generously of their time and money, bribing officials for the release of Christians from the dungeons, and finding shelter for the many homeless. Tatiani became thoroughly familiar with the maze of catacombs of Rome wherein she helped many of the faithful to elude their pursuers, took risks for her fellow Christians, which she preferred to the safety of her own comfortable home. Her familiarity with what amounted to the underground of ancient Rome was coupled with access to authority which she could easily disarm with her captivating charm to effect escape or release of a hapless victim of the unrelenting persecution.

Tatiani's father put his trust in one of the many sycophants of the emperor and was ultimately betrayed by this tool of royalty and dragged before a tribunal in humiliating fashion without proof other than the word of the royal foil who bore witness against the benevolent parent. If the accused had so chosen, he could have denied the accusation and perhaps won his freedom because there was no real evidence against him, but when the question was put to him as to his innocence or guilt, Tatiani's father forthrightly stated that his only guilt lay in a love for his fellow man through Jesus Christ, the Savior. Realizing that this statement alone had condemned him, he chose to say nothing more in his defense and was condemned to death. He chose to die rather than deny Christ.

Tatiani was quite soon thereafter seized and brought before the emperor himself who saw in the pretty young maiden an opportunity to discredit Christianity. He surmised that with an approach befitting her station she could be won over by his imperial persuasion and be made to return to paganism, thus achieving a triumph over her followers that could not be attained by her being put to death as her father had been. Emperor Severus used his utmost oratorical skill, but when he saw his words were being wasted, he decided on another plan.

Tatiani was taken under armed guard as an enemy of the state and ceremoniously placed in the midst of the idols in the royal temple where she was ordered to recant and bow to the stone figures. Tatiani did nothing but look around in defiance of those who had crowded to witness the transformation that never came about. It was then that she was flogged unmercifully, lashed to the point where she fell to her knees and she begged God not for help but for a display of his might. The earth commenced trembling as though an earthquake had struck and all the stone idols came crashing onto the floor. The pagans scattered in terror, but when order was restored, the nineteen-year-old maiden was taken out into the streets where she was tortured anew and then put to death. Her remains were discovered and placed in a chapel in 1634 under Pope Urban VIII. She is commemorated on January 12.

January 13

Saint Maximos (Kafsokalyvitis)

The incredible saga of the monasteries of Mount Athos is the summation of the life's work of some of the most noble spirits of Christianity. Among the many holy men of Mount Athos whose affinity to God has led to their sainthood, and perhaps the most noteworthy and certainly the most unique, was Maximos, a man whose asceticism and peculiar lifestyle set him apart from his peers. A confirmed non-conformist, Maximos epitomized the rugged individualism of the monks whose behavior was generally considered eccentric by the outside world. Sensual society that deemed monasticism irregular at best would have undoubtedly seen Maximos as hopelessly deranged. And yet, if it had seen his pure spirit it would have knelt before him.

Admitted to the sacred confines of Mount Athos at the age of seventeen, Maximos, over a span of nearly eighty years, evinced a piety and wisdom that endeared him to countless pilgrims seeking his counsel and blessing. He never ceased to inspire those about him. Although decline had set in on Athos after it was plundered in the thirteenth century during the Fourth Crusade, a revival occurred during the following century. Maximos, part of the revival, along with such stalwarts as Saint Gregory Palamas, upheld the doctrine of hesychasm. In fact, he carried hesychasm to the extreme that became his trademark.

Maximos availed himself of the vastness of the Athos peninsula—a promontory stretching thirty miles out into the Aegean Sea, with a width in excess of six miles. When he found it impossible to communicate with God in the monasteries, even in any of the sketes or caves, he fashioned a crude hut in which to meditate and pray. When the hut seemed no longer impervious to anything but purity, he would burn it and build another. This habit caused him to be dubbed Maximos Kafsokalyvitis (hut-burner). Living in his hut, enveloped in prayer, Maximos thus experienced a greater form of self-denial than simply the solitude and austerity of an anchorite.

Just as Moses had gone up to Mount Sinai and Elijah to Mount Carmel, Maximos ascended the holy mountain of Athos—which rises abruptly out of the Aegean for nearly seven thousand feet—an ascent which few have dared to venture. Heedless of the dangers and the biting cold, he scaled the lofty peak, and in the stark seculsion that can be found only on a mountain top, he prostrated himself before the Lord. After a week passed, a vision of the Virgin Mary appeared to him. The Theotokos told Maximos that he would henceforth know spiritual perfection through the Holy Spirit.

Maximos descended the sacred mountain with the wisdom of ages stored within him, and with the sweet serenity of the Holy Spirit in his heart. It was as though he had been reborn, glowing with a presence that suggested an intimacy with the Divine.

Word of his transformation brought scores seeking his blessing and healing through the Holy Spirit. As a result, he was so beseiged that he sought the refuge of his dismal hut.

Maximos withdrew to the seclusion of his hut and would have lived out his days there, but he was prevailed upon to grace the community with his presence. Instrumental in drawing him out of seclusion was a noted hermit, Gregory of Sinai, who like many others had gone to Mount Athos for the express purpose of seeing the holy Maximos.

Mount Athos contains many miracle-working icons and in the fourteenth century, Maximos was a living icon. This gentle link with Divinity lived to be ninety-five years old. Even after his death he continued to serve those of the faithful seeking comfort at his grave site. The fires of his huts have long since gone out, but the flame of his holy spirit will never be extinguished.

The Church remembers St. Maximos Kafsokalyvitis on January 13.

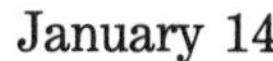

January 14

Saint Savvas, the Serbian Prince

It was during the thirteenth century that Savvas, son of King Symeon of Serbia and heir to the royal throne, forsook the glory and power of the throne to dedicate himself to the Savior. One of three brothers, Savvas was trained and educated to be a monarch. However, with all due respect for his royal responsibilities, Savvas considered service to the Church to be of greater importance. Since either of his two brothers could assume the throne, he felt free to serve Christ. Later, he did not regret this decision to serve the King of Kings.

Savvas was not certain how he could best serve the Church. He above all wanted no special favor because of his royal position. It happened that some monks from Mount Athos arrived in Serbia to solicit funds from King Symeon. Symeon had been charitable in the past, but on this occasion he gave not only his money, but also his son. Savvas secretly planned to go to Mount Athos with the monks in order to become a monk himself. He persuaded the monks to take him without his father's knowledge. Savvas argued that he was not betraying his father, but that were he to be denied permission to accompany them, they would be betraying the Lord whom he desperately sought to serve.

Savvas faded into the obscurity of Mount Athos among the thousands of monks who enjoyed not only spiritual freedom, but total independence from the state without fear of intervention. After being tonsured a monk, Savvas soon established himself in the brotherhood as a man of great intelligence and profound devotion to the word of the Lord.

Meanwhile King Symeon had instituted a broad search for his son. Two years after Savvas' secret departure, the hunt came to an end with the revelation that he had left of his own volition to become an ascetic. Although the king's emissaries advised Savvas that his only course of action was to return to his rightful place at the side of his father, Savvas sent the emissaries back with a letter for his parents. In his letter, which was reputed to have been four hundred pages long, Savvas not only extolled the virtues and importance of monasticism, but in a torrent of passionate prose he also revealed to them the true meaning of Christian love and the depth of his devotion to Jesus Christ.

Greatly moved by his son's impassioned letter, the king transferred the royal authority to his two sons and then journeyed to Mount Athos to experience first-hand what had been so eloquently described to him. Shedding the royal purple for a monk's habit, the king found for himself a serenity he had never known before. Soon many of his countrymen joined him and his son, eventually founding Chilandari, the first Serbian monastery on Mount Athos.

Impressed by the holy work of Savvas, the patriarch of Constantinople prevailed upon him to return to his native Serbia to serve his people not as king, but as archbishop of Serbia. With considerable reluctance Savvas left Mount Athos to respect the patriarch's wishes and assume the spiritual leadership of his native land. His service was one of distinction; the Orthodox Church of Serbia flourished as never before in its history. But more than this, the countries known as the Balkans, which includes Serbia, are indebted to a number of missionaries for their steadfast Orthodox faith. To one of their own, who might have served as royalty, they owe a special debt of gratitude, that is, to St. Savvas, but for whom the light of Christianity might have dimmed.

In an era of Christian upheaval, the Crusades and the barbarian menace to the north, St. Savvas brought stability to the Greek Orthodox faith and in turn to the welfare, spiritual and temporal, of a region that was no stranger to turmoil and vacillation. He is all the more revered for choosing to serve the King of Kings rather than be a monarch himself.

Savvas eventually returned to his beloved Chilandari where he died peacefully on 14 January 1236.

The Thirty-Eight Fathers of Mount Sinai

Less renowned than the cloister of Mount Athos in Greece, the Monastery of Saint Katherine in Egypt is as much hallowed by time and location as it is by the sacred purpose it represents. Located at the base of the holy mountain of Sinai, it goes back almost 2,000 years to the Savior himself as a spiritual beacon for those who believe in God. It serves not only to remind us that at the summit of this mountain God spoke to Moses, but also to venerate the Son of God who died to save the world. Manned down through nearly twenty centuries by Orthodox monks, it has an illustrious history of service and sacrifice in the name of the Lord far greater than any other institution on earth.

Following the destruction of Jerusalem in A.D. 70, a small group of extremely devout men went in search of a secluded spot in which to contemplate and pray, and the bleak desert area was selected over all others because Mount Sinai was sacred ground. The Holy Spirit seemed to hover there because of God's presence when Moses had delivered his people from bondage, but there was little to indicate why God had chosen this barren terrain as a meeting place with the prophet Moses. The dismal surroundings held out little comfort, and that from the rude beginnings of crude huts there should come a cloister now nearly two thousand years old and still going strong is nothing short of a miracle itself.

How the Monastery of Saint Katherine lived beyond its infancy in such forbidding surroundings in these ancient times is told in the history of this citadel of God by intrepid souls who defied the elements in creating this spiritual outpost of Christianity. They defied the hostility of the wild tribesmen as bravely as the stoutest of warriors, and with little or no assistance from the outside world, they ignited a torch of the truth of Jesus Christ that has been undiminished by the ravages of time and by enemies of Christendom. It took remarkable courage and ingenuity to gain a foothold in this somber place, but divine inspiration must have made it all possible.

By the middle of the fourth century, literally thousands of monks were living in the caves and grottoes in the shadow of the Holy Mountain in a spiritual colony that had little use for the comforts of life afforded by buildings and houses. They were constantly harassed by nomadic tribesmen whose sporadic raids threatened the gradual ruin of this loosely administered colony. Saint Helen, the mother of Constantine the Great, was concerned about the welfare of this scattered cloister, which became one of her favorite projects, and in A.D. 325 she financed the erection of a huge tower in which the monks could seek refuge in times of peril.

The nomadic hordes grew in number and in their hatred for the holy men of Sinai. Massing their tribesmen, they converged on the tower; before they could be driven off they had slaughtered thirty-eight monks. The Church has set aside January 14 as the day commemorating the martyrdom of these pious men. The day also commemorates the slaying of hundreds of unarmed monks in another bloody attack in the Sinai plain of Raitho.

The tower erected by Saint Helen had saved many of the brave souls who stubbornly refused to leave the holy ground, but it soon became evident that the tower could not withstand the onslaught of increasingly savage hordes. The colony seemed doomed. The Emperor Justinian, however, one of the most benevolent rulers of the Byzantine Empire, vowed that the faithful monks would never face extinction in the land of Moses, and he lost no time in erecting a magnificent monastery in the midst of an impregnable fortress that discouraged any further raids.

Many of the structures now lie in ruins, but the main monastery, built in A.D. 536, is largely intact and has afforded a haven for men who have engaged in an uninterrupted service to the Lord for centuries. Orthodox monks who take up their holy work there now are little different from those of earlier centuries, except that they now have not only a sacred ground on which to worship but a monastery steeped in ancient and hallowed tradition.

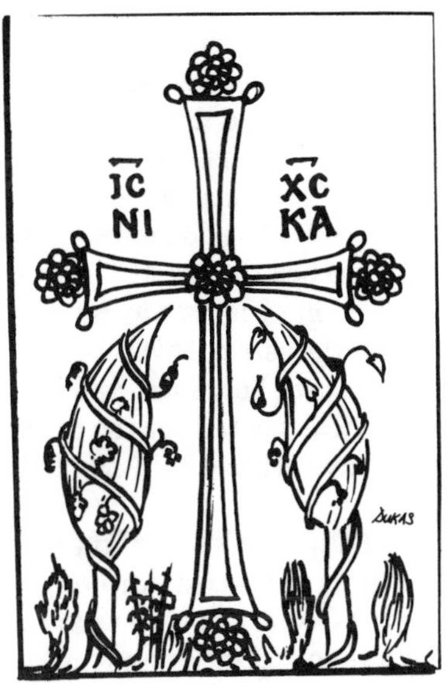

January 15

Paul the Hermit of Thebes

Long before monasteries had been formed by pious men to express the will of God, those that combined in holy efforts had started out by individually isolating themselves from the rest of the world and, thereafter, collectively banding together in cloisters. In the late third century, the man who had generally been acknowledged to be the first self-appointed hermit was Saint Anthony, but he in turn came to discover that he really had not been the first and who discovered that the first genuine religious recluse was a man from Thebes named Paul.

It was not until after Anthony's example of isolation in the name of the Lord had been followed by others, with the result that there came into being the first of countless monasteries, that it was made evident that Paul had preceded Anthony by several years in this ascetic way of life. And it was only through a divine intervention that Anthony and the world came to know the truth as to the identity of the originator of asceticism in isolation.

Born in the city of Thebes, Egypt, Paul was orphaned at an early age and was brought up by devout Christians who saw to his complete religious education. He had been left a considerable estate but gradually withdrew from the social set whose Sybaritic preferences he deplored. He could have enjoyed the favor of the Emperor Decius but he chose to follow the dictates of his Christian conscience and forsook his estate for the quiet and solitude of the desert. He was only twenty-two years old when he abandoned his worldly goods and sought out a cave in which he could meditate and pray. Close by the entrance to the cave was a spring from which he drew water as he needed and next to which was a tree which was virtually a tree of life for him. Not only did he clothe himself with garments fashioned from the durable leaves of this tree, but he sustained himself much of the time with its fruit. It is said he was given bread by a raven, much as Elijah subsisted on bread borne to him by a raven sent from God.

Perhaps in spite of his meager diet rather than because of it, Paul lived well beyond 100 years, although there is much to be said for abstinence particularly from foods that do anything but prolong a man's life. Paul had already reached the age of 114 when the ninety-year-old Anthony had a vision in which it was revealed to him that deep in the desert was a predecessor. This revelation prompted Anthony to seek out the unknown holy man, and after telling his fellow monks of the vision, he departed for the desert and eventually made his way to the cave where Paul had lived for nearly seventy years.

As Anthony approached the cave, Paul, who knew of the coming of the visitor, called the delightfully surprised Anthony by name, and they embraced in the glory of God whom each was serving so nobly. After many hours of gentle conversation and meditation, Paul announced that his time was near and asked if he could be buried with the cape of Athanasios of Egypt, now in the possession of Anthony, as his shroud. Amazed as much by the fact that Paul knew of the cape as by the fact that he knew that death was at his door, the visiting monk returned to the monastery and brought the cape back with him to Paul's cave.

Several of the monks had volunteered to accompany Anthony on his return trip but he preferred to go back alone, much as he would have liked to have his entire monastery meet this impressive hermit of the desert. When at last he got back to the cave, he perceived Paul kneeling in the shadow in prayer, and he remained discreetly outside, not wishing to disturb his friend of the cloth. The minutes passed, and Anthony would peer from time to time into the cave, but when he observed the praying figure he paced outside the cave, cape in hand.

As more minutes passed, Anthony grew apprehensive and went right to the kneeling Saint Paul the Hermit, only to discover that he had died much as he lived, in kneeling before God. As he had requested, Paul, the original hermit of God, was buried with the cape of Athanasios draped about him. He died on 15 January 341.

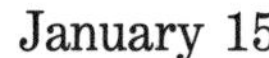
January 15

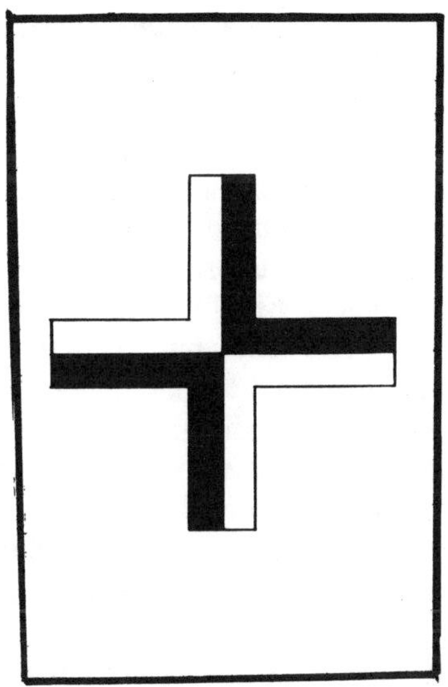

John Kalyvites

The popularity of the name John, made it a name common in many families. In one family there was a son named John whose common name identifies him in a most uncommon manner, appropriate to the most uncommon life he chose to lead in complete devotion to the Savior seldom equalled in intensity and unsurpassed in loyalty. Thus a man comes down to us in ecclesiastical history by the name of St. John Kalyvites (=hut dweller), whose life story is a study in Christian resolve and calculated denial.

This particular John was born to parents whose names were Eutropios and Theodora, both of whom were devout Christians and whose station in life was lofty enough to place them in the company of Emperor Leo. The youngest of three children, John had every advantage, but he might as well have been born of paupers. When he was old enough to make a choice, he scorned the fun and games of the more-or-less idle rich in favor of more serious pursuits, enjoying most the company of monks who had paused in his city enroute to the Holy Land and one of whom remained for a time with John's parents while the others went on.

The parents were content to entertain their guest for as long as he wished, but the monk extended his stay principally because he fascinated young John who piled him with questions about Jesus Christ and the Kingdom of God. The monk in turn was pleased at the boy's religious bent, spending hours in spelling out the concepts of the Christian faith and the beauties that lay in the worship of Jesus Christ. The monk finally left to continue his pilgrimage only after promising the boy that he would return and take him to the monk's monastery called Akoimetoi (Sleepless).

Making no mention of his intent to eventually go to this monastery, whose name derived from the fact that the monks, organized in groups, prayed and meditated in turn around the clock. John went on with his education but with a request that he be given a Bible. The parents agreed because they could afford it since a hand written Bible was expensive, a possession few youngsters possessed. It is said that the boy's Bible was illustrated with holy figures, and made from the best of materials. John savored every word of the Bible while keeping up with his other duties and awaiting impatiently for the monk to return as promised.

John's anxiety grew as the days passed. Finally, after a year had passed, his friend the monk appeared. Determined to keep his future course a secret, he arranged to meet the monk aboard ship, getting the passage money from unquestioning parents. Once they had arrived at the monastery, they had no trouble asking the abbot to waive the mandatory one year period, despite the boy's extreme youth; and John was tonsured a monk without delay. He joined his fellow monks, embarking on a program of extreme austerity.

John's vow of poverty and chastity included fast days that were ongoing and not restricted to sacred observances. John's diet, restricted to meager portions of bread and water, was so severe that his gaunt appearance alarmed the abbot who implored him to take substantial nourishment.

John continued his fasting, but as he continued to shut out everything and everybody to think only of the Lord, his will weakened to the extent that he allowed himself to turn his thoughts to the parents he had abandoned without warning. Finally, he was driven to ask the abbot for permission to see his parents once more. The abbot was only too willing to grant permission, assuring the young man, who now looked much older than his years, that the Lord would understand.

John somehow bore up under the weary journey and when he appeared at what once was his home, the servants were about to turn him away, when his father, not recognizing the haggard creature before him as his own son, ordered them to let the poor monk in. Offered shelter in comfort, the unrecognized son asked to be given the use of a hut in a corner of the grounds. He remained there for three years. In all that time his own mother failed to recognize him.

After three years of deliberate deprivation and isolation, John had a vision in which an angel of the Lord appeared to tell him that he was about to be received into the Kingdom of Heaven. He sent the Bible to his parents, who came rushing to his side. But in a matter of days the son, finally recognized by his parents, died.

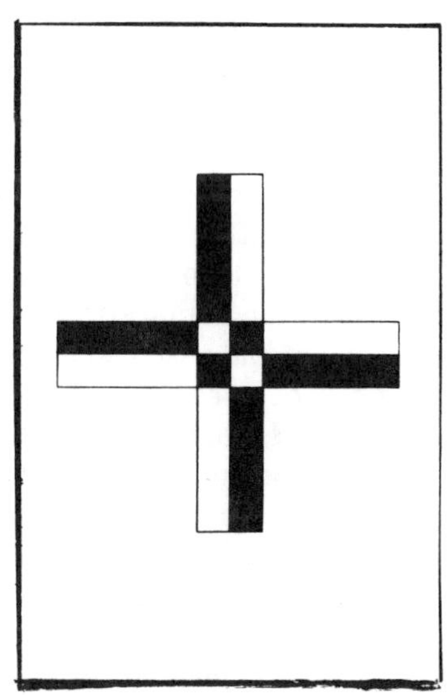

January 16

Saint Damaskenos

The anguish of the American people over a small band of its brethren being held captive in an Islamic nation only serves to underscore the gallantry of the Greek nation which for nearly four centuries was hostage to a ruthless Ottoman horde even more merciless and wanton than its present-day counterparts. Further brought out are the stark historical facts that for the thousand years of its existence the bulwark between Christianity and oblivion was the Byzantine Empire, which was overrun by the Ottomans only after being weakened from within even by such well-meaning misadventures as the Crusades.

The Turkish invasion sent many Greek families scattering to Balkan regions, which accounts for the fact that the saint now known to us as Damaskenos came from generations of Bulgarians of Hellenic origin. Damaskenos was born in the village of Gabrova, Bulgaria, a country which had long since taken to its soul, in loving embrace, the Holy Orthodox Church. His beginnings were humble enough to remain in early eighteenth-century obscurity, and it was only after he had come to make his presence felt in the defense of Christiantiy that it was learned that from early youth he had felt the call to the service of Christ, a call which his devout Orthodox parents seemed to have anticipated with strong emphasis on his religious training in childhood.

The prestigious citadel of God known as Mount Athos had beckoned Damaskenos from his remote Bulgarian village, and when he appeared on the Holy Mountain with his more-than-adequate credentials, he was assigned to serve in the monastery of Hilandar. The monastery was not lacking for men of brilliance and devotion, and it took exceptional talent to keep a dedicated monk from melting into the crowd and comparative obscurtiy. Damaskenos had remained for but a short time when it was made evident that his was not destined to be a face in the crowd, and after a relatively brief but outstanding service he was singled out for greater duty in his native country.

Having returned to a Bulgarian monastery affiliated with Mount Athos, the resolute Damaskenos was made overseer of an auxiliary building known as the Metochion, which in addition to serving as a spiritual retreat also saw to the administration of an agrarian economy which over the years had assumed a prosperity that was a national pride. The new overseer was aware of this enterprise that was so eminently successful, but unaware of the fact that the entire affair was slowly being wrenched from its original high purpose of providing for the poor and diverted instead to the high-handed Turks of the area.

Damaskenos discovered to his dismay that the coffers that were being filled by the honest labor of the peasants were being emptied systematically as loans to Turks who made no effort to repay and had no intention of so doing. When questioned, the monks as much as admitted they considered it a tribute to the conqueror and never pressed for payment of these loans in the interest of peace and harmony in the community; but to Damaskenos it was an extortion he could never countenance.

Damaskenos called for an immediate halt to the lending of money to anyone, asserting it to be the task of money-changers, and furthermore called for the repayment of all outstanding loans, some of which had been on the ledgers for years. Even with their cunning and scheming the Turks knew that Damaskenos was well within his rights and the law in calling for them to honor their debts; but honor was lacking in the Turkish character, a trait for which they substituted deception and deceit in every form.

When Damaskenos showed no signs of relenting in his demands, the perfidious debtors hit upon a scheme to rid themselves of the honorable overseer and go back to their evil ways. A Turkish girl was somehow smuggled into the compound, and through subterfuge they arranged to storm the house of Christianity under the pretext of rescuing one of their own who swore she had been abducted. Damaskenos was sentenced to death for this spurious crime but was offered life if he would renounce Christ and become a Muslim. He refused and gave his life for Christ on 16 January 1771. As a postscript, a party celebrating his death with a cruise on the Danube was drowned when the craft capsized in high winds.

The Chains of Saint Peter

Memorabilia of historical figures are kept in museums or sold at auction from time to time and represent articles that in themselves have no monetary value but have such historic and/or sentimental value that something as ordinary as a letter will fetch a handsome figure at auction. Religious mementos, unlike antiques, are considered priceless and are jealously guarded by the Church. The Greek Orthodox Church goes beyond treasuring such artifacts to the extent that they are actually venerated and memorialized by certain feast days, much as the very lives of the persons with whom they are connected are commemorated.

One of the many memorabilia of the Church which are of such significance as to merit a feast day are the chains of St. Peter which, like so many other precious mementos attached to religious figures, have disappeared for all time. Versions of the story of the chains of St. Peter, differ between the Eastern and Western Churches, as a result of which the chains of St. Peter are said to be resting at the Vatican, but unfortunately according to Eastern Church historians the chains have long since been lost.

One of the greatest figures in Christianity, St. Peter, is well known to all as the stalwart apostle who denied the Messiah but went on to become the best remembered missionary of the twelve disciples.

The veneration of the chains came about after the passage in the New Testament, in the Book of Acts (12.6-8), which says: "And when Herod would have brought him forth from a jail in Jerusalem the same night Peter was sleeping between two soldiers, bound with two chains; and the keepers before the door kept the prison. And behold, the Angel of the Lord came upon him and a light shined in the prison; and he smote Peter on the side, and raised him up, saying "Arise quickly." And his chains fell from his hands."

This miraculous act merits a day of commemoration. The Greek Orthodox Church commemorates it on January 16 of each year to remind the faithful of the power of the Lord. Hymns have been composed to observe this solemn occasion and precious indeed are the chains that clattered to the floor, freeing a precious apostle of Jesus Christ.

Accounts of what ensued vary and over the centuries many different versions have appeared which serve only to confuse. However, the Greek Church historians state that the chains of St. Peter were snatched up from the prison floor by unknown persons who were followers of Jesus Christ. They realized the historical and religious significance of these chains and sought a suitable hiding place, revealed to no one but a few of the stoutest supporters of the Messiah.

Exactly where in the sprawling city of Jerusalem the chains of St. Peter remained was kept a secret, but it can be assumed that from generation to generation their hiding place was passed on. Nothing so sacred to Christianity would be ignored. It also is reasonable to assume that Christians were forced for better than three hundred years to keep their beliefs to themselves for fear of persecution and were careful not to risk exposing the whereabouts of something as precious to them as the chains of St. Peter.

It can be further assumed that is was not by accident that only after Constantine the Great had made it safe for Christians to assert themselves that the chains would suddenly surface. In any case, according to church historians the chains were brought to Constantinople where they were put on guarded display in a church erected, appropriately enough, as the Church of St. Peter. For centuries thereafter they were among the many treasures of Orthodoxy, along with the remains of saints and other sacred relics.

It cannot be said for certain how long the chains of St. Peter remained in that one particular spot, since the moving about of precious relics was not uncommon. However, they could not have remained at St. Peter's Church after the church was completely destroyed and reduced to rubble in the final conquest of Constantinople by the Ottoman hordes that brought an end to the glorious Byzantine Empire.

When the dust had settled over the city and the invaders had exhausted themselves in their destructive onslaught, valiant efforts to recover the chains from the ruins proved to be in vain.

January 17

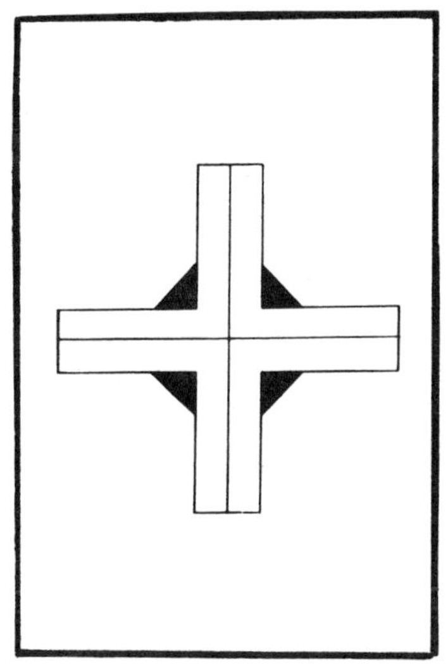

Saint George of Ioannina

The Ottoman forces overran proud Greece nearly half a century before Columbus discovered America, yet at the turn of the nineteenth century the heavy hand of the oppressive Turk was still being felt by every Greek Orthodox while Christian nations looked the other way as their children were being taught of the glory of ancient Greece. A martyr of the nineteenth century, such as St. George of Ioannina, offers mute evidence that the conquest of Greece was not a political act of aggression so much as Islam's futile endeavor to assert its power over Christianity. Only the indomitable courage and deep faith in Jesus Christ, as expressed by St. George and the Greek nation as a whole, prevented an erosion of the Christian Church and spared the rest of Europe the Turkish tentacles so tightly wrapped around the Greek peninsula.

Born in Epiros, Greece in 1802, of humble peasants known by the names of Constantine and Vasiliki, both devout Orthodox, St. George was orphaned at the age of eight. His older brother and sister raised him until he was into his teens and able to fend for himself. Alone in the world, he was easy prey for Turks.

Young George found himself in the employ of a high ranking Turkish officer named Hatzi Abdul, second in command of the army of Pasha Imin. Hired on without pay as a stable boy, he grew to maturity in charge of his well-traveled master, amazingly enough never losing any of his Christian faith which an understanding master never sought to undermine. Nevertheless, those about him called him Giaur Hasan in derision. But eventually the scornful term Giaur was dropped and the Turkish name allowed to stand.

When Pasha Imin was placed in control of Ioannina in 1836, George, ever the faithful servant, accompanied his master to that community whose citizens could not tell whether he was Greek or Turk since his clothes were furnished by his master and he was in the company of those who served him. Seeking out his fellow Greeks, he met a girl named Helen, orphaned like himself. Soon after they were married in the Greek Orthodox Church.

An ill tempered number of the so-called Hotza Turks, on the alert to intimidate Christians, went rushing to authorities to lodge charges against George, since it had been assumed for many years that he was a Muslim. Accused of apostasy for having defected to Christianity, George was hailed into court for trial, in the course of which he appealed to his employer to substantiate the fact that he had not abandoned Christ at any time in favor of Islam. The officer appeared before the magistrate and, after assuring them that in all the years the young man had never been anything other than a Christian, secured his immediate release.

Despite the fact that the success of the Greek War for Independence was tentatively assured, the Turks were in full charge of Ioannina and even more determined to avenge themselves for their increasing losses. By the time George's happy marriage had produced a child, the full fury of the Turk had yet to be spent. George ignored the mounting danger of being trapped into a compromising position by a wily Turk, choosing to ignore them altogether and go about his business.

One night George fell into a sleep so deep that he could not be awakened until late the following day. In the course of this profound slumber, he had dreamed that he would be put to the test for Christ and would become a martyr for his sake. When awakened, George appeared as a man possessed of a divine spirit. He dressed in his finest and for no accountable reason went into the heart of the city.

Not knowing why he chose to go there, nor caring, George walked aimlessly for quite some time, long enough for a group of fanatic Turks to hatch a plot against him. Before the evening was out, he was arrested on renewed charges for treason. Formally charged and brought to trial, he faced a parade of false witnesses whose testimony was irrefutable in the eyes of those who judged him. There was only one way to escape punishment, he was told, and that was to disavow Christ. This young man, who from the age of eight had had no real Christian guidance, firmly refused to turn his back on Jesus Christ. He was hanged on 17 January, the Feast Day of St. Anthony.

January 17

Saint Anthony the Great

The Synod of Nicaea, convened by the Emperor Constantine in A.D. 325, was attended by the most important leaders of Christianity from all corners of the Roman Empire. Second in importance to no other council in church history, this synod was called to answer many crucial questions of theology and dogma. Among the issues discussed was the highly controversial doctrine of the Alexandrian priest Arius, who questioned the divinity of Jesus Christ. The Arian doctrine concerning the relationship of Christ to God the Father was vigorously denounced by the leading prelates as heresy. Among those who spoke in opposition to the Arian heresy was the saintly monk Anthony. His eloquent defense of the Orthodox belief in Christ as true God earned him the title of St. Anthony the Great.

His humble parentage, early orphanage and illiteracy dictated that St. Anthony be lost in the crowds of Egypt, there to live and die in complete obscurity, but divine edict decreed otherwise and he, virtually unaided, made a place for himself. When referred to as "great" or "near great," the group into which St. Anthony falls has to be the one referred to as "great." Ascetics had appeared years before he came upon the scene, but when a knowledgeable Orthodox Christian is asked whom he considers to be the dean of the ascetics, the name of St. Anthony is most apt to be mentioned. Over the years ascetism has been generally associated with spiritual attainment and if any name deserves to lead all the rest, it could easily be the name St. Anthony.

Anthony was born of extremely humble parents in the year A.D. 251 in Coma in middle Egypt. He received no education and when he was orphaned at eighteen he had not yet learned to read and write. In spite of this handicap he sought to learn the meaning of his existence. One day he was greatly impressed by a sermon based on a text from St. Matthew in which Christ said: "If you would be perfect, go, sell what you possess and give to the poor, and you will have treasure in heaven; and come and follow me." Anthony then sold his meager belongings, gave the money to the poor, and went into the Egyptian desert. There he met a group of monks who took him into their care.

In the desert Anthony applied himself diligently to prayer and study. Before he had mastered reading and writing, he is said to have committed to memory several passages from the Bible just by listening to the monks reading to him. Following a period of many years of self-denial, during which he not only acquired a scholarly intimacy with the Scriptures but also a proximity to God, he emerged as a man of piety. As a result, his counsel was sought by both monks and laymen.

When the Synod of Nicaea was convened, Anthony was seventy-four years old and was recognized as a man whose wisdom commanded respect. For this reason, he was invited to attend this historic meeting despite the fact that he held neither title nor power. His eloquent defense of the Orthodox doctrine concerning the person of Jesus Christ was instrumental in weakening the position of Arianism. His witness led to the eventual and complete elimination of Arianism.

Returning to his Egyptian desert monastery, St. Anthony applied himself to refining the rules of monasticism and to establishing a chain of monasteries. He attracted hundreds of monks to asceticism and greatly furthered the propagation of the Christian faith. Anthony's inspired leadership led to the creation of a monasticism in which active participation in the spread of Christianity was fostered through writing and counseling. At the same time, this form of monasticism did not neglect private meditation and prayer.

The monastic rules of St. Anthony, the "patriarch" of monastic life, have served as the basis for countless monasteries. The years of hardship he endured in the desert belie the guidelines set today for longevity; St. Anthony lived to the age of 105. He died in his desert retreat in A.D. 356. St. Anthony, whose name is synonymous with a monasticism of devotion and vigor, is honored on January 17.

January 18 (also May 2)

Saint Athanasios

Although Saint Athanasios was, according to English historian Gibbon, who was the author of the classic *The Decline and Fall of the Roman Empire,* more capable of ruling the Roman Empire than all of the sons of Constantine, nevertheless for all his greatness he remained one of the most tragic figures of the early Christian era. Of small stature and boundless vigor, Athanasios rose to prominence in the hierarchy, yet remained at heart an unworldly and unyielding monk. He was at the center of religious strife in a critical period of early Christianity and was in and out of favor with the emperors perhaps in one of the stormiest career of any clergyman.

Born in Alexandria, Egypt, in A.D. 297, Athanasios was associated with the Alexandrian chancery at an early age, having been ordained deacon in the year 319 and subsequently made a priest. His brillance was shown in his sermons *Against the Arians,* written to answer the widely spreading heresy of Arianism which had been condemned in 318 by a local synod. According to Arius, an elderly priest of Alexandria, Father, Son, and Holy Spirit were three separate essences or substances, which is contrary to Orthodox teaching. The spread of Arianism prompted Emperor Constantine to convene the First Ecumenical Synod in Nicaea (A.D. 325), where Athanasios brilliantly opposed the false doctrine of Arius. Nevertheless, the controversy was to last for another two centuries. The conciliatory tone of the Synod of Nicaea was not enough to put an end to the heresy; Arius would not comply with its decisions and thus fled to Palestine.

At the age of thirty Athanasios was made bishop of Alexandria. Although Arius assured the emperor that he accepted the Creed of Nicaea, the suspicious Athanasios defied the imperial order for Arius' reinstatement. For this he was banished, taking refuge in Treves, France, the place of his first exile, from which he returned in 337 after Constantine's death. The same year though, his enemies conspired to have him again banished by a synod in Antioch. Athanasios, eluding those who would have him imprisoned, traveled to Rome to plead his case before Pope Julius I. Although a council at Sardica favored Athanasios, he did not return from exile until 345, after the death of the usurper Bishop Gregory.

Once again his enemies sprang into action and at a council in Milan in 355, Athanasios was deposed. Thus, after ten years of fruitful rule, he took refuge with the monks of the Egyptian desert whom he greatly admired and whom he had befriended. While with the monks he wrote the *History of the Arian Heresy,* which displays his vehemence and ironic humor.

In 361 Athanasios was again restored as bishop of Alexandria and immediately resumed his struggle against Arianism. After a series of lengthy and complicated discussions, councils, synods, and other forums of debate, a credal formula was adopted which satisfied those whose middle view led them to be called Semi-Arians. Peace had hardly arrived when another storm came in the form of the regeneration of paganism under the Emperor Julian the Apostate. In the autumn of 363, Athanasios was again put to flight, only to return a short time later, after the death of the emperor. He enjoyed a comparative calm until he was removed by Emperor Valens during another resurgence of paganism. Four months later, the aging bishop was recalled and allowed to live out his life in comparative peace.

Greatly admired by the Orthodox and hated by the heretics he so adamantly opposed, Athanasios stirred the emotions of the Christians as perhaps no other Father of the Church. His theological doctrine is clear and uncomplicated in the strictest Orthodox tradition, and his encouragement of monasticism was a labor of love. He died 2 May 373.

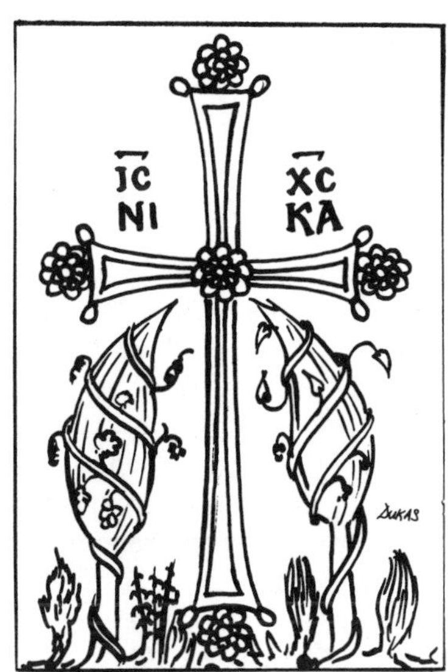

January 19

St. Mark of Ephesos

Early in the fifteenth century, the incursions of the Ottoman Turkish forces into the Byzantine Empire menaced the very existence of Christianity. Indeed, Orthodox Christianity in the Balkans and the Middle East might very well have lost its indentity but for the efforts of its stalwarts, chief among whom was Mark of Ephesos. Although Orthodoxy owes a debt of gratitude to many devout and brave souls who helped to preserve her ancient faith, deepest thanks must be reserved for St. Mark.

Scion of a distinquished family, Mark was born in the year 1392 with a lineage which promised him prominence from the moment of his birth. His father served with distinction in the imperial government and his mother was the daughter of one of Constantinople's outstanding physicians. The family honor and tradition were carried out by Mark, but on a higher plateau he chose to live and work for the glory of God and his Son. Displaying rare brillance of mind and profound religious conviction, he ascended the ladder of religious leadership and was elevated to the post of metropolitan of Ephesos, a prestigious spiritual center of Orthodoxy. Among his accomplishments was an impressive series of writings on church affairs which for insight, perceptiveness, and devotion may have been equalled but never surpassed.

At this time the Turkish threat was very great: the borders of the empire were being systematically reduced by the invaders who, in fact, were within striking distance of the Byzantine capital. The Orthodox Church was thus compelled to seek assistance from the pope of Rome, whose army of trained mercenaries would, they hoped, provide much needed military support. In response to this appeal, Rome convoked a council in the cities of Ferrara and Florence. Representatives from all over Orthodoxy, including the

Orthodox of Russia, the Holy Land, and the Ecumenical Patriarchate, were in attendance. The two great figures of Eastern Christendom, Emperor John VIII and Patriarch Joseph of Constantinople, had traveled to Ferrara for the council and had brought with them the Church's most eloquent defender, Mark of Ephesos.

The meetings were to extend for months, from 1438 to 1439, primarily due to an impasse stemming from the pope's insistence that no military assistance would be forthcoming unless the Orthodox Church agreed to a unity with Rome under the papal stipulation. This thinly disguised extortion no doubt contributed to the death of the disillusioned Patriarch Joseph, which in turn threw the meetings into greater turmoil. The pressure to submit to Rome, exercised directly by the Byzantine emperor and indirectly by the papal agents, was so great that most of the Orthodox representatives signed the Articles of Union. The emperor believed that the Byzantine Empire could only be saved from the Turks with papal assistance.

Mark of Ephesos, however, staunchly refused to submit to Rome. Storming out of the council in protest, he vowed never to submit to what he thought was little other than tyranny. He returned to Ephesos to lead a movement against so-called unity which Rome contrived. Mark firmly upheld the purity of the Orthodox faith which had not yielded to any external influence since the time of Christ. He was instrumental in rallying the faithful to a clear defiance of papal pressure and a reaffirmation of Orthodox principles. Subsequent events saw the failure of this infamous attempt for unity, the exile of some of the metropolitans, and the return of those who had strayed from the Orthodox faith. In a time when Orthodoxy sorely needed a show of spiritual fortitude, Mark of Ephesos scorned the mailed fist. For this he was banished by the emperor, whose concern for his city was greater than his concern for the purity of Orthodoxy. After two years of banishment, Mark of Ephesos returned to great acclaim in Constantinople where he died in 1444.

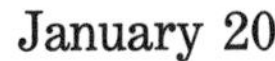

January 20

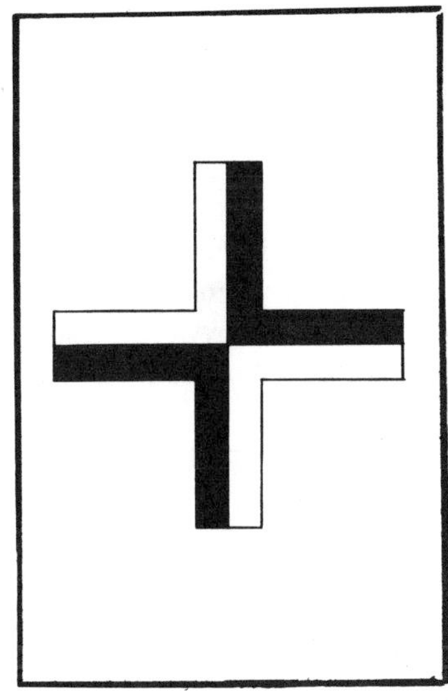

St. Euthymios the Great

Of the vast army of saints down through the ages, one of the few who merited the honor of being dubbed "the Great" was a comparatively obscure Armenian whose life for Christ commenced in the fourth century and carried over into the fifth, embracing almost 100 years of a glorious life in the most pious example of being cast in the image of the Creator.

This saint was born to a couple named Paul and Dionysia after the Lord had answered their fervent prayers for a child just as they were about to give up this cherished hope after many years of a barren marriage. The great joy of having been blessed with a son was as great as the elation they experienced when visited by an angel of the Lord who advised them to name the child Euthymios, a synonym for joy and exaltation. This divine visitation foreordained that the offspring was to be a cradle-to-the-grave servant of God.

Euthymios received his early religious training at the hands of no less a person than the bishop of Melitene, Armenia, whose name was Ephrotes and whose repute as a holy man had already been well-established when Paul and Dionysia brought their child to him. The good bishop did not fail to notice the touch of grace that was already evident in his young charge and schooled the boy in all aspects of Christian theology.

At an age when most young men were applying themselves to the acquisition of material wealth and standing, Euthymios gave himself over completely to the service of Jesus Christ and was ordained a priest by his mentor of many years. The bishop had hoped that Euthymios would remain to assist him in the work of the church, but Euthymios felt the call to a greater service in acquiring not a standing in the community but a posture which could bring a closer proximity to God and because of this holy urge was drawn to the Monastery of St. Polyeuthes.

It was at the monastery that Euthymios found the solemn joy of the nearness of God through meditation, prayer and service, and felt for the first time that inward mysticism which was to stand him in good stead in a long lifetime of service to God and to his fellow man. It was a full five years of complete immersion into asceticism of the cloister before he finally emerged into the company of men, carrying with him an aura of holiness fully evident in his every gesture and deed. He had retreated to submit to the will of God and returned to find the will of God was within him.

His closest friend and confidant was another holy man named Theoktistos with whom he discoursed at length on matters of religion and at whose insistence he finally ventured out to be of service among the people. The very presence of Euthymios in a town square commanded the respect of all around him, including those who had little or no religious belief. To the Christians whose belief was genuine, however, he seemed like a messenger sent straight from Heaven, and he proceeded to brighten the lives of the villagers wherever he went.

At one point the will of God that was within Euthymios was made clearly evident even to the skeptics. A young Arab, paralyzed by an accident, was carried to this holy man for help, and the help he received was witnessed by a small band who stood in wonderment at what actually took place. Without ceremony and the usual laying of hands, Euthymios simply knelt in prayer for God's assistance with the stricken lad, and when Euthymios stood up, the young Arab stood up with him. If there were any disbelievers among the onlookers, they had a change of heart when the former cripple walked away.

The only other recorded instance of the power of Euthymios tells of an incident in which the Empress Eudokia, widow of the emperor Theodosios II, came to Euthymios for help. The holy man told her that her time was not far off and that she should abandon the heresies of the Monophysites. A few months later the transformed empress died.

Euthymios died on 20 January 473 at the age of ninety-six with a man named Savvas, destined for greatness himself, at the side of his deathbed.

January 21

Saint Neophytos

The ancient Greeks were looking in the right direction when they gazed toward the summit of lofty mountains such as Mt. Olympos as the dwelling place of their gods; but for centuries the focus of the Greeks was short. It was the apostles of Christ who extended their sight to the Kingdom of Heaven. Not long after St. Paul's appearance on Mars Hill before a gathering of the Athenians, Zeus and his fellow gods were supplanted by human beings who literally dwelled on the mountain, tranquilly searching for the company of God through the power of Jesus Christ. Hundreds of years after the appearance of Christ, another Mt. Olympos, this one in Asia Minor was transformed from the campsite of imaginary supernaturals to the quiet abode of pious monks.

The slopes of Mt. Olympos came to be occupied by many pious men, monks, hermits, and prelates, whose combined spiritual efforts were to glorify the Christian religion. In some instances, miracles were worked through the Holy Spirit. In the era before Mt. Athos became famous, Mt. Olympos achieved great renown and produced many extraordinary spiritual figures, among whom was the little-known Neophytos.

Neophytos was born into a society of early Christians whose depth of faith and whose sacrifices were of such magnitude that it is little wonder that all Christians of the first three centuries were not recognized as saints. The quiet courage of Neophytos in the face of unspeakable horror set the example for his contemporaries in their unshakable faith.

Under circumstances which would have discouraged one of weaker will, Neophytos enthusiastically accepted the word of Christ at an early age. Although Christians were cruelly persecuted at that time, he pursued the happiness of the Christian religion with undiminishing zeal. From very early youth he participated in the church services which the faithful held underground to escape their persecutors. He grew to comprehend fully the word of God and the truth of Jesus Christ. One day an angel of the Lord appeared in a vision to the parents of the young Neophytos and advised them that their son would be called to the service of God. The very next day Neophytos approached his parents and said that he felt he should enter the monastic life to find God.

Neophytos chose the heights of Olympos, thousands of feet above sea level, as his new dwelling place. When not in the company of the many monks who sought sanctuary there, he lived in a skete of his own where he strove to attain the "perfect life" through piety, asceticism, prayer, and meditation. His commitment to God was total, yet never did he lose sight of his responsibility to his fellow Christians, whom he served with care and devotion. While reading the Scriptures one day, he was visited by a holy messenger who informed him that his parents were ailing and near death. Ignoring the fact that the most coveted prey of the pagans was a holy man of Mt. Olympos, he hastened to his parents in the city of Nicaea, comforting them until each had passed on.

The watchful eye of a centurion brought the gentle Neophytos to trial and swift punishment for his Christianity. When Neophytos refused to disavow Christ and worship the pagan idols, he was subjected to inhuman tortures. Afterwards he was thrown into an arena in which the wild animals refused to attack him. Neophytos earned the martyr's crown when a soldier's lance ended his earthly life on January 21.

There have been countless imitators of St. Neophytos, many of them well-meaning and deserving; but most of whom very soon discovered that mountain-climbing did not necessarily bring a closer proximity to God and, thus discouraged, turned to more worldly and safer pursuits. Neophytos enjoyed a proximity to God at any earthly level and his sacrifice would have been made in the name of the Lord at any height or any depth. Scaling a height for the Lord was one gesture; giving his life to Christ was another.

January 21

Saint Maximos the Confessor

To the average communicant, the dogmatics and abstract theological philosophy of the Christian religion are preferably left to the clergy. They are content to go to church on Sunday to worship Jesus Christ but they need to be reminded that except for men such as St. Maximos the Confessor there would be a variety of doctrines in the Orthodox world instead of the one true, solid, and virtually unaltered Greek Orthodox faith which St. Maximos, among others, refused to see splintered.

Born of nobility in A.D. 580, Maximos was that rare combination of statesman, philosopher, and acknowledged religious leader who was well established when he quite suddenly resigned his post as chief secretary to Byzantine Emperor Heraklios. Discontent preceeded Maximos' action but he did not abandon this lofty post solely because of this, but primarily because he preferred to devote all of his time to the Savior. The underlying cause of his departure was his anticipation of taking issue with Heraklios who was leaning toward acceptance of Monotheletism, an heretical interpretation generating the false notion that our Lord and Savior Jesus Christ had but one will — the divine. That was diametrically opposed to the long accepted Orthodox doctrine that Christ had two wills — the divine and human.

Maximos not only turned his back on the class into which he was born, but gave away his wordly goods for distribution among the underprivileged before entering a monastery. No ordinary monk, he wielded a powerful pen and began to write denouncing Monothelitism, He was elevated to abbot of the monastery and, relieved of temporal chores, stepped up his campaign against the heretics whom he assailed with unrelenting rhetoric which remains to this day as masterpieces of literature. He saw to it that enough copies of his treatise were distributed to the hierarchy, as well as clergy and influential laymen.

From time to time, nomadic Persian tribes would besiege the isolated monastery, with attacks upon the cloister increasing with such alarming frequency and intensity that finally the beleaguered Maximos slipped out to take refuge in Alexandria. The patriarch there, however, proved to be as troublesome to Maximos as the Persians had been because under the influence of Emperor Heraklios he had embraced Monotheletism.

The death of Emperor Heraklios in no way weakened the position of Monothelitism since his successor Constans not only accepted the heresy but issued his infamous "Typos" Declaration and thus formally accepted it. The heresy was like an infectious disease, spreading throughout the empire until it had infected Patriarch Sergios of Constantinople, to be passed on to his successor Pyrros, as well as several members of the hierarchy and a number of public figures. This imposing array of opposition placed Maximos in a difficult position, but undaunted he sought to regroup his forces and rid the Church of this divisive heresy.

Maximos carried his noble cause to Rome, where he found favor with the city's bishop who was in total agreement with him. The pope formed a council of all the bishops of Italy who issued their unanimous denunciation of the heresy. This action so displeased Emperor Constans that he summoned before him the bishop of Rome, the crusading Maximos, together with an aide by the name of Anastasios, and others. After listening first to the bishop of Rome, the emperor's answer was banishment. He also sent Maximos into exile.

There was no doubt in any one's mind by whose order Maximos was systematically put to torture, particularly when he was told that the punishment would end when he embraced Monotheletism. Maximos would not bend to the royal will no matter how severe the punishment. His anger growing with each refusal, the wretched emperor ordered that the right hand of Maximos be severed and that his tongue be cut out as well to assure he would never again preach or write. Maximos, now eighty, survived this horrible mutilation but continued his crusade through his disciple, Anastasios, until he died. Maximos was vindicated in 680, some years after his death, when the Sixth Ecumenical Synod, convened by Emperor Constantine, outlawed the heresy of Monotheletism.

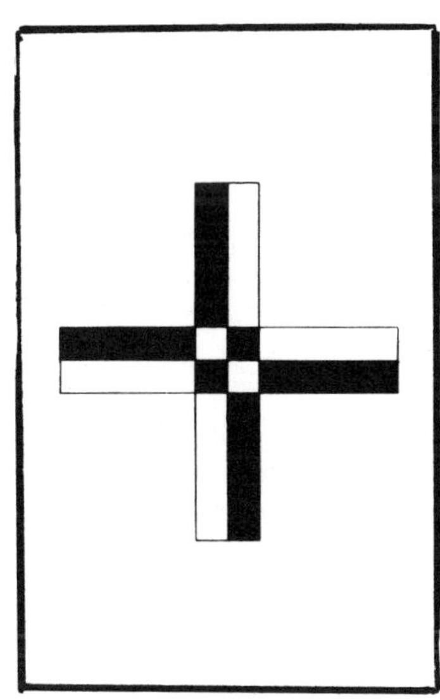

January 22

Saint Timothy

To a man called Timothy fell the solemn honor of being the recipient of two letters from the great apostle St. Paul, who wrote these sacred epistles in his final hours before his martyrdom, while a captive of Nero. Now known as the Pastoral Epistles, they are the two books of the New Testament entitled First Timothy and Second Timothy. In them are set forth regulations for many aspects of church worship and a bestowal of apostolic trust upon a young man with whom St. Paul chose to "labor and suffer reproach" in spreading the word of Christ, and whom St. Paul embraced as a son.

With the mantle of responsibility for spreading the word of Jesus Christ having been spread by no less than St. Paul over the shoulders of the young Timothy, it is enough that the great St. Paul's letters to him form a part of the New Testament and thus make sacred the very name Timothy. But if any reverence be fully accorded St. Timothy, it is because he assumed that sacred responsibility with such dedication that chapters of the Holy Bible bear his name, a name synonymous with Christianity itself.

He was born in Lystra in Lyconia of a pagan Greek father and a Jewish mother named Eunice. His grandmother was a Christian and it was perhaps through her influence and teaching that he came to follow Christ.

When the Apostle Paul visited Lystra, the young Timothy was already a full member of the Christian Church and after the two discussed the many difficulties Christianity was facing, the younger man expressed a desire to serve as a missionary, despite its hazards. It was after the departure of Barnabus and Mark that Paul summoned Timothy to accompany him as a colleague in the cause of Christ.

About a quarter of a century after Christ had died, Timothy

and Paul traveled to Europe, accompanied by Silas, in a missionary task of staggering proportion. In most areas theirs was at best a thankless job, but with the zeal born of a profound love of the Savior they succeeded in securing a foothold in spiritually darkened corners. They brought this about with administrative skill in the face of odds which might have discouraged less hardy souls. In a fury of religious oratory, they summoned thousands to the fold and established churches of God where for centuries people had worshipped mere objects or beasts out of fear and superstition.

When Paul was summoned to Athens, he commissioned Timothy to carry the word of Christ to Corinth, Thessalonike, and Phillipi. To these areas Timothy displayed his talents to the fullest in establishing a nucleus of Christian churches which became the cornerstone from which Christianity has grown to its present day proportions. With the help of subordinate apostles, he instilled in the populace a love of the Savior. Under his leadership churches were built, the form of worship was set forth, and capable ministry for all services was established.

Overcoming obstacles strewn in his missionary path, Timothy made his way to Ephesos. There he was established as bishop of that city and took on the formidable task of putting Christ into the hearts of people who lived in fear and awe of the pagan god Artemis.

The pagans grew more and more resentful of the presence of Timothy and out of their hatred evolved an aura of terror. One evening, when one of their eerie rituals had spilled out into the streets and had carried them out in front of the Church of Christ, Timothy emerged to denounce them, whereupon the frenzied mob stoned him to death.

Timothy died a martyr for Christ on 22 January A.D. 72.

January 23

Ss. Clement and Agathangelos

The hapless conspirator against a queen of England (while dangling at the end of a hangman's noose) was disemboweled while there was yet life within him, a practice to which the royal house ordered a halt once and for all. But in the third century, an indomitable Christian defender of the faith met with all manner of cruelty calculated to bring him to the brink of death and back again by a succession of cruel monarchs who took fiendish delight in torturing a man whose only guilt was the preaching of love of the Savior.

The name of this venerated saint was Clement, more than half of whose noble life was spent in degradation and heinous abuse. Nevertheless, he held out to the end of a quarter century of intermittent torture in a display that only a man endowed with a divine grace could have endured for so prolonged a period of agony and remain steadfast in his allegiance to Jesus Christ.

Clement was a boy of twelve when his mother, a devout Christian who had foreordained the life of suffering for her son, fell ill and followed her husband in death, leaving Clement to the care of monks in a monastery near the city of Ankyra (Ankara). It was not unusual for monks to be entrusted with the care and education of a young orphan until he could fend for himself in the outside world. But the more Clement remained in the cloister, the greater he felt the urge to serve Jesus Christ. By the time he was twenty, his eight years of training convinced his elders that he was destined for greatness, although none could have foreseen the burden the brilliant young man would have to bear.

Clement served the city of Ankyra with such distinction that the Christians looked on him as their spiritual leader, one whose incessant efforts for the children and the underprivileged led to his appointment, at the tender age of twenty-one, to the post of bishop of the city of Ankyra and its province. The public exposure of such a Christian luminary inevitably drew the attention of envious pagan elements whose mounting hostility was ignored by a bishop pledged to preach the faith of Jesus Christ.

The youthful Bishop Clement was not yet twenty-two when he was snatched from his growing number of Christian friends by the vengeance-seeking pagans who set a course of utter misery for the plucky bishop that was to last an agonizing twenty-eight years. The records show that Clement was subjected to abuse and debasement under two Roman emperors, the infamous Diocletian, 284-304 and the diabolical Maximianus, 286-305, in a parade of horror fashioned by no less than nine regional rulers.

In a relay team of torturers that seemed endless, the indestructible Clement faced a formidable array of persuaders who succeeded only in convincing themselves that their quarry was the superhuman product of sorcerers. They did not realize that he drew his strength and will to resist from the Divinity they blindly refused to acknowledge. The redoubtable bishop was taken from city to city in the empire where he was not only tortured, but held up to ridicule and scorn for his beliefs. This was calculated to stem the rising tide of Christianity; but rather than be discouraged, the onlooker was drawn closer to Christianity at the sight of the Christian valor of a hierarch who refused to abandon the Messiah.

Clement's parade of infamy led him to Rome where he was cast into prison. There he met a fellow Christian named Agathangelos whom he embraced with the mutual love of the Messiah and each other. While authorities pondered the next move, the two Christian prisoners comforted each other. When finally led from the prison, they appeared so calm and resolute it was decided not to risk embarrassment in the capital city. Instead they were taken to a small town in the province of Galatia where they were systematically put to every form of torture; they were stretched on the dreaded rack, whipped at the stake, seared with hot irons, and eventually flung on beds of nails.

The last of the rulers wearied of this deadly game and had Clement and Aganthangelos returned to Ankyra where Clement had served as bishop. They were beheaded, bringing to a close one of the grimmest chapters in ecclesiastical history on January 23.

January 24

Paphserios, Theodotion, and Paul

To three brothers of the third century, extreme devotion to the Savior was a family affair, a family exceeded in numbers by the family of St. Basil but unsurpassed by anyone for heroism in the long history of the Church of Jesus Christ. These three brothers were named Paphserios, Theodotion, and Paul, each of whom rendered a service to Jesus Christ with a bravery that in the military would have covered their chests with medals, but each of whom made the supreme sacrifice for which he received not the gilded medals of the military but the golden halo of sainthood.

The three brothers, the sons of hard-working parents who could barely eke out a livelihood from the unyielding soil, were born in the area of Egypt now known as the Suez. What little gains they made with their small herds and sparse gardens were methodically taken from them by the tax collectors who made certain they could acccumulate the wealth from those whose small bribes made them virtually tax exempt. The wealth of Egypt in those days was concentrated in the hands of the royalty, corrupt merchants and tradesmen, and as the rich got richer, the poor got poorer.

The brothers labored from early childhood to keep the family from starvation but never lost heart, clinging to the hope that somehow their lot would be improved. They were also aided by a strong Christian spirit imbued by parents who never ceased to be thankful for their meager fare and were sustained by a faith in Jesus Christ. Of the three, the most defiant was Theodotion who railed at the misery forced upon them by an oppressive state and an insensitive aristocracy. The other two were more resigned to their fate and much more devout; as a result, instead of resentment they felt closer to the Savior and often voiced a desire to serve him to a greater degree.

When the parents died, the three sons decided to give up this harsh living, but for different purposes. Paphserios and Paul answered the call to serve Jesus Christ as monks but no amount of persuasion could convince their brother Theodotion to do the same. While his brothers went off to the sanctuary of a monastery, Theodotion took to the hills for a far different purpose, seeking not the company of monks but the company of outlaws whom he sought to join but only for the purpose of robbing the rich to give to the poor of his class.

Paphserios and Paul entered a monastery and over a period of years became devout servants of the Lord, servants who would venture forth from time to time to offer spiritual assistance to Christians who dared not hold services publicly for fear of being caught up in a wave of state persecution. Wherever they went they heard of the daring and resourcefulness of a bold highwayman named Theodotion who would rob tradesmen and merchants while managing to elude every trap set for him. Theodotion was doing more for the poor than his devout brothers were but not in the same approving manner that the Lord intended the poor to be helped.

Theodotion was in his hideout planning his next raid when word came to him that his brothers had been taken prisoner to stand trial for their Christianity, a trial which could have but one outcome. He made for the city in which the tribunal was to sit in judgment, and disguising himself, he walked about to see what he could do to effect his brothers' release or escape. It was not as easy as robbing a caravan. The distraught Theodotion went to the trial to see what judgment would be passed on his brothers, but as he looked about, he realized the hopelessness of the situation.

When Paphserios and Paul were brought forward, Theodotion could hardly restrain himself from rushing forward to acknowledge them in an embrace, but for the moment he sat still, anguished at the sight of his beloved brothers being at the mercy of a merciless tribunal. There was the usual reading of the charges, after which the chief magistrate railed at the brothers, belaboring them with abusive language and condemning them to death. At this point Theodotion charged forward and embraced his brothers, turning to identify himself and berating the onlookers as fools. He joined his brothers in death, but somehow it is felt that he was forgiven as was the thief alongside the Savior on the Cross. All three brothers share a commemoration on January 24.

January 24

Saint Xeni

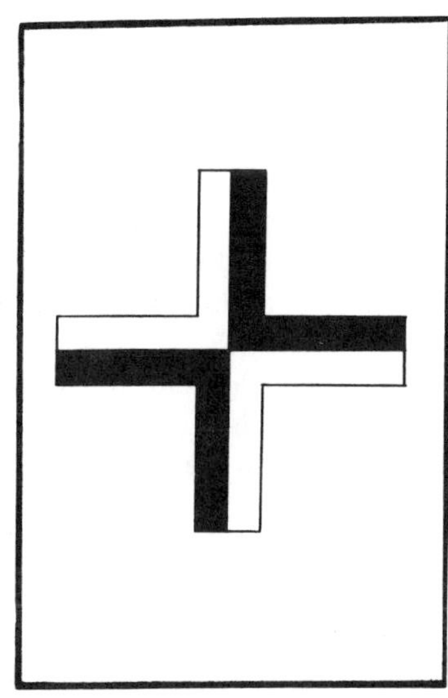

Child prodigies are not restricted to artistic expression in areas such as music, literature and art but have been seen in the expression of a deep religious commitment, a prime example of which was St. Xeni, who evinced a sense of piety at an age when children were expected to play with blocks or games of hide and seek. A serious child almost from birth, she hid from nothing but evil and sought no one but the Savior. William Blake, who was a poet, artist and visionary, claimed he saw God in a tree when he looked out the window one day at the age of four. At the same age, there is no question that there was a touch of divine grace in Xeni, although she was never known to have remarked that she saw God.

Xeni is known to have been born into an upper class family of Rome and to have been baptized with the name of Eusebia. She also has been known to have taken life very seriously, harboring a piety which went undetected even by her parents, who placed more emphasis on her social training than on her spiritual guidance, despite the fact that they were dedicated members of the Christian faith. Church attendance for her family was regular and sincere but lacked the intensity felt by the daughter, which escaped the notice of the parents even when she joined them in their many acts of charity, which they could well afford.

Considered unsmiling and distant by youngsters who tried to reach her heart, the quite personable and lovely Eusebia endeared herself to the community as a whole who construed her quiet solitude as difference and not the indifference seen by those who sought to probe the inner reaches of her mind which was preoccupied with thoughts of the Savior. As she grew into her teens, however, the comparative isolation which she found from time to time grew more and more elusive as families gathered closer to hers with sons who would have her as a bride.

It was the family that arranged the nuptials, and she was barely seventeen when a husband was selected for her from among the many eligible young men of Eusebia's social level. She had made a decision for Christ and rather than create any unpleasant scenes which might mark disobedience to her parents' will, she observed that calling she heard to a higher will, and she decided to quietly slip away. With the assistance of a servant and confidante, she arranged passage on a boat bound for the Holy Land and left unnoticed with some regret that she had to leave her parents in this manner but with high hopes of fulfilling her lofty ambition.

Eusebia's first order of business was a visit to the tomb of Jesus Christ where she paused in prayer for divine guidance and for forgiveness for having offended her parents. After several such prayerful visits, she, for reasons known only to her, left the Holy Land to go to the island of Kos in the Aegean where she met a highly respected monk named Paul, who saw at a glance the grace within this gentle creature of God whom he dubbed "Xeni," meaning the stranger, which is what she considered herself, and the name she adopted from there on.

Paul sensed that there were great things in store for this visitor to his island and arranged to have her settle in an isolated hut which afforded her privacy and the solitude she needed for prayer and meditation. She emerged from isolation after a period of time with an aura of the Divine so evident that Paul urged her to make herself known on the island to do what she could for a people that knew little but poverty. She not only brought to these islanders a rare kind of spiritual guidance, but a rarer still power of healing which made her the cynosure of all who came to revere her in life as one sent from heaven.

When her friend and benefactor, the monk Paul, was made bishop of the area, he asked Xeni to become a deaconess of the Church, an invitation which she hesitated to accept until a contingent of islanders prevailed upon her to put aside her doubts and assist the bishop who would in turn assist her in doing God's work. Forewarned in a vision of the imminence of her death, Xeni walked out of the village quietly to her bed and fell asleep in the Lord on January 24. The beam of light that shone brilliantly in her room as she died left no doubt as to her ascent to Heaven.

January 25

St. Gregory the Theologian

Of the twenty centuries since the birth of Christ no single century has had crowded into it so many great events as the fourth century, which witnessed a fragmented Christendom of God. Were it not for the efforts of such men, Christianity would not have become the spiritual haven of mankind it is today. The fabric of Christendom was woven into its strength and beauty of character by the threads of men such as St. Gregory the Theologian, who became one of the four great doctors of the Church during this era, along with Basil the Great, John Chrysostom and Athanasios the Great. He is further remembered as one of the three so-called Cappadocian Fathers, an honor he shares with Basil and Gregory of Nyssa. He is also recognized as the champion of Orthodoxy against the heretical doctrine of Arianism.

The son of a bishop for whom he was named, Gregory was born in Arianzos in Cappadocia, Asia Minor, in 329. He was educated in Caesaria and then in Athens, where he met Basil with whom he became close friends linked in a common resolve to serve Christ. At the suggestion of Basil, the two friends became monastics at a retreat in Pontos, where each embarked on a spiritual journey that was to lead them both to greatness. It was with some degree of reluctance, however, that Gregory left the monastery to be ordained into the priesthood to serve as an assistant to his father, the bishop of Nazianzos. The son's brilliance as a preacher outshone his father's. When barely thirty years old, he won acclaim throughout the region as a mighty warrior in the fight against paganism and heresy.

It was largely through the influence of Gregory that his friend Basil was made bishop of Caesaria. In the process, he himself was made bishop of the relatively unimportant town of Sasima, a post he never sought and in which he never served, preferring to remain with his father in Nazianzos. He took over the church of Nazianzos after the death of his father in 374. With the loss of his father, he had a longing to return to asceticism in some retreat, there to meditate, pray, and interpret the Scriptures. He was allowed to go to the seclusion of Seleucia in Isauria, where his tenure as an eremite was short-lived.

After the death of the Arian Emperor Valens, followed closely by the death of Gregory's friend Basil, Gregory was called to Constantinople. He was to head the reorganization of the Orthodox Church which had been torn asunder by the heresy of Arianism from within and by the harassment of pagans without. In the course of this holy work, he achieved distinction as an orator, traditionalist, and a crusader that earned him the title of "Theologian" despite the opposition of Maximos the Cynic, who had been set up against him by the bishop of Alexandria.

When the Orthodox Emperor Theodosios came to power in 380, Gregory assumed the direction of the magnificent Church of Hagia Sophia, the most prestigious house of God in all Christendom. While director of this mighty church, Gregory took part in a synod held in Constantinople in 381 to settle the differences among the prelates of the Church. Known as the Second Ecumenical Synod, it resolved the issues and voted to accept Gregory as patriarch of Constantinople. It further added its official support to the Nicene doctrine which was championed at the First Synod in Nicaea.

For as long as he held the post of spiritual leader of Orthodoxy the gallant Gregory served with honor and dignity. Moreover, he was the instrument of God in unifying the Church into a cohesive unit that could withstand any internal or external pressure. He grew weary of the personal attacks that are the occupational hazard of a patriarch and after a moving farewell address, he retired to live out his days in meditation, writing, and prayer. He died 25 January 388.

But there can be no underestimating the value of the unrelenting service of St. Gregory to the Savior. St. Gregory earned the title of "Theologian" by reason not only of his knowledge of theology but by direct application of that knowledge to an eminent degree.

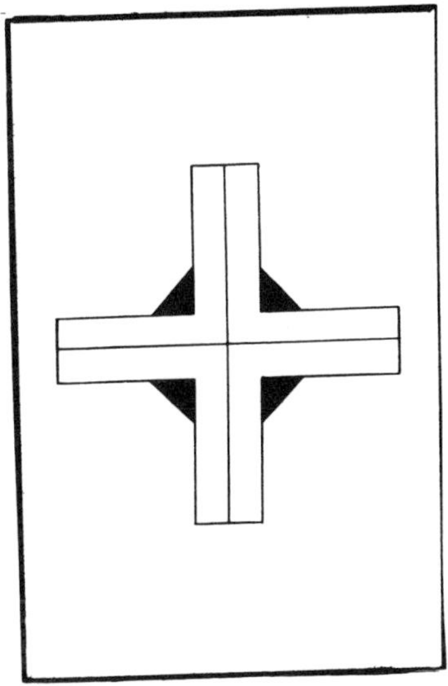

January 25

Puplios the Ascetic

The mystical land of Persia was not very fertile ground for Christianity, which had to compete with assorted cults and mystical cultures that varied from tribe to tribe and in the nearly 800 years since Xerxes the Great had seen little or no advance in its civilization. Although the number of Christians of twentieth-century Persia were sparse indeed and rarer still were the saints of Christianity from this hostile land, there was a man named Puplios who was dubbed the ascetic and for very good reason.

Born in Zeugma, Persa, Puplios mastered a number of languages out of sheer necessity since the area was populated by tribes who spoke different tongues.

The region which Puplios grew up was populated by people whose language was Syrian and whose culture was far in advance of those of their brethren in the interior. Christian missionaries had come and gone for more than three hundred years but not with the success that had been reached in the name of Christ in countries such as Greece, whose advanced culture allowed them to abandon their false idols in favor of Jesus Christ. It is to the everlasting credit that Puplios was to attain the stature of a Christian saint in a small Christian body that was frail in comparison to its stronger brothers to the west. Not only that, he was one of the hardy Christian souls of that era who was not a tortured martyr but whose proximity to God was such that it was not martyrdom but extreme piety which placed him among those favored by God.

As few as the Christians were in that corner of Persia where Puplios was raised, fewer still were the number who could lay claim to any sizable estate. By the standards of the day, Puplios was a wealthy man, whose father had herds of cattle, sheep, and goats and whose abundant acreage boasted of gardens and vineyards. Chores on this kind of property were endless but Puplios not only was of great help to his father but also found the time to become a very literate scholar, in the course of which he found the truth of Christ. His spare moments were spent reading the Bible in its original language of Greek, which he had mastered with other languages. He found himself ever yearning to forsake the temporal pastures in order to be alone with God.

When his father and mother had passed on, Puplios had to decide between his inheritance and the Savior, but it was an easy choice. He disposed of his holdings by doling out everything he had to the poor except enough money with which to build a monastery. It was within the confines of a monastery that he hoped to reach the heights of spiritual attainment. He not only bought the materials needed but helped in building a durable edifice in which he was joined by monks in numbers sufficient to fill the cells and take up the holy work to which he had pledged himself.

Puplios had built individual cells so that each monk was assured his private moments, but in each door was a grille into which Puplios would peer and if the monk was not engaged in prayer or meditation, he would rap for admittance and ask to join in prayer for a short time, then remind the monk that he should carry on alone what each had done together—pay tribute to God. His asceticism called for extreme self denial.

Puplios' monastery took on aspects of holiness which otherwise would have been denied were it not for the strict discipline observed by all the monks, especially Puplios who demanded more of himself than he did of others. His austerity was such that he developed a lean hardihood that suggested that divine nourishment sustained them. If there were any shortcomings in the ranks of the monks of Puplios, obesity was not one of them. The aura of holiness was so evident that many were attracted to the monastery where they were welcomed by men of God. When visitors left, they were much more enriched in their spiritual lives than when they had first entered the grounds.

Fasting and prayer alone were not the only observances at the monastery of Puplios, who had become abbot and leader of the monks. The services held were inspirational to all, monk and visitor alike, and when conducted by Puplios the spirit of Heaven seemed to descend on the gathering. He died on A.D. 380 and lies somewhere along his beloved Euphrates River.

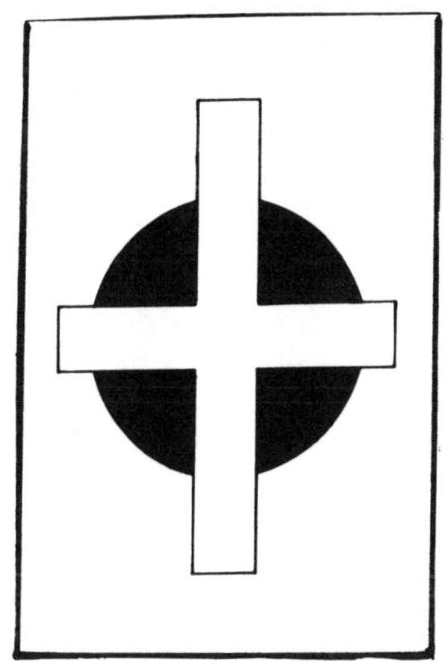

Xenophon, Maria and Sons, John and Arkadios

A tragically splintered family that regrouped after years of involuntary separation to serve Jesus Christ jointly, as they had separately with such dedication as to achieve individual sainthood, comprised one of the proudest families in the era of the Byzantine Emperor Justinian, the monarch generally considered to be most responsible for the magnificent Cathedral of Hagia Sophia of Constantinople. The father of this renowned group was named Xenophon, a well-to-do senator. His wife, Maria, bore him two sons named John and Arkadios, both of whom shared with their parents an intense dedication to the Messiah.

When it was decided that the sons complete their studies in one of the most advanced schools of the empire, they took passage on a ship bound for one of the greater institutions of Beirut, Lebanon. The vessel must have been something less than seaworthy, for in a sudden storm the craft virtually disintegrated in heavy seas. It is not known how many survived, but it is known that both John and Arkadios managed to cling to separate pieces of timber and were parted by mounting swells and swirling currents that eventually placed them miles from each other.

John managed to clamber onto a heavy timber which, after several days of drifting, washed ashore near the city of Melphythan, not too far removed from the ancient city of Tyre. Meanwhile, Arkadios was carried to a point of land several miles south of the city of Tyre, there to kneel in prayer of thanksgiving for his deliverance and for the salvation of the soul of his brother, whom he presumed had been lost at sea. Several miles to the north John was offering identical prayers, unaware that, like himself, the life of his brother had been spared.

The battered John, barely alive after his ordeal, was nourished back to health by the monks of a monastery of the desert. They so impressed the devout John that, after fully recovering, he decided he belonged by divine edict in this sanctuary. Turning his back on his past life, he took up the rigorous regimen of monasticism and ultimately proved himself to be a monk in the highest tradition of complete service to Jesus Christ.

Two years elapsed before Arkadios, who had a vision following his recovery that somewhere his brother was alive and well, began a search for his brother. During this search Arkadios also came under the influence of monks and entered a monastery, ultimately demonstrating the same complete dedication to the Savior as his brother did. As time passed Arkadios doubted his brother's survival, but he never weakened in his faith.

An itinerant monk happened to visit Constantinople where he sought out Xenophon and Maria. The monk suggested to them that the survivor of a shipwreck known to him as Arkadios, whom he had met in the Monastery of St. Savvas of Jerusalem, might be their lost son. Xenophon and Maria immediately set out for the Holy Land, and it was more than mere chance that at about this time their other son, John, decided to visit the Holy Land to pray at the tomb of Jesus Christ. An unseen hand led all four members of the family to the tomb of Christ where they met in tearful but joyful reunion and knelt in prayer together after long months of doubt and misgivings.

After visiting the Garden of Gethsemane for further prayers in praise of the Lord and his blessing upon them, the family went as a group to the monastery where Arkadios had served, and each told of what had transpired in the intervening years. After many hours of the rapture of reunion the family regained its composure; and following a consultation, they decided that the lives of the parents, as well as the sons, would be given over to the Lord.

Xenophon sent a letter of resignation from the senate and appointed an executor to see that his entire holdings be given to charity. He then undertook to become a monk at an age when most men of his means would have chosen to live out their remaining years in comfort. Maria, willingly chose to follow the example of her husband and sons and with greater joy than she had ever known, entered the service of Christ in a nunnery not far removed from the Monastery of St. Savvas where her husband and sons were to serve. Their names, each of which has been invoked with miraculous results, are remembered on the same day, January 26.

January 27

Demetrios of Constantinople

The average Christian looks upon those who have been sainted with reverence and awe but always at a distance, because he cannot identify with those who have taken to seminaries, monasteries, and cathedrals for an ultimate recognition by the Church Fathers as exalted and venerated saints whose lives were a total devotion to Jesus Christ. But now and then there appears a man who has been sainted without having worn the cloth, lived in asceticism, or performed the services required to "qualify" one for canonization. It is refreshing as well as reassuring for a Christian to read of a man no different from himself who made God's honor roll by answering a call to assert his true Christian spirit in a moment of glory for which any man can become a saint.

Such a man was the eighteenth-century hero of Christianity who has come down to us as St. Demetrios of Constantinople, a man who quite possibly never gave a thought to the prospect of becoming a priest or a monk or any full-time servant of God but whose thoughts did turn to the Savior quite often enough to mark him as a devout Christian as well as a faithful churchgoer. He shared with all his fellow Greeks the ignominy of submission to a yoke of tyranny and oppression forced on a proud people for four centuries by Turks who in the 1800s debased Christianity while flaunting their own Muslim faith.

Demetrios was about twenty-five years old when he achieved a degree of prominence in the city of Constantinople as a business entrepreneur of no small talent; as a result of which he found himself looked upon with favor as proprietor of one of the best hotels and taverns in the entire country. He catered to some of the country's most famous figures as well as to visiting dignitaries from other lands and was considered not only an eminently successful man but one of the prized eligible bachelors of the land. With all this he never allowed himself to relax his concern for the Church and was a deeply religious follower of Jesus Christ.

Competitive businesses soon sprang up in emulation of his success, but all of them, which were mostly organized by Turks, were doomed for failure, and Demetrios prospered more than ever in spite of them. As his prosperity increased and his competition lessened, there set in an envy among the failures that grew more ominous as time passed. There was a particular group of truculent young Turks who banded together in a common hatred for the handsome Demetrios and plotted his downfall.

As fate would have it, there was a scuffle among just such a gang of malevolent Turks outside the hotel operated by Demetrios. Demetrios went into the street to quell the disturbance. In the melee one of the young hoodlums stabbed another, whereupon the finger of suspicion was pointed at the hated Christian, and he was ultimately charged with the murder. The rights of a Greek in those days were practically non-existent, and despite his innocence Demetrios was hauled before a tribunal.

Demetrios served as his own counsel, calling on witnesses on the scene whose credibility was dismissed in the face of the perjured testimony of his enemies, each of whom swore it was the hand of the Greek that wielded the death blade. No amount of eloquence of the innocent man, nor the overwhelming evidence of the fraudulent aspects of the whole sordid affair, had any effect on the vizier who sat in judgment.

As much to serve their own vindictiveness as to embarrass Demetrios, a compromise was offered by the vizier, who proposed that in exchange for what they considered the proper gesture, the charges would be dropped. It was suggested that he disavow Jesus Christ and embrace Islam openly, an act for which he would be completely exonerated. It was anticipated that no man in the eighteenth century would give up his life for Christ, especially in a Muslim country where he could be allowed to continue his prosperous way of life. To the everlasting credit of the gallant young Demetrios, he scorned the proposal, choosing to die for Christ. He was executed in Constantinople on 27 January 1785.

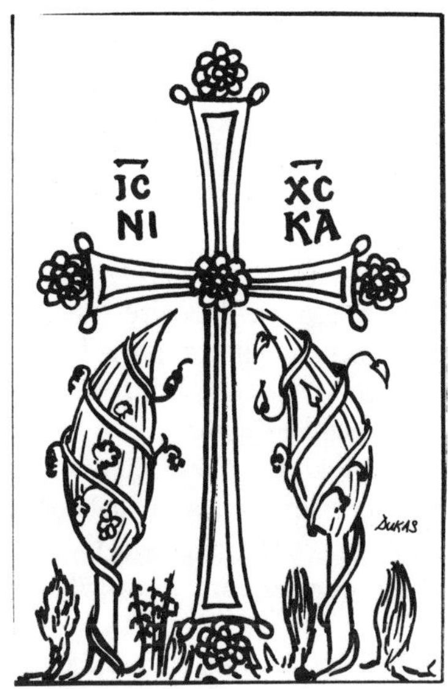

January 28

St. Ephraim the Syrian

One saint whose holiness of life was recognized unanimously by every sector of Christendom was a humble Syrian named Ephraim. He is revered not only by the Orthodox Church, but also by the Roman Catholic and the Eastern Rite of Syria as well. Although he was born in Syria in A.D. 306, Ephraim's impact on the Christian religion was such that sixteen centuries later, in 1920, Pope Benedict XV decreed that this pious Syrian be listed among the "Fathers of the Church." This is a distinction which is reserved for the most deserving of the untold numbers who have toiled in the service of Christ. This unheralded and relatively unknown saint left a legacy of prose and lyrical hymns which are treasured by the Orthodox Church. Ephraim's prayers and hymns are as much a part of the worship of the Church as are the icons themselves are.

Although Ephraim's father was reported to have been a pagan priest, he evidently did not object when Ephraim's mother embraced the Christian faith. Thus, even though his father was a pagan priest, Ephraim was raised as a Christian. In spite of this difficult and sometimes embarrassing situation, Ephraim became completely absorbed in the study of the Christian faith with such dedication and objectivity as to place him among the Fathers of Christianity.

The intellectual powers of Ephraim came to the fore when he was a student of Bishop Iakovos, a teacher with considerable influence in the city of Nisibus, Syria. Bishop Iakovos delighted in the literary and musical talent of his gifted pupil and fellow Syrian and greatly encouraged him.

After intensive study of all fields of knowledge, including philosophy, theology, and hymnology, Ephraim turned to creative efforts in literature and music. This established him as one of the most gifted and prolific contributors to sacred expression in the annals of the Christian Church. Not one to stray from his high purpose, Ephraim did not turn from his creative work in order to acquire a mastery of other languages. As a result, all his masterful dissertations and beautiful hymns had to be translated from the Syrian tongue.

Tonsured as a monk by his friend and confidant, Bishop Iakovos, he was eventually ordained a deacon. Despite this prominence in church affairs, he chose no advancement in the hierarchy, preferring the monastic life which afforded him greater opportunity to express himself in word and in song.

Ephraim was reported to have attended the First Ecumenical Synod in Nicaea (A.D. 325) with Bishop Iakovos. Later he became director of a Syrian theological school, where his genius as teacher, lecturer, writer, and hymnographer earned him a world-wide reputation.

When the persecution of Christians intensified in 363, he was forced to seek refuge in the community of Edessa on the banks of the Euphrates. There he continued to develop his creative talents for the glory of God and consequently the people of Edessa referred to him as "The Lyre of the Holy Spirit." The quiet reticence of St. Ephraim might have kept him out of the public eye but in his case he was so immersed in the all-consuming light that emanates from a divine gaze that he was unquestionably among the leading Orthodox theologians of his time.

Throughout his lifetime Ephraim continued to write works of poetic beauty in which he expressed his Christian faith. Furthermore, according to St. Gregory of Nyssa, Ephraim had "written commentaries on the Old and New Testament with such insight and wisdom as had no other Father of the Church." Among those who concurred with this opinion was St. Gregory's brother, St. Basil. In spite of the accolades which he received during his own lifetime for his great accomplishments in Christian expression, Ephraim preferred the simplicity of monasticism, eschewing the pomp and trappings of high office. He died on 28 January 373.

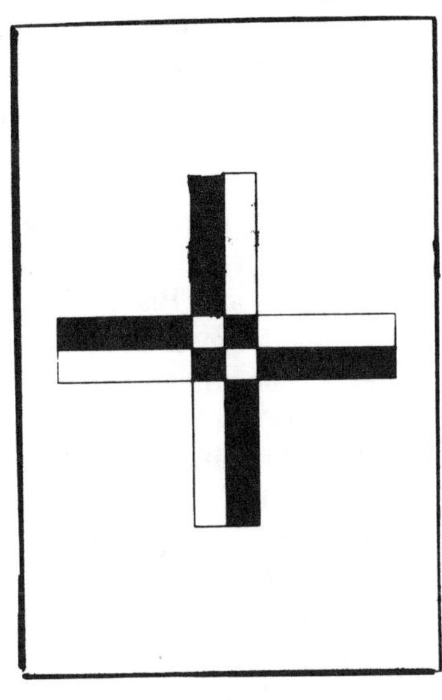

January 28

Saint Palladios

One of the most astute and literate churchmen of the fourth century, St. Palladios was destined to live in the shadows of his more renowned friend and confidant, St. John Chrysostom. He is known but to God and the knowledgeable historians who have placed him on record as one of the most prolific religious writers of all time, a man who lives in obscurity in spite of the masterful church works he left behind.

Palladios was born in Galatia, Asia Minor, in A.D. 365 at a time when great religious leaders were asserting themselves and strengthening the Christian Church. His was a time when great hierarchs were shaping the course of mankind through the worship of Jesus Christ, a task in which he took no small part and to whom all of Christianity is indebted. A supreme orator, he was an even more supreme writer, using the power of the beautiful Greek language with such mastery that his rhetoric in the name of the Savior lived on for centuries to come.

Not content to apply his intellect, which alone could have made him a standout, Palladios sought to prepare himself through the discipline of asceticism, thereby attaining spiritual greatness. But spiritual attainment is hard to reach to its fullest extent in the clamor and distractions of urban life and that is why he chose, like so many others, a life of extreme asceticism. To this end he remained in a number of monasteries, moving from one to another that he might acquire knowledge from them whose service to God varied slightly from place to place as time forged the habitual observances of men pledged to God. By the time he had completed his rounds of cloisters in both Palestine and Egypt he was acclaimed as a true man of God whose relentless pursuit of spiritual perfection thrust him into the van of protagonists for the Savior.

Following a period of isolation, he entered the city of Palestine in the year 400, there to be greeted warmly by all who saw him. Shortly thereafter he was appointed bishop of Helenopolis by no less a person than his friend, the one and only St. John Chrysostom, with whom he was to join hands in many of the important church councils.

When Chrysostom, who was not one to compromise even for royalty, was exiled by the emperor, Palladios went to Rome to seek the assistance of both Emperor Honorios and Bishop Innocent of Rome. Armed with letters of appeal from both of these dignitaries, he went boldly before the Byzantine emperor to plead the case of Chrysostom, but in the end was rewarded with exile. At the insistence of Bishop Theophilos of Alexandria, who for years had been at odds with Chrysostom, the noble Palladios was put to flight and sought refuge in a remote monastery of Egypt.

Following the death of Theophilos tensions eased and Palladios was allowed to return to his post in 412, free to resume his administration and his writing. From 419 to 421, Palladios launched a series of articles which were termed the "Lausiac History." The name is derived from the fact that he was commissioned to write these articles by a man named Lausos, who was not only a devout Christian but a man of high position in government and close friend of Emperor Theodosios II.

The "Lausaic History" concerns itself with monasticism and Palladios drew on his vast experience. The insight to be gleaned from the detailed pages he painstakingly wrote gives the reader the true meaning and utter devotion of the men whose monasteries were truly citadels of Christianity. Without them, it was evident that Christianity would have suffered, and the good will so earnestly sought by the Savior would not have emanated from cloisters to permeate the countryside and urban centers and thus strengthen Christianity.

Perhaps his great work was his biography of St. John Chrysostom, a detailed account of this great patriarch's achievements. Palladios not only brought out the greatness of this holy man but defended his stand against the opponents whose bitterness and rivalry had brought about his exile. Following this he made a detailed study of the religions of far-off India, a work used to this day by clergy and lay alike for reference. But most important works were his many treatises on every aspect of Christianity to which he applied himself to the end of his days. He died on 28 January 431.

January 29

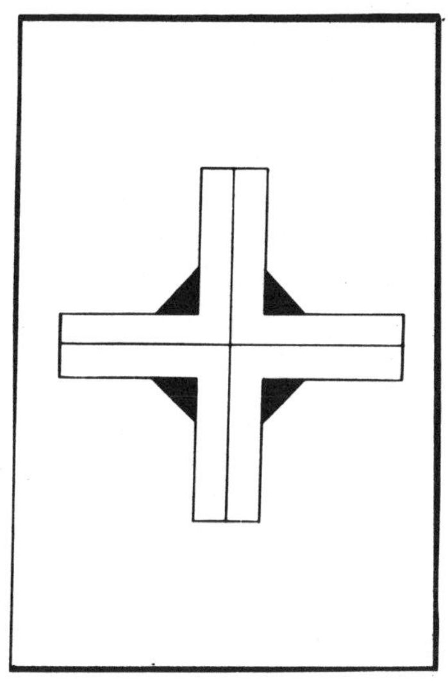

Demetrios of Chios

Love conquers all, including a man's rationality, as in the case of a young Greek islander of the nineteenth century who came to realize that the temporal love for a woman is a poor substitute for the spiritual love of the Savior. Even a king's abandonment of the throne of England for the love a woman cannot lessen the terrible guilt of a Christian who walks away from the presence of the King of Kings and the throne upon which he sits in eternity for the pleasure of a woman's company for the fleeting moment on earth that is called a lifetime.

Demetrios of Chios, to his everlasting credit, demonstrated both man's frailty and Christian courage in an episode that stands out as an example of the true Christian. He was the kind who never wore vestments nor outwardly served the Lord in his lifetime, but stepped out of a crowd of ordinary men in an hour of glory which has placed him among the immortals known as saints of the Church. For having loved not wisely but too well, he recovered his Christian sense of honor in time to more than make amends—but at the cost of his life, the most precious gift he willingly offered to Jesus Christ.

Born in 1780 on the island of Chios in the northern Aegean Sea, Demetrios left his small village of Paliokastro while yet a young man to seek his fortune in the city of Constantinople, still a glamorous metropolis in spite of the Turkish occupation. It was a place where men of intelligence and talent were much sought after, especially by Turks who lacked the artistic and commercial skills of the Greeks whom they had overrun. The business community was under the influence of Greek tradesmen and artisans, allowed to prosper by the Turks who knew on which side their bread was buttered—all of which led to greater harmony in the marketplace. It was on theological grounds that the Turks endeavored to assert the supremacy of Islam over Christianity, mute testimony to which was the conversion of the beautiful Church of Hagia Sophia into a mosque with its incongruous minarets.

The handsome and industrious island boy was soon an outstanding cosmopolitan as he worked his way into a place of prominence in the business community. Demetrios enjoyed the admiration of Greek and Turk alike in his everyday display of business acumen and personal charm. In this mixed society he turned more than one female head of both religions, showing courtesy for all. Unfortunately, he was finally stricken with a fetching Muslim girl for whom his love was so consuming that he dared to seek her hand in marriage. The girl returned the strong love that Demetrios bore for her; but Islamic law, as well as the sense of Turkish superiority over the entire land, precluded fulfillment of the mutual love.

So intense was the love of Demetrios that he set aside his Christianity, forsaking it, that he might have for his wife the one creature he so adored. He lost sight of the fact that he would not only make himself an apostate by embracing Islam, but a social outcast of the Greek community as well. He decided that the sacrifice was worth it, too blinded by love to see that it was unworthy of such a Christian as he and that his true Christian spirit would once again surface, bringing him misery instead of bliss.

Within weeks Demetrios realized his grievous error and in near panic called upon his brother, Zannis, to tell his Christian friends that he now realized the gravity of his folly and the disgrace he had brought upon them. After this, he went to his parish priest to confess his sin and to plead for forgiveness, vowing to abandon his shameful and sorrowful display and to openly disavow his acceptance of Islam as the act of a man who had lost his reason. The sincere repentance moved his priest who assured him that the Lord would forgive him, but that at the same time the Turks would deal harshly with him.

It mattered little to Demetrios when he was arrested for mockery and treason, because he felt an inner peace he had never before known. His parents tried to bribe officials, a common practice to this day, but to no avail; and the gallant Demetrios was beheaded on 29 January 1802, as much of a martyr as any who gave their lives for the Savior.

January 29

Saint Philotheos

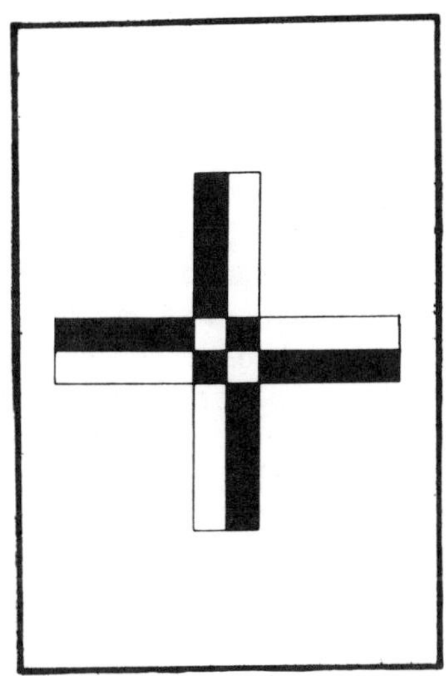

It is ironic that Asia Minor was the land in which most of the blood of the martyrs was spilled, only to eventually be trod by opposing religions and cults whose members were a far cry from the teachings of Jesus Christ, all of which lends credence to Cowper's remark that God moves in a mysterious way. It is also ironic that seven martyrs whose blood was shed in this region surfaced in ecclesiastical history with no precise dates as to when they made the supreme sacrifice. It is enough to know of their heroic action and that at least their names have been handed down to us to be venerated. It is safe to assume they acted for the Savior in the early centuries of Christianity.

Known as the "Seven Martyrs," chief of whom was St. Philotheos, they went under the name of Hyperechios, Abibos, Julianus, Romanos, Iakovos, and Parigorios. The next to the last name is familiar to not only the Greek Orthodox, but to the world at large, since it is the name of the present Greek Orthodox Archbishop, but the rest are unfamiliar. Nevertheless, they all comprise a group venerated as saints by the Greek Orthodox Church, and although not one was an exalted hierarch, each was a servant of God.

Much has been made of the well-known saints who have served the Lord to the fullest, but these obscure seven gave as much. And it is enough to know that they were aggressive, youthful, and dedicated and beyond that possessed outstanding courage. They are not to be found in high places, nor has it been recorded that they spent so much as a day in a monastery. They are not known to have been ascetic, hermits, or eremetic pillar dwellers, making themselves known in spectacular fashion. Better still they were the average men of their time with whom the average Christian of today can identify.

If one were to take an educated guess, it would be that this glorious group of Seven lived during the reign of Emperor Diocletian, known as much for his arrogance and cruelty as for his pagan intransigence. The accounts given of this gallant seven is commensurate with the treatment meted out by Diocletian.

While many earnest, well-meaning Christians remained passive, others like the Sacred Seven were activists whose overt devotion to the Lord is what kept Christianity growing in the face of superior odds. Undaunted, they carried the word of Jesus Christ to any who would listen and although none was singled out as an orator of supreme persuasion, they served by example in the conversion of pagans to Christianity. Service to the Savior is not always measured in terms of asceticism, priesthood or monasticism, but is as valuable when a man approaches another and asks to listen to the story of Jesus Christ. We leave the work of the Lord in the hands of the clergy today, but when clergy was scarce, or virtually non-existent in some hostile areas, some one had to shout out for the Savior and these seven shouted and were heard.

Persecutions would ebb and flow with the whim of the emperor, whose fiendish delight was never better satisfied than when Christians, were put to torture. It was during one of these assaults on hapless Christians that special effort was made to capture the Seven who had become a team, inseparable in their crusade for Christ. They were rounded up and separated from others who had been caught. They were placed in a squalid dungeon where they were intermittently beaten as a prelude to their final torture.

Eventually led from prison they were told that hanging or beheading would be too easy a death for them. The Seven did not flinch. They were taken to a public square before a howling pagan mob. Their friends had not deserted them, but they could not prevail against the odds and chose not to look upon this bestial scene. They took to other places, even more determined to spread the word of the Savior.

A wooden wall stood at one end of the square and the now suffering Seven were placed against this barrier to be nailed to the wall, much as their Savior had been nailed to the cross. Not content to have nails driven through their arms and legs, the pagan executioners then produced long spikes which were driven through the heads of the dying Seven, and with blood streaming until their hearts had stopped, the fanatic mob howled in delight. It is doubtful if such inhumanity has been surpassed, even with burnings at the stake, and the holocaust of recent memory. The martyrdom of the Seven is commemorated on January 29.

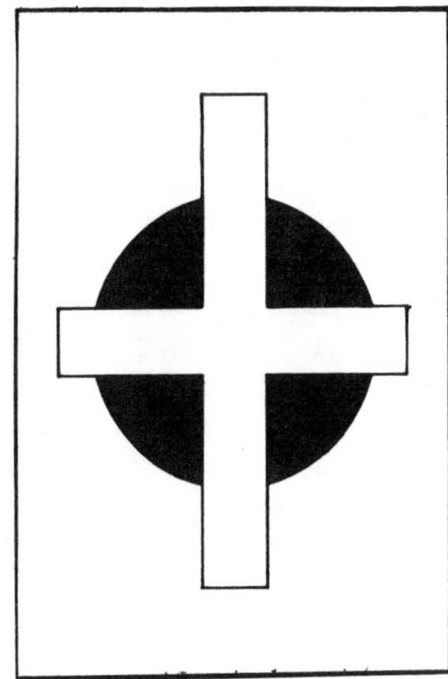

January 30

The Three Hierarchs

The eleventh-century Christian appears to have been much more deeply concerned about his religion than the generations which preceded him and those which have followed. He enjoyed a greater freedom of expression than the predecessor who worshipped Jesus Christ at the peril of his life, and his life was not crowded with the social changes brought on by the invention of the printing press and the machine age. Unencumbered by ideologies spawned in revolution and knowing only one Mother Church, his popular topic of conversation was religion, which invariably came down to a debate about who was the greatest figure in Christian history. These rather innocent and well-intended arguments, which by today's standards appear ill-considered, very often assumed serious proportions, to the point that a formal consideration was necessitated and resulted in the rather unusual celebration of three of our greatest theologians on the same day.

There are heroes galore in the Christian Church, any one of whom could be selected as a favorite, and of the favorites that cropped up in private or public discussion there were three that were most commonly mentioned. These three, who had the remarkable coincidence of serving the Lord in the fourth century, were St. Basil the Great, St. Gregory the Theologian, and St. John Chrysostom. The debates that began in the home or market-place soon spread into the Church and its councils and found their way into the upper echelons of the hierarchy, not out of proportion but out of an evolution of ideas wholly natural to the eleventh-century Christian structure.

With an absolute state rule there was little challenge for the brighter minds of the time in government, civil service, as a result of which the intellectuals as well as the dedicated found themselves drawn to the Church. The tax collector commanded little respect, but the cleric was a man very highly esteemed, and it was to this spiritual servant that the average citizen turned for many services, some of which were outside his sphere of authority. It was quite natural then that a religious question would be brought to the priest and that the controversy would pyramid beyond him to the highest and most respected prelates.

Honored as "Doctors" of the Church, Sts. Basil, Gregory, and John were intellectual giants of equal stature, serving God and man with an equally high level of devotion and spirit. They were theologians and philosophers of the highest order, as well as gifted educators, orators, and spiritual leaders whose influence was such that seven hundred years after they appeared they were still so highly esteemed as to touch off a dispute as to who just might be greatest. After years of polemics, the burning issue reached a climactic conclusion in 1081, during the reign of Emperor Alexios, and then only by what would appear to be the result of divine intervention.

One of the most highly respected prelates of the day was Bishop John of Galatia, known throughout the Byzantine Empire for his considerable wisdom and spiritual integrity, a man who had refused to be drawn into an argument which by then divided the Christian community into three different camps in a sorry display of ill-advised but unavoidable dispute. Some of the greatest minds of the Church became involved in a matter that was spinning out of control and which posed a serious threat to the solidarity of the Faith.

Bishop John of Galatia received a vision in which the Three Hierarchs in question appeared to him to deplore the current disagreement and to ask him to step into the breach with an announcement of their visit and their admonition that the three were equal in the sight of God. Whoever disputed this would, therefore, dispute God. The elated Bishop John went to Constantinople to announce the divine visitation and the tumult was transformed to quiet accord when this relatively simple solution to what up until then had been an uncompromising strife was revealed. Almost overnight harmony was restored. A formal declaration of the equality of the three saints was issued and January 30 was designated as the feast day celebrating the equation of St. Basil the Great, St. Gregory the Theologian, and St. John Chrysostom.

January 31

Saint Elias

Had not the "Great Schism" of 1054 sundered the Christian Church, there is little doubt that the western half of the Roman Empire would have joined the Eastern sector of Orthodoxy in canonizing a gallant seventeenth-century Greek whose demonstration of faith bolstered the faith of a God-fearing nation harshly oppressed by avowed enemies of Christianity. The inglorious conquest of Greece by the merciless Ottoman hordes had cast an ominous shadow over the cross of Jesus Christ. However, at no time in four centuries did the oppressor conquer the Christian spirit of an embattled people, nor weaken the will of its defiant spokesmen, among whom was the courageous man of God now known as St. Elias the New.

The shattered remnants of the glorious Byzantine Empire had disappeared by the time Elias was born in the mid 1600s, but in the heartland of Christian Greece, in the Peloponnesos region, there was virtually no change in the lifestyle of villages whose strength of faith was as unyielding as the rugged mountains they inhabited. In this atmosphere of recalcitrance Elias plied his trade as barber, but not content to limit himself to topical discussions of the day in the confines of his shop, he became an activist in 1676 and soon found himself in heated debates with Muslim Turks in matters both political and religious.

In venturing to speak for the rights of the people of his district, Elias found himself in the embarrassing position of having sparked a retaliation that threatened the safety of those whom he sought to protect. In a confrontation with a group of incensed Turks, he reversed himself for some unknown reason, and in an effort to appease his opponents donned a Turkish fez as a gesture of good will. The astonished Turks took full advantage of this unexpected turn of events, embracing and regaling him to the point where, in a confused state, Elias gave himself over to Islam in a shabby display of ill-considered peacemaking. This apostasy was short-lived, however, and an extremely contrite Elias crept back to Christianity.

Unable to face his fellow Christians, he left Kalamata and made his way to the great cloister of Mt. Athos on Greece's eastern slope, and there confessed his grievous sin and asked that he be admitted to do penance and atone for his disservice to the Lord. After a period of eight years of complete dedication to God in an ascetic tenure of meditation and prayer, he was consecrated a monk, taking the name of the prophet Elias of the Old Testament. He had more than fulfilled his obligations to the Savior when he asked to be allowed to return to his home town and reassert himself as he had originally intended, this time with a strength of will forged by eight years of an asceticism that had brought him a nearness to God.

The people of Kalamata hailed his return as a triumph of the spirit of the true Christian. Elias felt gratified at long last and plunged himself into the role of activist that he had surrendered, but this time with a renewed vigor and with a voice that rang with authority. Once more an aura of defiance permeated the community, to the great delight of Elias but very much to the dismay of the Turks, who were now goaded into an elimination of the Christian leader.

A militant group of Turks accosted Elias on the streets and demanded that he answer to the name Mustapha Ardunis, a name given him when he had ostensibly defected to Islam years before. When Elias responded that his defection had been as meaningless as the name they had applied to him, the Turks seized him and dragged him through the streets to the magistrate, meanwhile beating him without mercy. The battered monk was thrust before a less than judicious official whose scowl grew more menacing as he heard the holy man being accused of having made a mockery of the Turkish faith. If Elias had repeated his sorry act of previous years, he could have walked away without further abuse, but this time he wavered not in the least and proclaimed himself a servant of Jesus Christ.

A hangman's noose failed to kill the condemned Elias, and he was cast into an arena in which a charging bull's horn pierced his stout heart. He gave his life for Christ on 31 January 1686.

January 31

Saints Kyros and John the Unmercenaries

Two eminent physicians of the third century fused their talents as healers together with such devotion to the Savior that it became obvious that it was both a combination of their skills as well as God which enabled them to affect cures which fell short of nothing but miracles, marking them for all time as saints of the Greek Orthodox Church. Their names were John and Kyros, venerated for their undoubted divine expression of the will of God more than their earthly achievements and sacrifices.

Their place in ecclesiastical history commences with Kyros who was born in Alexandria during the third century reign of the infamous Emperor Diocletian. As soon as he had acquired his credentials, he lost no time in applying himself to the care of the ailing and afflicted, doing so with such a degree of success that his eminence as a physician earned him a reputation which spread throughout the sprawling city. With his growing eminence as a doctor, there came about even greater respect for him because of his devoutness and humility in attributing cures to God with his admonition that "of the Most High cometh healing." His was not so much a home as it was a clinic, crowded with the sick or injured who sought his help, firm in the belief that if his potions were ineffective then he had the power to invoke the will of God in effecting a cure. He came to be known as the "Holy Physician."

At the urging of the patriarch Apollinarios of Alexandria, who had learned of a pagan plot against the holy physician, Kyros fled from Egypt into Arabia, where at least he would be out of harm's way and still be able to carry on his noble work. It was there that he met another young physician named John, a doctor who had in his own right achieved a high reputation for his medical skill. John joined his newly acquired friend Kyros not only in holy work but in holy orders. Both men were tonsured as monks, continuing, their healing art through the power of Jesus Christ as well as their own knowledge, coming to be known as the Anargyroi (Unmercenaries) since they charged no fee for their services. This partnership in Christ continued for a number of years until it was decided that, in spite of the risks involved, they would be of greater service to Alexandria, where they returned.

Kyros and John had been in Alexandria for a short time when they got news of the plight of a woman named Athanasia in the neighboring village of Kanopos. In this hotbed of paganism her crime had been simply her devotion to Christ, for which she was cast into prison, along with her three daughters. The girls, ranging in age from eleven to fifteen were innocents caught up with their mother in yet another web of Christian persecution about which an outraged Christian community could do little.

Confidence was placed in the ability of Kyros and John to successfully intervene on behalf of Anastasia and her daughters. The holy pair pleaded the case for the mother and daughters but their eloquent words fell on deaf ears. The final answer of magistrate Syrianos was that John and Kyros direct their appeal to the family they hoped to defend but only to disavow Christ. Realizing the hopelessness of their position, the holy pair exhorted the family to pray to the Lord for courage, after which they all fell to their knees in supplication.

The final act was to force Anastasia and her three children to look upon Kyros and John as they were tortured with pagan bestiality. Their freshly opened wounds felt the further sting of salts and acids. Even the pagans tired of this demonic display and on 31 January, Kyros and John, together with Anastasia and her three children, were executed.

Their story does not end there. The remains of the sainted physicians were retrieved and enshrined by Patriarch Apollinarios who foresaw that miracles would occur at the site. A portion of the relics were removed to Menuthi, Egypt, to be enshrined in a chapel which proved to be an additional site of miraculous healings. The city of Menuthi was renamed Abukir, taken from the Greek Abba Kyros, or Father Kyros. This was no mere coincidence, and the famous shrine is still to be found centuries later in the Egyptian City of Abukir. It can also be noted that more than a thousand years later, in 1798, a famous battle took place at sea just off the Egyptian coast near this shrine. In this naval engagement Admiral Lord Nelson emerged victorious. The unseen hand of Kyros might have been of some consequence.

February 1

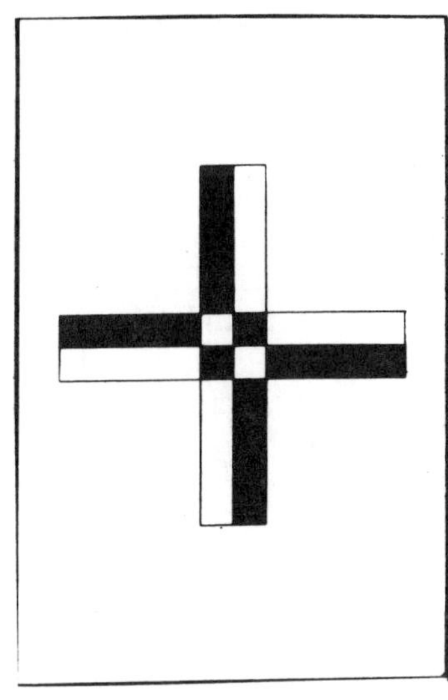

Saint Tryphon

A third-century shepherd named Tryphon became the lamb of God while yet a boy of seventeen, a martyr, and servant of the Lord without formal education or training but endowed with a spiritual grace that superseded the highest learning. Tending a flock offers no credentials for sainthood, but neither does it preclude immortality inasmuch as the shepherd symbolizes loving care and the serenity which come from a proximity to the Lord. It is doubtful that fate would have cast him in any other role but that of a humble herdsman like those who, we are told, shall inherit the earth.

Tryphon was born during the reign of the Emperor Gordianus, who not only was of Hellenic descent but was also extremely tolerant of Christians, who were considered enemies of the state for their allegiance to the Son of God. When Tryphon was only seventeen he was touched with the grace of the Holy Spirit and found that there was within him a genuine power of healing. There have always been faith healers in our midst who are soon enough discredited, but this lad had a bona fide divine gift which he did not try to exploit and which was made known to others in spite of his reticence. Tryphon divided his time between herding and isolated prayer but was constantly called upon by true believers who sought the benefit of his awe-inspiring spark of divinity.

The Emperor Gordianus had a lovely daughter who suddenly became stricken with a malady which the royal physicians diagnosed as fatal. The distraught emperor in desperation sought the help of soothsayers and self-appointed healers to no avail, and was in utter despair when someone told him of the young shepherd. Tryphon was summoned to Rome from Phrygia, but by the time he arrived the girl was in the throes of death; his task seemed hopeless. He took up a vigil at her beside and, after bow-ing his head in prayer for divine intervention, he took the girl's hand. The healing power of the Lord coursed through her debilitated body and within a few days she was restored to good health.

The grateful emperor lavished on Tryphon gifts whose worth assured him a place of honor far from his humble abode and his lonely hillside, but he chose to turn over everything given him to the poor and return to his flock as impoverished as the day he left. He resumed his ascetic life as a herdsman and, though there is no record of his having been tonsured a monk, he patterned his life after those who dwelled in cloisters, apparently preferring to remain close to nature, content to glory in the serenity which few have known.

At the death of Emperor Gordianus, a tyrant named Decius, who was as cruel as his predecessor was lenient, issued among his first official orders a decree that all Christians had to disavow Jesus Christ as their master or suffer torture and death. Intent on asserting himself as lord and master of all in the realm, he set in motion a reign of terror designed to eliminate Christianity. It was a campaign of barbarism that made the agony and brutal death of Christians commonplace.

The governor of the Phrygian province, a loathsome myrmidon named Akylinos, who curried the emperor's favor by sending him Christians in excess of his quota, exulted in the capture of the renowned Tryphon and dispatched the hapless Christian to the emperor, a prize victim worth several lesser followers of Jesus Christ. This pious prey of vengeful paganism was given the usual interrogation and then commanded to disavow Christ and acknowledge only the gods of the sovereign. Refusing this, Tryphon was put to inhuman torture but refused to recant. He was thereupon led to the executioner's block, where he prayed for God to take him before the blade could descend. He died for Christ while the axe was yet lifted high.

Three hundred years after his death on 1 February 251, the great Emperor Justinian, in the year 552, erected a chapel in his memory, and in A.D. 575 his successor, Justin, honored Tryphon with the erection of one of the finest monasteries of antiquity. The rustic St. Tryphon is considered the patron saint of laborers of the field.

February 1

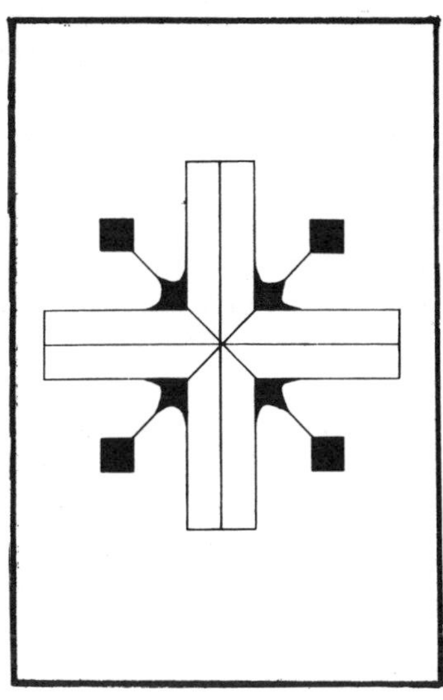

Saint Basil, Archbishop of Thessalonike

A chapel of Hiliandarion on Mt. Athos bears the name of St. Basil, but it is not for the greater Father of the Church who is memorialized on January 1, but for a lesser known figure of Christianity who is known to us as St. Basil, archbishop of Thessalonike. Destined to live in the shadow of Basil the Great, this namesake of Thessalonike was nevertheless a hierarch of Orthodoxy in the highest tradition of Christianity.

St. Basil reached sainthood by no accident of birth, nor by a martyrdom for the Savior, but by dint of an outstanding record in the service of Jesus Christ. No causes or conflicts propelled him to the forefront of Christianity as a protagonist for the Church. No clashes with the all powerful Byzantine Empire sent him into exile for an offense for which he was to vindicate himself, as others in prior years attained prominence in the notoriety that followed defiance of royal will. Like the untold number of others whose service to Christ was uneventful, his pursuit in the path of Jesus Christ would have been ordinary except for one thing. He was no ordinary man.

Basil of Thessalonike was not to make his presence felt until he was tonsured a monk in 875 at Mt. Athos, under the auspices of the eminent St. Euthymios, a sponsorship which in itself indicated that great things lay in store for this future saint. His mental prowess, complete command of theology and Christian resolve had attracted the eye of St. Euthymios who took the aspiring theologian under his wing while in Athens. He was chosen out of the several qualified candidates in that great city and he more than justified that choice in the years to come.

Over the centuries thousands of monks have come and gone from Mt. Athos, but Basil of Thessalonike was a rarity. He was one of the very few whose intellectual and spiritual capacities were such that the Church, ever closely tied to the eremitic monastery where numberless have been lost in a anonymity, singled out this brilliant mind and removed it from the sea of deserving but lesser minds astir on that sacred promontory. Full in the knowledge that he could be of greater service to God and mankind as a member of the general community rather than the sequestered eremites above whose ranks he had risen in the sight of Heaven, he was the unanimous choice of the synod to succeed Archbishop John of Thessalonike in the year A.D. 904.

As archbishop of Thessalonike, Basil brought about a reawakening of the Orthodox spirit that for years had been darkened by methodical observance, uninspired communicants and a lethargic clergy. Under his dynamic leadership there was a gradual reassertion of the Greek Orthodox spirit, bringing with it not only a renewed faith but a full return to cultural traditions of ancient Greece. Moral values were reasserted and brought to a level that rivaled the cultures of the golden city of Athens. Thessalonike was soon the equal of its sister in every glorious aspect except for size.

A gifted and prolific writer, Basil authored many volumes, chief of which was his concentration on the lives of saints. He found time to write not only of the great men of the Church but, in a study of detailed dedication, wrote a voluminous account of the life of his spiritual mentor, St. Euthymios. This work capped the others, all of which earned him the title "Synaxaristes," that is, a biographer of saints.

Known also as Basil the Confessor by reason of his staunch defense of the Christian faith, he had remarkable success not only in reviving a sagging Christian spirit but in bringing back to the Church those who had strayed. Attendance at the various churches, meager at times excepting for the high holy days, rose to full attendance almost regularly, thanks largely to his innovative programs and a personal approach to every person he could reach. His sphere of influence went beyond the elderly and the needy, reaching into the sophisticated social circle of the more affluent who found themselves proud to be associated with him. Not even the patriarch, himself, was more venerated than Archbishop Basil. His thunderous orations were exceeded only by his masterful writings and administrative excellence, all of which were aimed at the glorification of God. His long, productive life finally came to an earthly end on 1 February 950.

Presentation of Our Blessed Lord into the Temple

The celebration of the birth of Christ on December 25 is marked by a period of extreme joy in which Christians the world over attain a euphoria referred to as the "Christmas Spirit," which is so genuine it is contagious but altogether too short-lived. Nevertheless, that joyful spirit, highlighted by the exchange of gifts, has an emotional carry-over which tends to obscure the fact that forty days later the baby Jesus was presented at the Temple in accordance with ancient custom. This solemn occasion is regrettably more than just obscured; it is overlooked, but since it comes in the wake of the greatest religious celebration on earth, Christians cannot be judged too harshly for the apparent oversight. In any event, the birth of a baby occasions such great joy that anything that follows shortly thereafter is of necessity anticlimactic.

The Vesper Service contains a prayer from the service of the Presentation of the Infant Jesus which reads: "Lord, now let your servant go in peace according to your promise, because my eyes have seen your salvation which you have prepared in the presence of all people, a Light to show to the Gentiles and for the glory of your people Israel." The eyewitness referred to in this short prayer was a man named Symeon who was privileged to hold the infant Jesus in his arms to be presented to the Father.

According to the Scriptures, Symeon was a man not only of holy spirit but of infinite patience as well, a highly intelligent scholar and deeply religious who knew from his interpretation of the Old Testament that the Messiah was to come. He prayed not only for deliverance, but for the opportunity to remain alive just long enough to cast his eyes on the Messiah. This was no small request made of the Lord because, although estimates vary as to his actual age, it is quite certain he was born so many years before Christ that he had to be quite ancient by the time of the Nativity. Symeon is estimated to have been at least 150 years old and only because God gave him that many years in answer to earnest prayers was he allowed to live to that great day.

Born in a cave, the Son of God was held in the arms, not of some young hero, but of an ancient ascetic barely able to hold himself erect, let alone carry the Infant, for the age-old ceremony of presentation at the temple. We read in Luke (2.22-40) of how the old man's patience was finally rewarded by being led by the Holy Spirit to the infant Jesus, whom he fondly embraced as a Savior. There is no true Christian who would not exchange the mythical Midas touch just to be able to touch the garment of Jesus Christ at any time in his thirty-three-year life span, but this old man Symeon was privileged to cradle the Savior in his arms.

The practice of presenting a child to God in the church originated in the ancient temples of the Jewish faith and is continued by the Orthodox Church in the unbroken tradition of centuries which Orthodox prefer to call "being churched." The true believer of Orthodoxy believes, as did the third-century St. Cyprian, that "he cannot have God for his father who has not the Church for his mother," a religious admonition that bears repetition and should be borne in the minds of Christians throughout the year. The presentation on February 2 is one reminder that Christian duty comes before all else.

The same prayers are offered to God for infants of both sexes, but in Orthodox tradition, a male child is brought into the sanctuary in the hope that he will be one selected by heaven to answer a call to serve as a priest one day. The female infant, however, is brought only to the entrance of the sanctuary, not in a discriminatory gesture, but simply because, since a female does not serve as a priest in the Orthodox Church, she is not offered to God with the prospect of being called to serve as a priest.

This does not smack of the chauvinism that is being misapplied by well-intentioned women of the world today. Since Mary Magdalene, the presence of women has been very much felt in the Christian faith, to which countless heroines and martyrs who have been sainted bear witness. There is ample proof throughout the New Testament that women are on the same level with men in the eyes of God, who chose as a Savior a male child. The presentation of the Lord on February 2 is a presentation of all who believe in him.

Stamatios, John, and Nicholas, Neomartyrs of Spetsai

When the call to arms was sounded by an intrepid Greek hierarch of Patras in 1821 to shed the yoke of Turkish oppression, the response was an explosion of pent-up patriotism that reverberated in every corner of the Greek peninsula and its beautiful islands, among which was the very lovely isle of Spetsai, which down through the centuries has yielded mariners in times of war and peace. Like all its sister islands, Spetsai, at the outbreak of the Greek War of Independence, was the home of men who knew and loved the sea as well as they knew and loved their country and God and who were more than willing to fight for their homeland, their religion and their independence.

From the island of Spetsai, the site of many heroic naval battles in the long history of Greece, there emerged three heroes who epitomized the gallantry of Greek warriors and who valued not only their love of country but their love for Jesus Christ more than their own noble lives. Their names were Stamatios and John Ginis, who joined their uncle Nicholas in a daring sea venture in which they anticipated the considerable risk involved but certainly could not have anticipated that they would be called upon to make the ultimate sacrifice for the Lord and find eternity in sainthood. The brothers were the sons of Theodore and Aneste Ginis, a highly respected family that owned a shipping firm of considerable consequence by island standards of that day.

In the second year of the revolution, the island of Chios had been isolated with a reign of terror by the Turks, who had formed an impenetrable ring of barriers to repel any approach by outside revolutionaries, and the Greek populace that had taken to the hills was on the verge of starvation. Stamatios and his brother,

John, linked with their uncle Nicholas in a bold plan to bring relief to the people of Chios loaded a ship with provisions, chief of which was that staple of Greece—olive oil. With exceptional mariner's skill, they approached the island under the cover of darkness in an area considered inaccessible by any large craft because of the dangerous shallows. Lying at anchor they set about hauling their lifesaving cargo to shore with small boats, seeking out members of the underground to help cache the supplies, unaware that among the group was a traitor who stole away in the night to betray the Greek colony. Their job had no sooner been done than the Turks swooped down on the hardy mariners. In the ensuing battle many of the ship's crew were killed and those who did not escape were taken prisoners.

The Turkish authorities saw this episode as an opportunity to assert not only their ruthless authority but to flaunt the religion of Islam as superior to Christianity. To that end they cast the two brothers in prison and lost no time in trying to bend the will of the unyielding uncle Nicholas. Recognizing the hopelessness of intimidating such a stout Christian, they led him to the town square and summarily executed him.

The two brothers were quite another matter, however, and believing them to be more pliable than the recalcitrant uncle, the Turks went about not only converting the heroes to acquiescent collaborators but to obsequious apostates as well. There had been a precedent here and there in acts of denial of Christ by hapless Greeks seeking to escape torture and death, who in reality never renounced the Savior in their hearts and whose apparent defection had no effect on the Christian community as a whole.

The conversion of a pair of brothers now held in the highest esteem would be of immense consequence and to that end the Turks programmed an agenda that would have converted lesser men. Suffering long and harsh imprisonment, torture and every manner of depraved indignities that could be heaped on a human being, Stamatios and John never wavered and at long last were murdered by the exasperated Turks. The feast day of the three gallant mariners is observed on February 3.

February 3

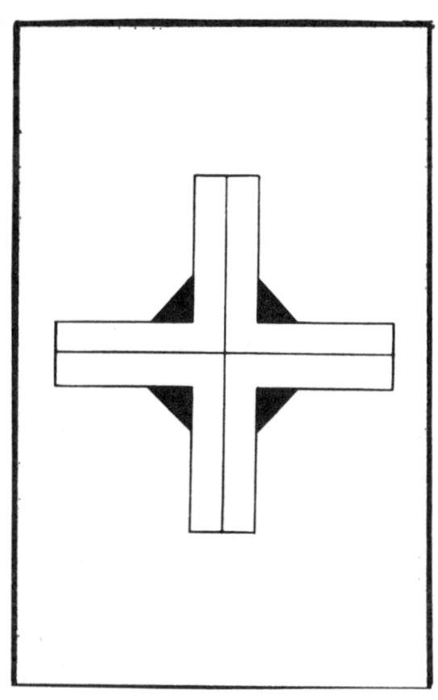

Vlasios of Caesaria

The superman of his day, by the highly improbable name of Vlasios, expressed the will of God in such spectacular fashion that it was bound to win converts to Christianity at a time when they were sorely needed. This obscure man exemplified by word and deed the intent and sole purpose of the appearance of Jesus Christ on earth when the future of the faith in the Savior was at stake and there was need for bold action. There is no question he was chosen of God to be one of those to put the faith in Jesus Christ on solid footing. The redoubtable Vlasios asked no question and because he acted through faith alone his sainthood was assured.

Born into wealth in Caesaria at a time when that ancient city boasted of wealth and culture, he grew up in the midst of pomp and splendor. Called by some a traitor to his class, he was the very soul of humility and the epitome of Christian charity. Because of his complete acceptance of Christ he knew nothing of the marketplace and the money changers, choosing the company of Christians much less privileged than himself. Caring nothing for the wealth left to him, he forsook the life of leisure and pleasure to be a servant of God with a rare commitment.

Vlasios could have cavorted with other wealthy friends in spending sprees but diverted every bit of his fortune before the feet of the Lord, there to be shared by the poor and undernourished, of which there were and still are so many to this day. With a willing heart he set up projects for the poor that were a study in administrative skill, logistical distribution and, above all, in humanity.

When the word was out that the generosity stemmed from Vlasios, he was approached by his affluent friends, anxious to determine what madness drove him to depart with his worldly goods. Vlasios saw in their concern an opportunity to convince them that far from madness, it was for the highest of purpose he was acting thus and he invited all he knew to a grand banquet, at which he not only acted as his own toastmaster but as a spokesman for the Savior as well. Pagan and Christian guests alike hushed in silence as he spoke of their obligation to those less fortunate than themselves, exhorting them to act in the same manner in the name of the Lord.

As impressive as the noble Vlasios might have been, it is doubtful that his affair was a successful fund raiser, although his words and deeds must have pricked the consciences of some of the Christians present. It is certain that although he may have won a few converts, he did nothing but incur the wrath of scornful pagans who looked upon Christian charity as a trivial application of support to the weak and defenseless. After the feast, the flint hearted pagans went forth not in gratitude to their host but to seek his denouncement for his overt offense to their own false beliefs. The more bellicose called for his Christian head and got it, although in the end they wished they had kept silent.

For his offense against the state and its false idols, Vlasios was called before a magistrate who might have been lacking in charity but was not lacking in the least in cunning cruelty. When the sentence was pronounced little did any one, know that the magistrate was summoning forth the power of God. Vlasios was brutually tortured but his body showed no sign of damage. The torture was repeated and each time the results were the same. The tortured man showed not the slightest scar, no matter how much flesh had been torn from him.

The futility of this form of punishment called for something else. An outsized cauldron was found, then filled with water which was brought to a boil. Vlasios was then tossed into this boiling water, only to climb out without so much as a blister. Suspecting that sorcery had rendered the boiling water harmless, the magistrate, to show no harm would come of it, plunged his face into it, only to pull away screaming in blindness and soon thereafter dying of his burns. The witnesses to all this fell before Vlasios in recognition of his Savior and were baptized without injury in the water that had destroyed the scornful magistrate.

Vlasios left the scene to go forth and preach as a dedicated missionary. His reputation preceded him and his work was made easier for what had happened. His missionary work continued for many years until he died in peace of old age.

February 4

Isidore of Pelusium

The archives of Christianity contain literature authored by the world's greatest minds, ranking in the forefront for the purity not only of their thoughts but for their prose as well, representing nearly two thousand years of unbridled enthusiasm for the word of Jesus Christ. Not the least among these classics are the near poetic expressions of devotion of a little-remembered monk who has come to be known as St. Isidore of Pelusium, a tireless chronicler of Christianity and constructive critic whose scope of influence reached a high as the Patriarchate itself. In a lifelong pursuit for perfection, he asked no more of the clergy than he demanded from himself—a strict adherence to clerical obligations in a rigidly disciplined pattern of behavior which stressed self-denial and total conformity in the sacred trust to which they were committed.

Born in A.D. 370 into an influential family of Alexandria, Egypt, Isidore was given every advantage, including a full education in a formal system which to him lacked the emphasis on religion so essential to his concept of a full life. By the time he had completed his studies, in all of which he excelled, he was attracted to religious endeavor, much as two of his kinsmen had been and had gone on to become the Patriarchs Theophilos and Cyril, both of Alexandria. He left the clamor of the city of Alexandria for the quiet of a monastic cloister known as Pelusium, a mountain retreat in which he began his remarkable life as a man of God. He embraced asceticism with the genuine zeal of the true monk and never ceased to consider that stern discipline and self-denial were as vital to the life of a cleric as breath and bread. At the core of his brillant expressions of faith was his uncompromising belief that a proximity to God demanded total austerity.

After he had been ordained a priest by his friend and admirer,

Bishop Ammonios of Pelusium, Isidore became abbot of his monastery. Under his direction it became the monastery he thought all monasteries should be, stressing the three essentials of prayer, virtue and faith. The observances were not mere gestures, as was true in some cases, but became the driving force in a meaningful relationship with God and man, with particular emphasis on maintaining a pious posture in every aspect of clerical efforts, all of which have the common goal of real service to Jesus Christ.

Isidore deplored the fact that the name of the great St. John Chrysostom, for whom he felt an esteem beyond measure, had been stricken from church records after he was exiled many years before by Theophilos. In a compelling letter of protest to the Patriarch Cyril, nephew of Theophilos, Isidore urged the restoration of the name of St. John to the annals of the Alexandrian Church. It is inconceivable that a hierarchy would have countenanced the act of vindictiveness that struck the name of so venerated a saint, but the deed had been done and it took considerable eloquence to convince Cyril to countermand his uncle's order. The restoration of the name and works of St. John was assured by the Patriarch Cyril, who agreed with his kinsman on this issue.

A literary genius in his own right, Isidore in his glorious lifetime wrote more than 3,000 commentaries in various forms on the basic elements of theology, philosophy, and Holy Scripture, comprising a massive output of masterful literature that makes up several sizeable volumes that weigh down the shelves of ecclesiastical libraries but add to them a lustre without which the light of Christianity would be appreciably diminished. In the centuries that have passed since he composed these masterpieces, countless thousands of clerics, as well as laymen, have benefitted from his genius.

A great portion of the writings of Isidore is in the form of a criticism of the clergy, ranging from the lowliest deacon to the patriarch himself, all of whom were called to task for certain abuses that existed in all echelons of the clergy. His pen brought the wayward into line and influenced a reformation in the church structure which restored order and respect.

Calling for observance of regulations set forth in the First Ecumenical Synod, Isidore wrote voluminously on dogma and monasticism, and when he died on 4 February 470, he left a treasure of undying Christian prose.

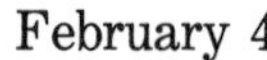
February 4

St. Abramios, Bishop of Arbela, Persia

Three centuries after the birth of Christ the ancient land of Persia continued to retain its inherent mysticism and conglomeration of religious cults and sects, each of which eyed the other with suspicion but, nevertheless, found a common ground in superstition. What made this strange land stranger still was the fanatic devotion to concepts that eventually spawned such ideas as flying carpets, Alladins, and Sinbads. That Christianity took a foothold in such a hostile environment is a tribute to the miraculous strength of Christianity itself. Nevertheless, a sizeable Christian community arose in Persia and became a vital and powerful force, in spite of the hostile environment.

If modern Persia be an unlikely land for a Christian missionary to trod, in the fourth century it was a miracle that Abramios could nurture the Christian church enough so that he stirred the wrath of soothsayers, cultists, and other misanthropes—so much so they banded together for the extinction of Christianity while countenancing each other. The task facing Abramios was insurmountable because although he had won converts at every turn, he appeared to be facing a populace that was a veritable Hydra because for every convert there appeared, not one, but a number of hostiles poised to strike back. The mounting hostility did not deter this courageous bishop who could have taken refuge with his band in friendlier confines, if indeed there were any to be found in this weird land, and awaited a miracle which would rival the parting of the Red Sea. But there was no miracle at hand, and with typical Christian resolve this all but abandoned bishop remained steadfast in his purpose and at his post. He must have known that inevitably the vipers which surrounded his hardy band of Christians would eventually take his life, but undaunted he continued to preach the word of Christ and ignored the ever present dangers. If ever there was a man who deserved sainthood it was the dauntless Abramios.

Abramios was named bishop of Arbela during the reign of Sapur II (371-379). Christian communities continued to establish themselves throughout the land. The spread of Christianity was so great that Bishop Abramios had difficulty keeping pace with the new communities and meeting their needs. He was most successful in winning large areas of the land to the cause of peace in the name of Jesus Christ. In fact, his successive triumphs became the envy of the soothsayers, magicians, and the religious fanatics of the occult. Soon they came to look upon Bishop Abramios as a threat to their own influence. In due course, his enemies bore down on the good bishop with a harsh and unrelenting vengeance.

In a country where treachery and sorcery flourished, it was no great task to bring Bishop Abramios to their own brand of justice. The corrupt rulers, whose authority was in the hands of religious and other demagogues, listened with nodding approval at the grave charges brought against the Christian bishop. When the charges mounted to treason, the judges had no recourse but to cast this very dangerous Christian into prison.

The prisons of ancient Persia not only agonized men's bodies but also tried their very souls. It was in such a prison of ancient Persia that the soft-spoken Christian Bishop Abramios was put to unspeakable torment. Under such dire circumstances one could understand how any man could give in to his tormentors and deny Christ. The unmerciful beatings continued to the point of death, but with cruel cunning he was allowed to recover just enough to absorb more punishment. At each point he was given the opportunity to denounce Christ and worship the sun as the Persians did. Each time the bishop reaffirmed his belief in Christ, the Son of God, who created the sun they saw fit to worship.

When the scimitar of an infuriated Persian severed the head of Bishop Abramios from his battered body on 4 February 347, the soul of Bishop Abramios ascended to Heaven.

February 5

Saint Agathi

An account of the lives of heroines of ancient times is made to read like the story of beauty and the beast with not quite the same ending, but the fact remains that in spite of the grandeur that was Rome, it does not take a full reading of Edward Gibbon to conclude that the moral decay which led to the fall of the Roman Empire stemmed largely from the lack of Christian principles. The femme fatale, which had no small part in the Roman decline, had no place in Christianity but did participate in the destruction of a follower of Jesus Christ, whose stand against immorality and paganism was taken at the cost of her life.

This martyred saint of ancient times was a girl named Agathi, who was born in Panormos on the island of Sicily into a prominent family of great wealth. The vast family fortune would have made her an attractive prospect for marriage if she had the face of a gargoyle, but in addition to being the potentially wealthiest heiress on the island she was also the prettiest. By the time she was fifteen, which was a marriageable age in that era, she was a much sought after prize, but in her earnest desire to serve in the Church she had vowed to preserve her chastity and become the bride of the Messiah. Her devout Christian parents saw no future for her in this but neither did they discourage her, accepting her decision as the will of God.

Agathi was not a hand-folding nun, but she was an active participant in church affairs, joining her parents whose immense wealth they were willing to share with the poor of the island, of whom there were many. These church affairs, while not sanctioned by the state, were nevertheless tolerated because of Emperor Philip who saw no danger imposed by people who sought not to govern but to live in peace. Unfortunately for Christianity,

Philip was succeeded by Emperor Decius, an avowed enemy of Christianity, who tolerated nothing but persecutions and brutality and whose appointments to rule in all the regions of the empire were restricted to men as fiercely opposed to Christianity as he was. This policy resulted in the replacement of the Sicilian governor by Consul Kyndanos who had a reputation for oppressive cruelty which preceded him.

When Kyndanos arrived in Sicily, Christians had already reverted to worshiping in secrecy. But before ferreting out the innocent Christians, he made it his duty to summon the beauteous Agathi, of whom he had heard because since the death of her parents she was considered the first lady of the island. It mattered little to Kyndanos that Agathi was a confirmed church member who was dispensing her vast wealth to the needy. He intended to put a stop to this and to make her his bride, never anticipating in his prideful confidence that she would dare deny the exalted ruler of Sicily.

Agathi obeyed the summons and the sight of her made Kyndanos all the more anxious to make her his bride, and acquire her wealth as well as her beauty. Agathi's reply was that she would consider the proposal only if he were to convert to Christianity, knowing she could not win him over for the Savior nor for the people. The would-be groom scoffed at this idea and reminded her that in obedience to him she would have to disavow Jesus Christ and worship his idols. She then told Kyndanos that it was useless to consider marriage anyway since she had taken a vow of chastity in order to serve the Savior.

Kyndanos hit upon the idea of exposing this chaste woman to the ways of more worldly girls and had her placed in the house of a woman named Frontisia, whose nine daughters did a flourishing business entertaining anyone who would pay. It is to the credit of Kyndanos that his twisted mind conceived this idea but a reminder for all time of his stupidity in presuming that a chaste virgin placed among harlots could look upon them with nothing but loathing. Frontisia had the girl sent back with the message that she was not only intractable but was turning away business.

When he had exhausted every form of persuasion, Kyndanos had the lovely Agathi tortured until she died. She was martyred on February 5. As a footnote it can be added that the tyrant who had her put to death was shortly thereafter swept off his horse while fording a stream, drowning in waters that carried him out to sea, never to be seen again.

February 6

St. Photios, Patriarch of Constantinople

At any time in world history the eminent St. Photios would have been an awe-inspiring picture, but in the ninth-century he was a fantastic mirror of mankind created in the image of God. Master of every form of human expression, a genius in militarism, politics, and theology, he tempered his every action with a genuine humility which eventuated in an ascension to the high office of patriarch. At home with prince and peasant alike, he was all things to all men, daring in political intrigue, artful in cleric and lay diplomacy, and extremely eloquent in defense of the faith in Jesus Christ.

A brilliant scholar, soldier, statesmen, and theologian, Photios was born in A.D. 820, a period when Byzantine culture was writing the brightest chapter in the world history. With prodigious talents suited to that era, his life spanned seven decades during which his glorification of God and man earned him the titles of "Great Star of the Church," "Father," "Doctor," "Confessor," "Isapostolos" (Equal-to-the-Apostles), and finally the ultimate in titles—that of "Saint." In this cultural atmosphere, however, strewn in the path of all men in public life were the many pitfalls of church-state power maneuvering, plots and counter-plots which Photios managed to survive in an unswerving approach to immortality.

The brilliant but checkered career of Photios began with military service during the reign of Emperor Michael III, son of Theophilos, and extended through the rules of Basil I and then Leo VI. From captain of the guard, a post in which he first displayed excellence, he was elevated to imperial secretary, the highest political office in the realm. This was an office whose prominence allowed Photios to display fully his abundant talents, among which were oratory, literature, philosophy, medicine, and theology. Inasmuch as church and state functions overlapped, the complete politician was of necessity a knowledgeable theologian; given this set of circumstances, even the high office of patriarch was within reach of Photios, who was yet a layman.

In a power struggle led by Bardas, uncle of the youthful Emperor Michael III, the incumbent Patriarch Ignatios was forced to vacate his office, whereupon there were set in motion formalities compressed into one week, for which many a patriarch labored a lifetime, to assure the succession to the patriarchal throne by Photios, the undisputed intellectual leader of the Empire. In the span of seven days, Photios was tonsured a monk by Bishop Gregory of Syracuse, then a reader, followed in rapid sucession daily by the successive offices of deacon, priest, and finally ecumenical patriarch on Christmas Day A.D. 858.

Photios had scarcely launched his career when another series of political maneuvers culminated with the assassination of the emperor and the succession to the Byzantine throne by Basil. Having been the favorite of the dead emperor, Photios found himself deposed by the successor, but in a short period of time was induced to return as royal tutor. Basil was not one to waste a mind such as that of the renowned Photios. When the reinstated Ignatios died, the Emperor Basil set aside all other considerations and gave the patriarch's seat to Photios, a choice he made clear should remain unchallenged by rival factions.

As the Byzantine Empire's chief vicar of Christ, Photios wrote one of the brightest chapters in the history of Orthodoxy, a chapter which unfortunately was tarnished by the troublesome dissidents whose clamorous voices all but drowned out a spokesman for Christ whose eloquence remains unsurpassed. The voice of Photios rang out loud and clear, however, when the authority of the Patriarchate of Constantinople was challenged, even threatened, by the western clerics of Rome. There ensued a power struggle within the Church equal to that of any in the state, and it was Photios' brilliant defense of the Orthodox faith that averted a subservience to the West by the East.

In the course of still another series of political intrigues under Leo VI, Photios was again forced into exile, and he retired to live out his last years as a monk in Bordi, Armenia, where he died on 6 February 891.

February 6

Saint Bukulos

Those honored by the Church as saints need not necessarily have submitted themselves to torture and made the supreme sacrifice for Jesus Christ in order to have drawn the attention of their fellow Christians to receive their due recognition. There are many who served for a lifetime and came to a natural end but who were so brilliantly outshone by their contemporaries that even though they have not been overlooked by the Church, their names are not too familiar to the average Christian.

In the days when the Apostles were roaming the earth in missionary labor for the Savior, there were those who were enlisted in creative action for the New Faith but one of many who came forward of his own accord to offer his services, to the extent that he became a saint, has been overshadowed by the Apostles, with the result that his name is little known and little mentioned. Such a saint was Bukulos of Smyrna, whose origins are unknown but whose deeds were well known to the apostles and who has come down to us as one of the most tireless workers for Jesus Christ that ever stopped forward in his name.

Drawn by the truth and love of the Messiah, Bukulos was not content to take a pious but passive posture in the Christian community but preferred to take the none too easy task of spreading the word of Jesus at a time when it took a stout heart as well as faith to take the abuse heaped by unthinking and derisive pagans. If today a presidential agent can be heckled with shouts of "Yankee, go home," one can imagine what an agent of the humble carpenter underwent in the unfriendly confines of hostile town squares. This did not deter Bukulos who was a young man when he went to the apostles with a commitment that could not be denied.

Bukulos came to the attention of St. John who saw in the newcomer an apostolic neophyte with great promise in a cause which sorely needed men who could not be swayed or deterred from their holy mission. Christianity was just taking hold, tenuous at best, and it involved a good deal more than bringing the light to people. It meant keeping that light by organization and development of a cohesive society which would not disperse with the first adversity. Bukulos had the administrative skill to form a strong Christian body that would worship together, so that when he went on to preach anew he would do so with the confidence that the previously formed group would remain intact.

The missionary zeal and administrative skill of Bukulos earned him the respect of the now several numbers of Christian communities, and, as a result the great St. John the Apostle ordained him bishop of Smyrna in Asia Minor in what is now Izmir, Turkey. Under his leadership, converts were added by the score everyday until Symrna very soon became a citadel of Christianity, a thriving spiritual community whose influence spread to the nomadic herdsmen and landowners who otherwise might have not known the inside of a Christian church.

Bukulos was unrelenting in his work for the church, but when the infirmities of his advanced years began to restrict his actions, he did not hesitate to appoint a successor, who happened to be the great Polycarp. Bukulos remained for a period of transition, and at long last, wearied from years of ceaseless effort, he took refuge in simple lodgings next to the church where he spent his declining years in prayer and meditation. He died of old age on February 6 and was interred close to the Cathedral of Smyrna.

Shortly after he was buried, a tree started growing from the earth under which he lay, and when investigation showed there had been no seed planted there, it was considered a manifestation meant to mark the spot where the holy man lay. As the tree grew, it became obvious that it was no ordinary tree, and its branches seemed to have a quality quite unlike that of any other tree that dotted the landscape. An afflicted pilgrim visiting what had turned out to be as much a shrine as it was a tree, placed his hand on the tree as he prayed and was cured. Thereafter, swarms of believing pilgrims came to place their hands on this tree and pray for divine help. The tree is still standing in Izmir, unmolested by the Muslims who respect the right of tourists to touch the holy tree of St. Bukulos.

February 7

Parthenios of Lampsakos

A fourth-century deacon of the Church would be considered more apt to become a saint than an illiterate son who elected to be a fisherman, choosing to cast his nets from an early age rather than thumb through books. But such is not the case with Parthenios of Lampsakos, the unlettered son of a well-read church deacon named Christodulos. Heavenly music can be heard from an instrument played by one who cannot read a note, and the highest reward of heaven can be given to a man who qualified as a spokesman for the Savior in spite of the fact that he could not read or write the words he uttered.

Parthenios, whose name translates into "one of purity," was born in the city of Melitopolis during the reign of the Emperor Constantine the Great who brought out the glowing light of Christianity from the shadows of persecution with an official proclamation known as the "Edict of Milan," an historic document issued in A.D. 313. This acceptance of Christianity allowed Christodulos to worship the Savior out in the open without fear of reprisal, but his fisherman son had observed the wonders of the Lord in the deep and had been open in his adoration of the Savior whether on the deck of his small vessel or in a church.

Apprenticed to a fishing captain at an early age, Parthenios was expected to take flight after his first voyage in the hazardous fishing trade and to run to the first school to beg for a book and literary knowledge. Not lacking for religious fervor to begin with, the young fisherman felt no fear when the first wave crashed into the vessel in a storm. His initial trip stirred within him a resolve to ply the ancient trade for his lifetime, during which he proved that faith, dedication and love can be found in places other than books; and while illiteracy is a definite deterrent to learning, an astute listener with a strong memory and willing heart can remain abreast of a monk of high intellect in the approach to eternity.

While still a very young man, Parthenios took over the fishing boat which the captain was about to abandon because of its age, and with loving care restored the vessel to seaworthiness. Returning from his first voyage as master of his own boat with an ample catch of fish, he decided to give a considerable portion of his supply to the poor, a practice which he made a lifelong habit. He took from each voyage only what he needed to sustain himself and maintain his boat.

It was shortly after his first display of lifelong charity that it was discovered that Parthenios was endowed with the divine gift of healing. From that moment forward, he was transformed into an instrument of the Lord at whose hands those with true faith were genuinely cured. This manifestation was wholly involuntary, and Parthenios sought to minimize his rare gift; but nothing could diminish either this gift or the increasing number of those who sought to benefit from it. Faith healers of questionable repute were usually discredited quickly and sought other pastures, but there was no doubt in this case which was investigated and authenticated by Bishop Philip of Melitopolis.

Bishop Philip was over-awed with not only what he perceived to be a divine gift, but with the amazing ability of Parthenios to quote flawlessly and at considerable length from the Scriptures and other religious articles he had committed to memory simply by listening. The bishop considered this fantastic memory yet another gift, and he prevailed upon Parthenios to become a priest despite the fact that he was illiterate. Implausible as it may seem, the new priest committed to memory nearly as fast as it was read to him enough of theology to fill volumes. But it was in the field, with his understanding heart and wondrous healing power, that the unlettered priest performed with such devotion to God and man that he was made bishop of Lampsakos. In this capacity, he was received by Emperor Constantine himself who saw in him not an illiterate fisherman, but a mighty servant of God.

The emperor saw a need for destroying the pagan temples and replacing them with Christian churches, and he assigned this task to Bishop Parthenios who not only accomplished this transformation, but in so doing won countless converts to the cause of Christianity. On his death on February 7, he was given a state funeral usually reserved for emperors and patriarchs.

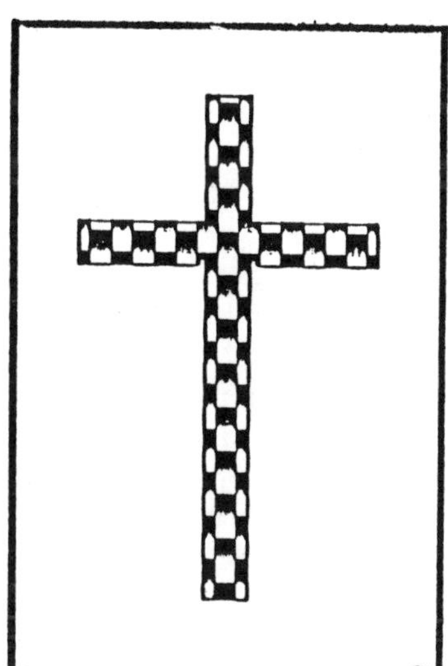

February 7

Saint Luke of Stiris

To rise above the crowd of thousands of monks who spent their lives on Mt. Athos is an achievement of eminent degree but an even greater accomplishment is to emerge from a tiny monastery of far less repute and become a saint. One monk who exceeded others to be hailed as a saint was a man named Luke, Stiris, from the tiny hamlet of Greece which was the site of a monastery which has received a prominent place on the holy map of Greek Orthodoxy. The illustrious name of Luke of the New Testament was undiminished by the much lesser known Luke of Stiris, who paralleled his biblical namesake in complete dedication to Jesus Christ.

Born at the turn of the ninth century on the island of Aegina, site of the shrine of St. Nektarios, Luke was raised in an environment of Christian love which he felt with such intensity that he turned his life over to the Savior when he was but a youth.

The technological distractions of modern times were lacking in the days when Luke lived, allowing ample time for a concentration on the Church or on the other hand allowing the less devoted to live meaningless lives in shallow pursuits. It is to the everlasting credit of Luke that he chose to study theology and the liberal arts, devoting his unoccupied time to a regimen of prayer and meditation.

While still very young he clearly demonstrated that the hand of God was upon him, particularly since he was able to go into prolonged fasting periods, denying him the essentials of nourishment, without suffering any noticeable debilitation. To all intent and purpose he was a virtual monk long before he was to retire to a cloister to formally become one. While others in his age group were playing their games, he chose to play at being a monk, only with him it was no game but an earnest apprenticeship for what was to come. In addition to his study of the classics and theology, the young Luke familiarized himself with the services of the church that he was as proficient in conducting a service as an ordained priest. He amazed all about him with his mastery of the Scriptures, and of a store of knowledge of the sacred music which was the envy of the most accomplished chanter.

Luke was anything but a green youth but more like a seasoned campaigner for Christ when he opted for the little known monastery at Stiris rather than the exalted cloister of Mt. Athos, for which he was more than qualified. From the moment he stepped into the confines of that monastery, he immersed himself into a depth of prayer and meditation that soon marked him as a man who enjoyed a proximity to God. Pilgrims who had been seeking spiritual guidance at the monastery were soon diverted to the newest member of the cloister, in whom they found a sublime serenity and astounding wisdom going away much more spiritually enriched that when they had entered. As the years went by, his fame grew.

The hierarchy sought to enlist his services formally into the church, where he might preach and rise to a post of prominence. Luke politely refused to give up completely the life he had chosen for himself but he made concessions along the way. He went forth from the monastery to be heard by multitudes wherever they might gather but next to his isolation he preferred to spend an evening with a family, engaging in quiet prayer and discussing the truth of the word of Jesus Christ. He is not known to have wandered too far from his beloved Stiris but his fame spread throughtout Greece to such an extent that visitors were constantly pouring into the village, leaving him little time for prayer.

St. Luke of the Bible was known as the glorious physician and by divine coincidence St. Luke of Stiris, without benefit of vaccines and medications, was able to heal the afflicted by divine intervention. He acquired this power of the Lord unwittingly, unaware himself until the sick and afflicted, who were seeking only solace, were suddenly finding themselves cured of maladies. It was this one awesome power that made the Monastery of Stiris a magnet for persons who traveled for miles around.

Unsolicited donations were given to the monastery by grateful pilgrims, particularly by those who had received cures. The money was given to the poor, thus giving the holy work of Luke added meaning. Luke died at a young age on 7 February A.D. 846.

Theodore Stratelates

The fourth century was for the Roman Empire a period in history in which the most admired men of public life were men of the military, particularly generals whose successful campaigns in the name of Rome touched off celebrations in which a hero's welcome would stretch over days of revelry. It is doubtful that this public acclaim would have ever been accorded a general who dared call himself a Christian, even were he to duplicate the conquests of Alexander the Great. Nevertheless, many generals and other high-ranking officers of the Roman legions had come to accept Christ in their hearts in a compromise of religious and political beliefs in the interests of their station and the protection of their families.

One such extremely popular commander of the armies was a man named Theodore who enjoyed not only public acclaim but the close personal favor of the reigning Emperor Licinius (320), who lavished awards and honors on Theodore to the extent that he became one of the empire's most influential and powerful personalities.

No one but his family and fellow Christians knew that in the privacy of his home and in the company of his fellow worshippers this mighty field marshal was but a humble member of the flock who knelt in prayer to the King of Kings. This unfortunate arrangement was a matter of expediency, but if it ever came to a clear choice of one at the expense of the other, the choice would, for this proud soldier, have been for Jesus Christ, as he was ultimately to prove at the cost of not only his lofty position, but his life as well.

Born in Euchaita in Asia Minor, Theodore was well-schooled from birth in the traditions of the military, displaying an excellence and an aptitude for military science and tactics that were furthered in a special school for military prodigies in the province of Galatia. Rising quickly through the ranks, he was yet in his twenties when he assumed command of the garrison at Galatia and resided at Herakleia, a strategic city on the Black Sea. His brilliant generalship in the sporadic battles prevalent in that area and his administrative excellence in maintaining the peace brought him the recognition of the Emperor Licinius. It also led to an invitation by the emperor which he could not deny but which would occasion his commitment to Jesus Christ, a declaration he was to make after yearning to do so after the many years he had kept silent.

The occasion was an invitation by Licinius to ceremonies to be held in the imperial city of Nikomedia in honor of Theodore, at which time he would receive the empire's highest award. The celebration called not only for the usual revelry but also for the observance of certain pagan rites attendant upon the award of the highest honor that could be bestowed.

Theodore realized that he would be unable to participate fully in the ceremonies, and that the time had finally come when he would have to declare and witness for his faith. Consequently, Theodore had only one thing in mind and that was to publicly declare for Christ among the many Christians in the city in which he had earned his fame.

The emperor had brought with him a number of gold idols that were to be set about the scene of the pageant, but at the direction of Theodore the golden images were broken into pieces and taken away to be distributed among the poor. When the emperor demanded to know who had perpetrated this outrage, he was taken aback when Theodore presented himself as the culprit, then and there to declare himself a Christian. He denounced paganism, he stated, as he had so many years ago when he accepted Christ, and was now ready to die for the Savior. The enraged Licinius pronounced that die he would, and Theodore was summarily put to death by crucifixion.

St. Theodore gave his life for Christ on February 8.

February 9

St. Nikephoros the Martyr

"As in the nature of things, those which most admirably flourish, most swiftly fester, those that are most blooming are soonest turned into the opposite." These words are taken from a naturalist of antiquity, Pliny the Elder, a Roman who was thirteen years old when Christ died, whose observations can be applied to a pair of third-century men whose friendship did, indeed, admirably flourish only to fester into a bitterness of feeling that makes for a story reminiscent of an ancient Greek drama. It is a study of the constrasting natures of two men named Nikephoros and Saprikios which culminates in a moment of truth in which each man reveals his true character in an unusual twist of stark reality.

Nikephoros was a deeply religious layman and Saprikios a prosaic priest who lived during the reign of the Emperor Valerianus, in Antioch, Syria, the city that first applied the term "Christian" to followers of the New Faith of Jesus Christ. The two were close friends, despite a difference in their respective temperaments, and were given to verbal jousts on various subjects, usually religious in nature, in the course of which, on one occasion, the usual good humor was lost in a sea of acrimony which developed after an unusually heated exchange. Even after they had stormed away from each other it appeared, in view of their past relationship, that the rift would be only temporary and that when tempers had cooled their friendship would be resumed.

Such was not the case, however, and it was Nikephoros, the layman, who approached his long-time friend, the priest, only to be rebuffed. Nikephoros sought, with genuine humility, to regain the lost friendship, even accepting full blame for the incident and apologizing for having offended one who was not only his friend but a man of the cloth as well. Saprikios stubbornly refused to be reconciled, even refusing to speak to the unhappy Nikephoros, who retreated to wait out his wrathful friend's displeasure, which he felt was sure to dissipate. But before this could happen Saprikios was seized in a new wave of persecutions and cast into prison to await trial and judgment.

When news of the priest's imprisonment reached Nikephoros, he lost no time in arranging through a bribing of the guards to visit Saprikios in the expectation that he would, under these circumstances, be reconciled with his friend and be of some comfort to him. But the priest was as adamant as ever, refusing not only the comfort offered him but refusing even to speak to the visitor. No amount of pleading could sway the priest, not even when he was reminded that should he be condemned to die, his lack of forgiveness could preclude his acceptance into the Kingdom of Heaven.

Saprikios was confident that his office of holy man would save him from the executioner, but he was included with all those who had been apprehended in a condemnation to be put to death. Nikephoros was in the crowd that watched as Saprikios was led to the execution block and noticed the priest's pallor when the death warrant was read. In an act of cowardice rarely seen in priests, the condemned man pleaded for mercy and offered to disavow Christ in exchange for his life. Even the hard bitten pagans were taken aback by this miserable act of wretchedness, and before they could react they beheld the other extreme in man's nature when Nikephoros sprang to the block in a dramatic interruption of the sorry proceedings.

Nikephoros called upon Saprikos to withdraw his shabby offer and then announced he was willing to die not only for the salvation of his weakened friend but to die for Jesus Christ, the Son of God. He called upon all to witness his death as a triumph of the spirit of Christianity, and for those in the crowd who believed as he did, to find forgiveness in their hearts for a man of the cloth who would ultimately find the courage, through their support, to publicly reaffirm his faith in Jesus.

After a brief consultation, those officiating at this inglorious ceremony, content to let one man die in another's place, called for the execution of the noble Nikephoros, who on 9 Feburary 259, went to a martyr's death in what must be one of Christianity's finest hours.

February 10

Saint Charalambos

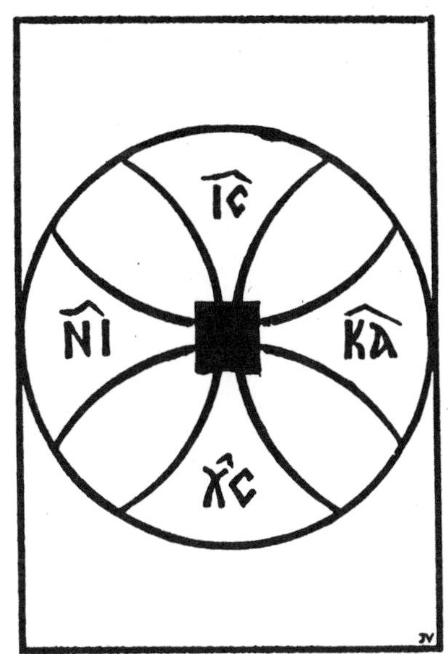

The invincibility of Christianity is epitomized by the superhuman endurance of the priest Charalambos, who suffered inhuman tortures and martyrdom at the hands of pagan tormentors. No single martyr was recorded to have endured as much physical punishment as Charalambos. He was an obscure Orthodox priest who earned his sainthood solely by his steadfastness to the Christian faith in the face of prolonged agonies. Although this seemingly indestructible servant of the Lord had that divine courage and steadfastness of faith which placed him among the saints, he was human and his flesh and blood felt the pain of torture as sharply as any ordinary man. Few Christians have been asked to pledge their allegiance to Christ under interminable cruelty. Charalambos proved faithful to the end. For his steadfast refusal to renounce the Lord, he is venerated as a saint in the highest tradition of the martyr.

Charalambos lived in the town of Magnesia in Asia Minor during the second century. He was ordained a priest at an early age to serve his home town in a province fiercely hostile to Christians. His reputation as a preacher and man of God placed him as the leader of the tiny Christian body that grew steadily under his influence in spite of great odds. A man of the people, Charalambos brought the light of the Lord's love to everyone in his community. In so doing he also brought down upon himself the envy and wrath of those in power.

The provincial governor, Lukianos, had little regard for the welfare of his people; for the Christians he had nothing but utter contempt. A confrontation between the governor and Charalambos was inevitable, as was the result of their meeting. After a brief exchange of formalities the governor unequivocally declared that Charalambos must renounce Christ or be punished. This set the scene for the longest period of human suffering in the name of the Savior. When he refused to worship the idols, his persecutors began a planned assault on his body. Loukianos unleashed his merciless hatred for Christians.

Charalambos was first lashed to a post in the public square to be held up to public scorn and ridicule. Then they slashed him repeatedly with sharp knives, taking care that no wound would be fatal. When Charalambos refused to denounce the Lord, they cut him down and dragged him through the streets by his beard. He endured the extremely painful grating of his skin by the pebbled surface as well as the merciless kicking of sandaled feet. Finally propping him up on his feet, they demanded that he renounce Jesus; once again he refused.

All of the various tortures applied to Charalambos are overshadowed by the cruel fact that he endured them all. After a systematic series of cruelties that spanned several months, the derision of the pagans turned to wonder at the power and the faith of this Christian. When their methods of punishment only served to draw converts to Christianity, Charalambos' enemies sought to put him quickly to death.

The local people, however, rose in opposition to his planned death. Charalambos had helped many afflicted people who were brought to him. The matter was brought up before Emperor Servius, who ordered the battered priest to be brought to Antioch, Syria. Once there, Charalambos was led through the streets with a horse's bit in his mouth. Then they nailed him to a cross. Not only did Charalambos refuse to relent, but he also refused to die. Then they ordered him to be beheaded. Just as his executioners were about to carry out the sentence, a voice said, "Well done, my faithful servant; enter into the Kingdom of Heaven." At that moment he died without a blow being struck, thus denying the pagans their revenge. The two executioners were immediately converted. He died for Christ in A.D. 192.

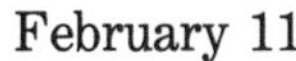

February 11

George the Serbian

In the early centuries of Christianity it was the Greeks who spread the Orthodox faith northward but in the fifteenth century the Ottoman hordes overran not only Greece but the lands north of it as well. An Orthodox Christian known to us now as St. George the Serbian fell victim to the oppressor, whose tentacles might have spread over much more territory had Greece and the Balkans been proven a softer prey, but their Christian tenacity kept the Muslims too busy, much to the good fortune of the rest of Europe. George was born in Cratova, Serbia, the son of Demetrios and Sarah. Raised in true Orthodox fashion, George was apprenticed to a jeweler and as his skill grew, so did his strong belief in the Savior. He soon surpassed his mentor in craftsmanship and was in great demand by the affluent who sought the best in this fine art. His work was of such natural beauty that his skill exceeded that of Turkish craftsmen whose envy grew with George's success.

A man of peace, George wearied of the difficulties his skill had brought him, he moved to Sophia. There he became a close friend of a priest named Peter whose influence imbued him with a boundless love of the Savior. Fashioning jewel encrusted goblets, cups, plates, and even dagger handles brought him into the homes of the most affluent Turks who admired not only his craftsmanship but his strikingly handsome appearance. He ignored the overtures made by Turkish girls who would have preferred him to men they found in Turkish households.

One of the dignitaries who commissioned George for several projects was the magistrate of the city who very soon discovered that his daughters were more interested in George than in his craft. The result was that he found himself a guest in that Turkish household very often. The magistrate, seeking to please his youngest daughter, offered her hand in marriage, knowing full well that Muslim law forbade intermarriage but was confident that this obstacle could be removed. But he underestimated George's Christian will when he sought to induce him to change his religion.

George's work very soon became subordinate to his beliefs and accordingly they were challenged by the magistrate for whom it became a matter of personal faith as well as satisfying his daughter's desire for a husband. George had to set aside his work and counter the Muslim persuasion with a defense of the Christian faith. What at first was a clash of personal beliefs developed into an acrimonious debate and, while George managed to maintain his composure, his opponent's reason gave way to rage. At the very mention of the Lord's name, the frustrated magistrate would only shout obscentities. George had no choice but to leave an enraged host screaming.

For a time there were no more protestations, but the silence that set in was but the calm before the storm. George was suddenly seized and brought to court on charges of treason. There was the usual exchange of unpleasantries, followed by a mockery called a trial. When the treachery had run its course, George was found guilty. Before sentence was pronounced, a malevolent judge offered the condemned man the so-called mercy of the court. He had but to deny Christ, become a Muslim and go forth a free man, ostensibly to marry the Muslim girl. The courageous Christian not only refused, but scoffed at such an offer, and again proclaimed his faith in Christ. When his friend Peter came forth to ask for real mercy, he was turned away.

George was sentenced to die. A pit was set ablaze with burning timbers, and into this inferno George was tossed. When the flames had subsided it was discovered that the death sentence had been carried out, but the lifeless body of the martyred Christian was intact. The astonishment of onlookers, struck dumb at this miraculous occurence, was such that they were content to leave the scene, since the Christian was dead. The magistrate was not satisfied with this amazing result and after ordering more fuel to rekindle the blaze, he had some animals tossed into the pit so that there would be such a mess of what was left, his victim could not be identified. The result was the same. The charred remains of the animals were undistinguishable but the unblemished body of the executed man remained the same. When the process was repeated with the same result, a fearful magistrate released the body to Peter. George the Serbian gave his life for Christ on 11 February 1515.

February 11

St. Theodora the Empress

Anyone bearing the name Theodora must feel an inner pride in having been so named. It not only means the "gift of God," but is also the namesake of one of the most noble souls in all Christianity. Theodora was the wife of Theophilos, emperor of the Byzantine Empire during the ninth century, when the empire was at its zenith.

Royalty has its advantages but the influence of a monarch's wife does not often hold sway, particularly in a complex issue such as Iconoclasm which for 150 years had divided the Greek Orthodox Church. Much as Theodora abhorred the idea of striping church interiors of icons, it is to her everlasting credit that rather than let herself be swayed in her determination, much as she chose to sway the emperor herself, she lived in the hope that the icons would one day be restored and that the issue would be settled in her lifetime although it had stormed for three lifetimes. If for nothing else this profoundly religious woman and empress could have been sainted for her unyielding stand on the issue when she could have chosen a course of resignation or indifference. Claims and counterclaims, lay and cleric, swirled about her and she had but to join sides with the iconoclasts and that in itself might very well have settled the question once and for all after a century and a half of dissension. It could very well be that it was Theodora's courageous stand that made a difference. Hers was not a voice in the wilderness. It emanated and echoed from the palace. The echo of her voice of protest never died and our churches are what they are today because she refused to be stilled. She was not a nun. She was an emperor's wife, but a handmaiden of God by her own choice.

During this period Iconoclasm was a strong, swift-moving force which swept the empire. The supporters of the iconoclastic movement believed that icons should be purged from the churches. They thought that veneration of icons was tantamount to idolatry. In fact, many Orthodox Christians had come to believe that icons, rather than being symbolic, were to be worshiped for themselves. As a reaction against this false understanding of the place of icons in Orthodox worship, many favored the complete elimination of icons. Believing that they were fighting against idolatry, some emperors issued decrees banishing icons from the churches and persecuting anyone possessing icons.

Theophilos was such an iconoclast emperor, but due solely to the efforts of his most noble wife, Theodora, he was the last. After 150 years, Iconoclasm was finally defeated.

During the reign of her iconoclast husband, Theodora secretly possessed many icons. She would kneel in prayer and meditation before her icons, firm in the belief that the time was at hand when the icons would once again resume their rightful place in the house of God.

Shortly after the death of Emperor Theophilos, one of the first official acts of Empress Theodora as regent for her son Michael III was to reinstate the icons. To do this she convoked a General Synod in A.D. 843. This Synod formally accepted the use of icons in Orthodox worship, affirming that the veneration is paid to Christ and the saints depicted on the icons, and not to the material substance of the paint and wood. This historic decision is celebrated each year in the Orthodox Church on the first Sunday of Lent, known as the Sunday of Orthodoxy.

Thus, Empress Theodora gave all her support to the recognition of icons as an essential element of Orthodox worship, and in so doing proved to be an instrument of God's glory.

In her lifetime Empress Theodora revealed her true nature to be more religious than civic, and because of her faith and devotion to Christ, the Church became as mighty as the empire. With her precious icons before her, she died on 11 February 859, a true champion of the Orthodox faith.

February 12

St. Chrestos the Gardener

When God created the earth, He saw fit to place man in a garden, the Garden of Eden; ever since the garden has become a symbol of serenity, peace, and kinship with God. In what better setting could man live the abundant life promised by Holy Scriptures to those who follow Christ than in a garden?

To know nature is to know God. It is largely because of this that the humble gardener Chrestos acquired intimacy with God which placed him among the saints of Christendom. His talent for tending the living things of the Lord paralleled his ability to attend to the needs of his soul and those of his brethren.

Saints abound in the early centuries of Christianity primarily because being a Christian posed a threat to life and in a primarily pagan world a Christian's life was cheap. In the eighteenth century it was another matter since Christianity was no longer a religious hazard and for that reason saints were harder to come by. For this reason the eighteenth century St. Chrestos, a Christian tiller of hostile soil, commands profound reverence in spite of his rather prosaic life and uneventful but genuine service to Jesus Christ. That he was able to retain this deep commitment to Christ while surrounded by those who delight in assailing Christians as "Giaours" or unbelievers, is convincing proof that his devotion to the Savior was total, and although his earthly body belonged to a sultan his heart and spirit were God's. To have been forced to live in this oppressive environment and yet stubbornly cling to his Christian beliefs indicate that Chrestos never flinched though he walked through the lion's den every day of his life. It was only after he had died for Christ that a closer look convinced the Church Fathers that to all intent and purpose his spiritual attainment would have been so greater had he spent an entire lifetime as an asectic.

Born in Albania, he found his way to Constantinople where he became the gardener for the Turkish sultan in 1748. Although he was an Orthodox Christian he nevertheless worked in the garden of the sultan. Because of this the Muslims envied him greatly. They considered him beneath their station and unworthy to set foot in the sultan's garden, let alone bear the responsibility of its upkeep.

Unheeding, Chrestos labored with such diligence that the garden flourished in beauty. His astonishing success with the plant life, which Chrestos realized was a gift from God, served only to intensify the smoldering envy of those about him. It seemed that the kind and gentle Chrestos, in nurturing his garden, also nurtured a hatred in others in the sultan's employ. So intense was their hatred that only the complete destruction of the good gardener could appease their wrath. The gathering storm was evident to Chrestos, but he knew his faith in God would shelter him.

Those plotting Chrestos' downfall knew that the only accusation certain to doom Chrestos was that of treason. His labors were such that he could be forgiven any human fraility. His enemies plotted to draw him into a discussion of his religion, and then bear false witness against him. Their evil scheme was accomplished. Chrestos was falsely accused of holding the Muslim faith up to ridicule, scorn, and derision before many witnesses.

Consequently, Chrestos was cast into prison, where he lanquished for two years under harsh treatment that would have wrenched the soul out of a lesser man. By brutal torture they sought to make Chrestos recant to save his life. Lashes and chains could not make this man disavow his Christian faith. They promised him the chance to return to his beloved gardens in exchange for a simple statement of conversion to the Muslim faith. Chrestos remained steadfast. He accepted the sentence of death knowing that his enemies had failed.

On 12 February 1752, he was beheaded. Not long afterwards he was proclaimed a martyr and canonized as a neomartyr, taking this place among the saints of God.

February 12

Saint Meletios of Antioch, Syria

The dominating influence in the Byzantine Empire during the eleventh century was the Orthodox faith due to the fact that there was no real separation of powers, no clear-cut separation of Church and State. It followed, therefore, that the emperors were an accepted power in the Church as well as the State, and that the bishops exerted influence on affairs outside of the Church. The Church and State worked together for the spiritual and general welfare of the people.

It was during the reign of Constantios (fourth century), son of Constantine the Great, that there came upon the scene Meletios, a man destined for greatness and for sainthood. While serving his post, Meletios established himself as a man of such great piety and wisdom that when the patriarchal see of Antioch was vacated, he was unanimously chosen to ascend the patriarchal throne. He was ultimately to prove himself a true man of God in his successful stand against one of the great heresies to ever menance the Church.

This menace was known as Arianism, so called for its principal advocate, Arius, an Egyptian presbyter. The heretic Arius sowed the vile seed of his philosophy throughout the Middle East and it soon found root in many areas. He held that Jesus Christ, the Son of God, was a created being, a member of the human race and, therefore, his divinity was open to question. Reasoning that there was only one God and therefore one divinity, the concept of a God-man in one person was not as the Church had long held. The eloquence of the Arians was such that it lured many bishops of the Antioch area into the fold. Meletios found himself battling against overwhelming odds. Because of his adamant refusal to even consider the new beliefs espoused by the innovators of his time, the worthy bishop was swept from office by a multitude of Arian followers.

The combined forces of Arianism were no match for Meletios. However, he quickly convened the Second Ecumenical Synod held in Constantinople in A.D. 381. At this synod, Meletios held his position sealing the doom of Arianism. His impassioned arguments for the divinity of Jesus Christ won over even the most stubborn opponents. He vigorously defended the time-honored beliefs of Christianity to the point of exhaustion.

While the deliberations were in progress, he ignored his failing health by working ceaselessly toward a unified and viable Church. Before the proceedings had been concluded, Meletios' frail health gave way and he died on 12 February 382, a martyr to the cause of Christianity. His efforts had not been in vain. The doctrine of Arianism was condemned by the Synod of Nicaea and Arius was excommunicated; the doctrine of the Holy Trinity was thus reaffirmed and the memory of Meletios made sacred for all time.

It is not unreasonable to believe that somewhere in the dusty archives of the Patriarchate there have to be reams, painstakingly written and perhaps modernized, of what took place in the long smoldering issue of Arianism, chief protagonist of which was the heretic Arius from whom the infamous name is attained. One can only wonder how many pages, perhaps long since gone in the dust of time, to say nothing of later Turkish interference, must have been written by the mighty Patriarch Meletios, mighty in mind, heart, soul, and devotion to God but frail of body. He placed his frail body on the altar of Christianity as surely as though it had been placed on the rack, and he had been tortured to death in the name of Jesus Christ.

Patriarch Meletios is a name to be revered and remembered. There are no statues erected in his memory but so long as there is a Patriarchate, and if by some evil chance the Patriarchate should vanish in a Turkish mist, his name remembered is statue enough to remind us of his ceaseless labors, labors that must have carried far into the night to help put an end to Arianism. He slammed shut the doors of the church right in the face of Arianism, but then did not live long enough to witness an official council seal, the doom of Arianism forever. He did not see it, but he had another vantage point.

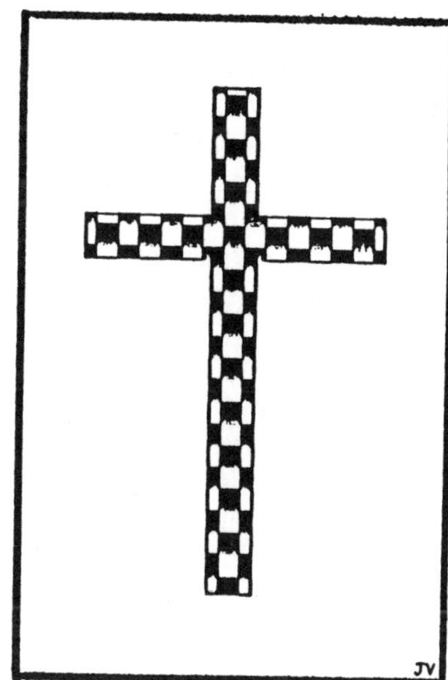

February 13

Saints Aquila and Priscilla

There are few saints who are commemorated twice in the Church's calendar, but such is the case of Aquila. He is remembered by the Church both singly on July 14 and together with his wife on February 13. The name of Aquila's remarkable wife who attained sainthood with him was Priscilla. Her name is synonymous in ecclesiastical history with piety and Christian zeal of the greatest magnitude.

Born a God-fearing Hebrew in a remote region of the Black Sea, Aquilla, together with his equally devout and highly intelligent wife Priscilla, settled in the ancient city of Corinth in the year A.D. 48 during the reign of Claudius, emperor of Rome. Aquila was a tentmaker, a trade which he shared with the great St. Paul. In fact, he met St. Paul in Corinth and this event changed the course of his life as well as that of his wife, Priscilla. After listening to St. Paul, Aquila and Priscilla converted to Christianity. As a matter of fact, St. Paul was so impressed by his new converts that he himself baptized them into the Christian faith. That St. Paul greatly loved them is evidence by the fact that they were mentioned several times in his Epistles (Romans 16.3; 1 Corinthians 16.19; 2 Timothy 4.19).

St. Paul, the greatest of the Apostles, carried the message of Christ to more people and more nations than any other apostle, and it was evident that throughout his magnificent crusade no one was closer to him than Aquila and Priscilla. The fact that this couple had such a close relationship with St. Paul is itself enough to insure their immortality. Yet they were much more than favorites of Christ's chief vicar. Their mutual affection stemmed from their common purpose of bringing the hope of Jesus Christ to all people, a glorious effort in which all three were to share joys and sorrows.

At a dangerous time for Christians when Roman agents were lurking in every corner and were bent on throwing Christians to the lions, Aquila and Priscilla labored for Christ without regard for their own safety. They were not fed to the lions, but the Church Fathers tell us that they were put to death for their steadfast belief in Jesus Christ. They were beheaded, as was their beloved St. Paul, because the law specified death by the sword for Roman citizens.

Not every one mentioned in the New Testament, nor associated with the great St. Paul has been made a saint, but the exceptions are the husband and wife, Aquila and Priscilla, a team whose missionary efforts on behalf of Jesus Christ are shrouded for lack of written record, except for the mention of their names by St. Paul himself. There are accounts, the Bible aside, of their having gone afield to preach the gospel, but exactly where and for how long, is a matter of speculation. The manner in which they died is also a matter of speculation as well. Despite scattered and unconfirmed reports that vary from author to author, one thing is a certainty.

Unlike others who had been approached by St. Paul but declined, Aquila and his wife Priscilla enthusiastically took up the cause of the New Faith and, with St. Paul as their mentor, took to the road to preach the word of Christ. Inasmuch as the ultimate end for those who dared to go forth for Christ was an ignominious and barbarous death, it is assumed that this husband and wife team finally came to a violent end by being put to the sword.

Whatever their end, however, there is evidence enough that, as proteges of St. Paul, they did preach the word of the Savior. Where they went and how long their mission lasted is subordinate to the fact that they both gave their lives over for Jesus Christ and can be numbered among the first saints of the Greek Orthodox Church.

This gentle pair was a source of great joy to St. Paul, the supreme apostle of Christ, and for that alone they merited a place in heaven. Moreover, they were an inspiration to countless Christians. It is because of the selfless devotion of men and women like Aquila and Priscilla that we enjoy the strong faith of Christianity today.

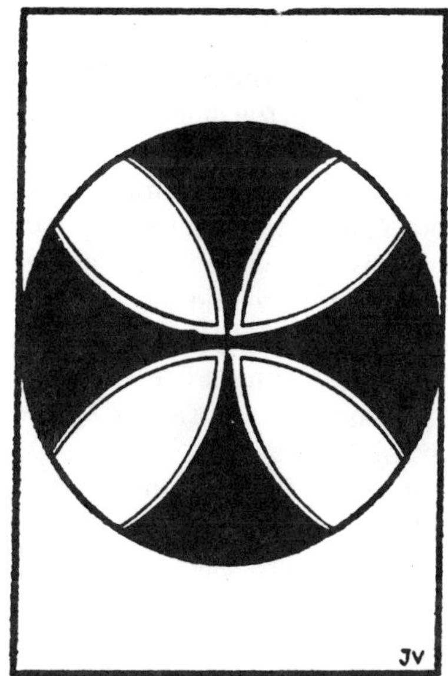

February 13

Saint Martinianos

If ever there was a "Golden Greek," it was the strikingly handsome Martinianos, whose features were something right out of Praxiteles, the unsurpassed sculptor of ancient Greece. His was a rare combination of the beauty of flesh and spirit, but there was no compromise when he chose the latter in total dedication to Jesus Christ.

Not even his parents anticipated the course of action he was to take at maturity. A dazzling appearance can be misleading so it came as quite a surprise when this golden youth abandoned the materialistic pleasures his popularity assured him in order to take up the severe austerity of monasticism. He was just eighteen years old when he made his decision for Christ. It was with some disbelief that his family and friends bade him farewell but if there was any skepticism as to his sincerity it was soon dissipated. Setting out on foot, he left his native Caesaria to trudge some distance to a remote site known as the "Place of the Ark."

This retreat might well have been a dry-land Noah's Ark, except for a small herd of livestock. Each monk had a cell of his own in which to meditate and pray and from which each would venture forth for prayer. Over the years Martinianos was to become known as the handsome hermit upon whom God seemed to continually smile for so great was his devotion and wholesomeness of body and spirit. Pilgrims who came to this ark were deeply impressed by this handsome holy man and felt much closer to God after but a few moments with him.

Martinianos had been there but a short time when one of his visitors, a lovely woman named Zoe, appeared to linger longer than most, obviously smitten by this handsome man. The ingenuous monk took no note of her feelings, accepting her as one of the more faithful who had come to pray with him. Zoe left the monastery determined to make him take notice of her.

Over her fanciest gown Zoe wore the clothing of a poverty stricken peasant and appeared at the gates of the monastery with a plea to see Martinianos just before feigning a swoon as though she had been ill. Carried to the monk's cell, she was administered to by the unsuspecting Martinianos and given permission to remain and rest when she seemed to have recovered. Left alone, she spent the night in a bare cell, but at dawn she took off her shabby outer garment and walked into the unsuspecting monk's cell in her full splendor just as he was refueling a fire. Looking up, the disbelieving monk beheld Zoe and was taken aback by her sudden appearance and by her exquisite beauty.

Zoe declared her love for him and lost no time in making known her intention to make the stunned monk her husband. When he managed to mumble something about his vows, she immediately switched her logic, drawing on stories from the Bible such as the marriage at Cana and the matrimonial bliss enjoyed by so many of the great biblical figures. Overwhelmed by erotic display, the monk was on the verge of embracing her when he regained his control and reasserted his vow of celibacy. Then in an act of repentance for having weakened, he thrust both of his feet into the fire to atone not for what he had done, but for daring to consider doing it. He endured the pain of the flames without a sound as a shocked Zoe looked on and later fled.

Later healed of his self inflicted wounds, Martinianos left the ark for an island so remote that he was its only inhabitant. He received sustenance from fishermen who would leave him with provisions from time to time, making certain that this holy man had enough to live on. He spent about ten years in stark solitude, meditating, and praying for a decade in uneventful bliss until something occurred to cause him to leave. Following a fierce storm, a young girl was washed ashore and was saved by the monk who helped her recover. Still handsome despite his added years, he took care to avoid the girl, whose gratitude soon enough blossomed into something more than thankfulness.

Given her choice, the girl remained on the island to assume Martinianos' devotion to the Lord. He left with the fisherman to take up missionary work on the mainland. After ten years, he settled in Athens, in the company of the city's archbishop, who never ceased to be amazed by the life his friend had led and how he had resisted temptation in keeping with the highest tradition. Martinianos died in Athens on 13 February 392.

Auxentios of the Mountain

The mountains of Greece and Asia Minor cannot even approximate the loftiness of the Himalayas, but they are just as formidable and closer to God because they are inhabitable and do not loom as bleak challenges to climbers who scale the icy pinnacles thrusting upwards just because they are there. While the mountains of Asia Minor do not offer the utmost in flora and fauna, a good many of them have the sacredness of a Sinai or an Ararat because they are the sites of holy manifestations from on high and holy dedication from earthbound men beneath the clouds.

Because their upward thrusts seem to symbolize a holy grandeur reaching out for the divine, men have climbed the mountians of Greece and Asia Minor to join the mighty mountain in reaching out, too, in a gesture towards God, affording an inner peace not to be found in the lowlands. Such a holy mountain climber, who ascended to be near God, was a man named Auxentios, who was not the originator of the idea but who set a fine example in altitudinal asceticism, attaining the spiritual fulfillment that earned him sainthood. In the case of Auxentios, it could be said that in his reaching up, God might have reached down and blessed him with a sanctified life which he wanted even as a boy.

Born into a family of the aristocratic military of the day where stress was laid on skill in the use of arms in defense of the state, Auxentios assumed his heritage with dedication and skill in the tradition which served Christianity in its own way by preventing the barbarous hordes from overrunning the country and destroying not only the state but the Church as well. Seen in this light, Auxentios served God and country admirably until he had seen enough of army campaigns and resigned his commission in order to find the real purpose of his life, which lay in the direction of

Jesus Christ.

The years of comradeship left Auxentios with no desire to seclude himself at the outset, so he found the company of intellectuals, holy men of the Church and pious monks of various monasteries, all of whom welcomed this avid pursuer of theology who demonstrated as mighty a pen as he had a sword. With a resolve to leave his prior service to the state behind him for a more dedicated service to the Savior, he absorbed the teachings of the Church with a mastery that soon made everyone about him forget he was ever a soldier. When he had learned all he could at the hands of the best of tutors in monastery and church, he came to realize that his penchant for companionship precluded the proximity to God he so very much desired. In an about face, he decided to go it alone in the seclusion that would allow him total attention to the word of God through prayer, meditation and penance. Eight miles distant from Constantinople was the mountain of Oxia which he scaled with a determination to roost at its top until he could feel the very presence of God.

Auxentios, in his lonely retreat on the mountain, gradually released his self concern until he was one with nature, animal and God. Already an accomplished authority on theology, asceticism, and its attendant principles, he came to feel a communion with the intangibles of the spirit not acquired through books. A solitary figure, he never felt alone, and in a few months time, he had acquired the appearance of a true man of God, so that when he descended for a brief period, he attracted those who felt the magnetism of this holy man and who found him not only possessed of wisdom but also of that spark of divine grace through which comes healing.

Auxentios was atop his mountain when word came to him that he was wanted in the capital by the Emperor Marcian, who had decided that this holy man of the mountain could resolve the issues raised by Nestorians and Eutychians, among others, causing confusion and disenchantment among the faithful. The holy man came to the city to join other dignitaries in rooting out these evils and without further ado returned not to his mountain but instead ascended Mount Skopa.

Auxentios is credited with having founded monasteries for both men and women, screening them carefully himself to keep out those who sought to escape the realities of life with no real purpose other than self-preservation. He died on this mountain on February 14 and lies in the Chapel of the Resurrection.

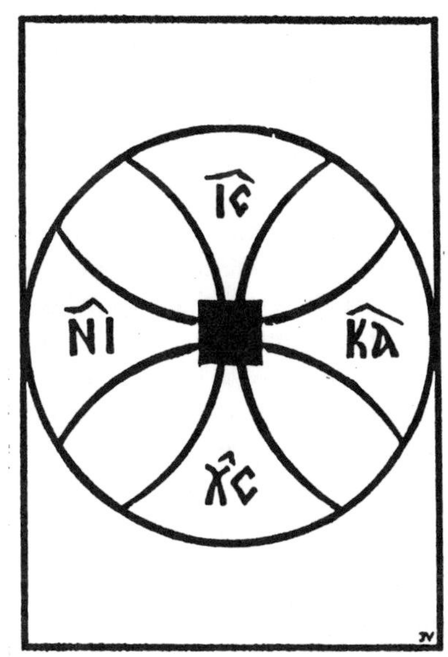

February 14

Saint Abrahamios

More than just crowd pleasers, the greatest of our missionaries were first and foremost eloquent speakers who knew whereof they spoke and since they were speaking of Jesus Christ even the most hostile of audiences gave an ear. One of the most compelling and convincing orators of his or any other time, St. Abrahamios labored for the Lord with a determination and ultimate success that is little short of phenomenal. While a count was never made, the number of conversions made by Abrahamios has never been surpassed.

Born in Kyrrhos, Syria, during the reign of Emperor Theodosios, when being a Christian was legal, Abrahamios prepared himself for service to the Savior by becoming a hermit. His eremitic existence interrupted only when he chose to go forth on occasion, to preach the word of Christ, and then retire to his isolation. In this way, he had made a lasting impression on those whom he reached.

Abrahamios had heard of a hotbed of paganism in a village on Mt. Lebanon. After pondering the challenge for a short time, he strode into the village and let himself be heard. At first he was greeted by catcalls and derisive boos but undeterred he went on preaching ever with refreshing enthusiasm. As the days wore on, the derision and scorn grew less in intensity and the converts increased in number until, after a few weeks, the entire village had been converted to Christianity. After the erection of a church, he was prevailed upon to remain as spiritual leader of the community.

Ever anxious to return to his isolation, he remained for three years and, when a suitable priest had been found, he took reluctant leave of the town and its Christian folk he had come to love. But the call of the desert was not to be denied, for it beckoned.

Many are the mysteries of the desert but for Abrahamios there was only a feeling of kinship. But Abrahamios' reputation lingered on, and he could not escape from it. As a result, he was called to serve as bishop of Karrhre, a diocese that was beginning to assert itself as a stronghold of Christianity.

He ventured into every corner of his diocese. Wherever he found traces of paganism or skepticism, he left abiding faith in Jesus Christ. Known for his piety, he practiced what he preached and was the most respected member of his community, a man who never lost sight of the cross that inspired him. With Christian love at the core of his every action, he virtually eliminated poverty and greed, bringing his Christian flock into an embrace of one another as well as an embrace of Jesus Christ.

Emperor Theodosios was so impressed by Abrahamios' commitment that he summoned the bishop to serve in Constantinople as his religious consultant and to conduct Sunday services. He was also a close associate of the patriarch who, together with Emperor Theodosios, saw in this resolute bishop that spark of the divine that drew so many near to him. As a result of his many successes in the field of conversion, he became the empire's official trouble shooter. He traveled throughout the empire wherever paganism still existed and always left behind Christians who had been taught the folly of their idolatry.

The many journeys of Abrahamios had impaired his health and his earlier days of fasting began to take their toll, but in spite of declining physical condition, his spirit remained as strong as ever and he continued his services as respected adviser to the court. A call came from one of the more remote regions for aid for Christians who were being assailed by pagans. Despite the warning that his frailty would no longer allow such demanding missions, Abrahamios went to the area in question and despite his weakness succeeded in exhorting the pagans to abandon the idols and live in peace as Christians among Christians.

This was to prove the last missionary effort of Abrahamios, who returned to Constantinople in triumph but in physical agony. He lingered for a short time, not once showing any weakness, but finally died. The entire city went into mourning and Emperor Theodosios himself ordered a state funeral, attended by lay and clerical dignitaries from all corners of the empire. According to his last wishes, Abrahamios was laid to rest in Palestine with mourners lining up at the roadside as his cortege passed through. He is commemorated on the day of his death, 14 February 422.

February 15

Saint Onesimos the Apostle

It is hard to believe that the name Onesimos was quite common in the days of Jesus Christ, common because it was a name given to slaves and is derived from the Greek word meaning "useful." St. Onesimos, a friend very dear to the mighty St. Paul, was a slave and retained the name that may not be a household word today but is nevertheless venerated, if only for the fact that Onesimos is the subject of one of St. Paul's Pastoral Letters, the one addressed to Philemon, as part of the sacred literature of the New Testament. St. Onesimos attained sainthood on his own merits in a lifetime of service to the Lord, which ended in martyrdom in Rome.

Onesimos was a slave to Philemon, whom he had robbed and from whom he escaped and somehow became acquainted with the mightiest of all the apostles, St. Paul, who converted the wayward slave and developed a fondness for him. Onesimos was a constant visitor in St. Paul's jail cell and doubtless would have remained at Paul's side to the very last had not the great Apostle decided to send the slave back to his master with his famous letter to Philemon. In this epistle, Philemon is called upon to forgive Onesimos and out of Christian decency to release him from bondage.

St. Paul and Onesimos had a strong bond of mutual love and understanding which was not unlike that of father and son, and the younger man was inspired to assume a position of responsibility in the dissemination of the New Faith, particularly since he could in some way compensate for the loss of the greatest voice of Christianity. He shared the belief of most Christians that without the work of St. Paul, Christianity could never have become the great faith that has stood for two thousand years and will live for all time.

Onesimos joined with Tychikos in carrying not only the letter to Philemon but the letter to the Colossian Church as well, together with a fulfillment of the promise to the imprisoned St. Paul to spread the Gospel to all corners of the land.

Ignatios of Antioch has extolled the virtues of Onesimos for his leadership as bishop of Ephesos at a time when the structure of the Christian Church was very fragile indeed. Onesimos is credited with having not only converted thousands to Christianity, but with buttressing the framework of the faith, providing leadership on all levels to withstand the onslaught of pagans and marauders in general. In this dedicated work he and Tychikos came to be known as "beloved brothers," who inspired a movement of brotherly love as the Savior would have wished. Philemon, the leader of the Lycus Valley churches, was delighted at the sweet success of his former slave, and recognized in him the greatness that was to make him a saint.

There are inferences in historical accounts that Onesimos was imprisoned on more than one occasion, and in different locations, for carrying the word of the Lord, all of which would indicate that he did not necessarily restrict his missionary efforts to the locale of Ephesos. In any event, he did play a large part in the early formation of the Church in areas hostile to Christianity, and he shared the lot of other missionaries who were subjected to indignities and suffering at the hands of pagans.

There is a passage in another of Paul's Pastoral Letters which refers to him as Onesiphoros, a probable confusion of names, but in this letter (Timothy 1.16-18) Paul gives warm praise to the onetime slave when he says: "May the Lord grant mercy to the household of Onesiphoros (Onesimos) for he often refreshed me; he was not ashamed of my chains, but when he arrived in Rome he searched for me eagerly and found me—may the Lord grant him to find mercy from the Lord on that Day—and you well know all the service he rendered at Ephesos." Paul can be referring only to the young man he so dearly loved—and his name was Onesimos.

It was inevitable that Onesimos would meet the same fate as his beloved St. Paul, but it is doubtful that when he was cast into prison there was any young man who came to refresh him as he had refreshed St. Paul. Be that as it may, Onesimos suffered martyrdom in Rome at the hands of the tyrant Tertilus when he was put to death February 15.

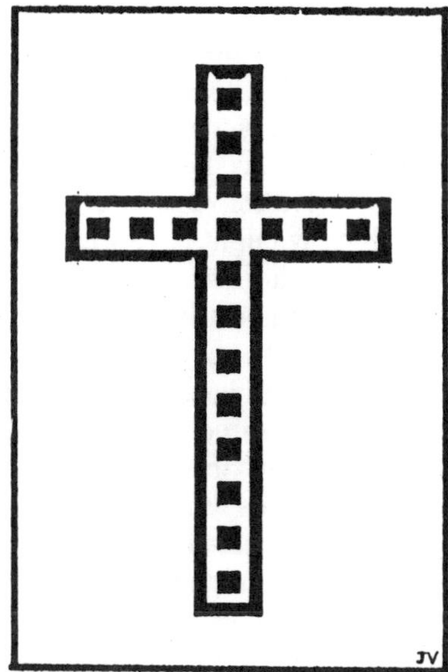

February 16

Flavianos, Patriarch of Constantinople

Blind obedience to the strong-willed emperors of the Byzantine Empire may have played no small part in the disciplined minds that saw to the empire's existence for more than a thousand years, and woe unto him who defied authority. There are times, as in the fifth century, when stubborn monarchs, whose will was opposed to the will of God, ran roughshod over even the patriarchs, as in the case of the Emperor Theodosios II (447) and the Patriarch Flavianos, who dared to defy an emperor in defense of established dogma. Without illustrious men of God such as Flavianos, who have stemmed the flow of dissension when it spilled over into heresy, the Greek Orthodox Church would have been splintered long before now.

Flavianos had succeeded Patriarch Proklos at a time when the heretic Nestorios had given way to an even greater threat called Monophysitism, which was such a radical departure from the established nature of Jesus Christ that knowledgeable theologians recoiled at the very thought of its consideration, denouncing it as heresy of the lowest order. Patriarch Flavianos, recognized throughout Christendom as a learned theologian and staunch defender of the true faith, formally proclaimed the Monophysite concept to be out-and-out heresy. With the full knowledge that the heretic concept had a certain appeal for those less familiar with church teaching (which included the emperor himself), Flavianos nonetheless decreed that those who persisted in following the heretic train of thought would be branded as heretics and would face excommunication.

At the heart of the matter was the solidarity of the Church which Flavianos knew would create new denominations as fast as newer and divergent concepts could be put forth until

Christians would be going in all directions, none of which could arrive at eternity unless it were by accident. The chart had been plotted for all time, and Patriarch Flavianos would countenance no detours or shortcuts, a profusion of which could only confuse the average Christian traveler whose salvation was at stake.

The emperor's acceptance of this heresy might have withered in the blast of the outspoken Flavianos, but there were sycophants in the royal court whose influence over the ruler was considerable and who considered themselves safe behind the royal robes. One of these courtiers, a chamberlain with the undeserved name of Chrysaphios, knew himself to be held in the same low esteem as his political cohorts by a patriarch whose proximity to God put a gap between the Patriarchate and the palace that could not be spanned so long as the given circumstances prevailed. This chamberlain had the ear of the emperor, goading him to exercise the royal power to discredit the patriarch, particularly after Flavianos had condemned through a synod a heretic named Eutyches, who happened to be a close friend of Chrysaphios.

In order to restore the discredited Eutyches, the emperor was prevailed upon by the eunuch Chrysaphios, to convene a synod staffed by bishops in sympathy with the Monophysites (a gathering of hierarchs who shamefully followed the dictates of the emperor in a blind obedience which assured their favorable consideration in the days to come). It then became a standoff between church and state, but the fact that the King of Kings was on one side, and a temporal monarch on the other, was of no help to the patriarch. This sorry series of events led to an even sorrier episode which no Christian likes to recall.

Flavianos was ordered exiled by a witless monarch in league with his character assassins. But before the patriarch could make his departure, he was set upon by a gang of hoodlums and beaten unmercifully at the bidding of those cloaked in anonymity, but known to God. The injuries sustained in the attack that followed what is now known as the "Bloody Synod" proved fatal, and the valiant Flavianos died after three days in exile. His sister petitioned the Empress Pulcheria, who had succeeded Theodosios, to convene a synod in Chalcedon in 451, at which time Monophysitism was discredited and the good name of Flavianos restored. The eminent patriarch was then returned to be buried with full honors. Chrysaphios paid for his crimes with his life at the command of Marcian, consort of Pulcheria.

February 16

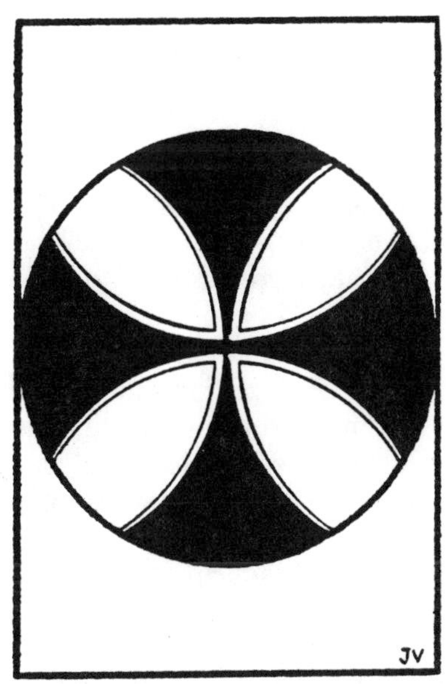

Saint Maruthas

Physician, diplomat, scholar and, above all, theologian, St. Maruthas was a man for all seasons and a man for all reasons, the most noble being his dedication to the service of Jesus Christ, expressing the will of God and man in various ways. In his lifetime, he assumed a variety of roles and was successful in every endeavor he undertook. His loyalty in the service of the Savior was his number one priority, always at the center of whatever responsibility he was assigned.

Born in the city of Sophia, Asia Minor, which bordered on the country of Persia, he became acquainted with the villages and customs of Persia. An excellent theologian, he paired his theological studies with those of medicine so that as a physician he could minister to the physical and spiritual needs of his fellow Christians. After some time, he was chosen to be bishop of Marjferqat whose odd sounding name was of Persian origin. Later, Maruthas was selected to serve as a good will ambassador to the Persian King Sapor II by Emperor Theodosios. As a man of the Church, a physician and diplomat, Maruthas was well known to the Persian king and thus was eminently qualified to bring peace and understanding between two nations with such disparate cultures and religious beliefs.

The first task of Maruthas was to convince a skeptical Persian king that the mighty Byzantine Empire had no design for conquest and that Persia would never be invaded by its superior neighbor. Thus reassured, Napor II was most cordial and flung open the doors of his country for any who cared to visit for exchange of ideas and improvement in relations. The tranquility brought about helped to keep the peace, something shattered from time to time by bandits. There were those in the Persian kingdom who looked upon the Christian kingdom with loathing, but they were forced to keep the peace.

Conditions vastly improved when Maruthas proved the good intentions of the Christian Empire. The daughter of Sapor II became gravely ill and when all hope for her recovery seemed futile, the bishop-physician-diplomat went to her side and after prayer and care, he brought about her complete recovery. The king was so grateful that he ferreted out the pagans who had held captive Christians and saw to it that they were restored to their families.

In A.D. 403, Maruthas appeared at the infamous trial of St. John Chrysostom who had been toppled from his patriarchal throne by sinister enemies from within. Maruthas was only one of the many voices that were raised in defense of the wrongly accused Patriarch but to no avail. The gentle Chrysostom was forced into exile but kept in constant touch with Maruthas. They even wrote to each other about the prospects of inducing the pagans of Persia to convert to Christianity.

Maruthas returned to his diplomatic post in Persia and convinced the Persian king that his subjects should be given a choice, after hearing Christian missionaries. Seeing no harm in this, and knowing that Maruthas represented good rather than evil, Sapor II issued a decree permitting Persians to listen to Christian missionaires if they so chose. He further decreed that there would be no intimidation of Christians by any one.

But, as always, there were those who were determined to rid themselves of the increasing Christian population and that the most direct way was to discredit Maruthas. They tunneled under the floor of the temple which the king attended and smuggled one of their conspirators under the spot where the king was sure to kneel. When he appeared for his usual ritual, he was greeted by a voice which seemed to come from the bowels of the earth. Transfixed, the king listened to the mysterious voice as it denounced Maruthas and exhorted him to rid himself of this hypocritical diplomat. The bewildered king went to Maruthas, who was waiting for him to emerge, but Maruthas had known of the plot and the infuriated king ordered the imprisonment of those who would have made a fool of him. After this sorry event, the conspirators who managed to escape disbanded and normalcy was restored. Returning to Marjferqat, renamed Martyropolis, Maruthas died suddenly on 16 February 420.

Theodore of Teron

The life of St. Theodore parallels that of St. Auxentios because both came out of the military ranks to enlist in the service of the King of Kings. Unlike his counterpart, Theodore was not born of high station and did not scale mountains, in addition to which the state which he served cut short his life. He had his own individuality and identity in an approach to heaven not far removed from that of other saints, however, in whose company he is very much at home.

The origins of Theodore are not known, but had he been born into a family of prominence, it would no doubt have thus been recorded, so it is assumed he was one of the thousands whose physical equipment was such that they were drawn into the military service. He is said to have made a striking figure, a six-footer whose military prowess and straightforward manner caused him to be selected for service in what was known as the "Terian Legion," an elite group noted for integrity and courage. The word Terian means "chosen" and Theodore was just that, except that at the time neither he nor his friends knew that he was chosen of God.

Although he had evinced an interest in Christianity while still a boy, Theodore had not become one until he was twenty-three, when after some secret sessions with a kindly monk, he was baptized into the New Faith in about the year 305. Once baptized, he was not the passive Christian that accepts Christ into his heart and then does nothing to indicate that he is a follower of the Savior, the best indication of which is worship in the house of God. Unbeknown to other members of the Legion, to whom Christianity was a mark of disrespect for the emperor, Theodore attended the morning liturgical services every day, kneeling with genuine humility before the cross.

Theodore managed to attend the Sunday services and to mark the holy days as well without incurring the suspicion of those who would have had him executed. Gradually, however, his faith in Jesus Christ was of such magnitude that he considered it a disservice to the Lord to withhold his abiding faith from anyone, so that he could no longer contain himself, and he openly vowed his Christianity and made no further attempt to demean himself by surreptitiously striking a posture of humility in church and thereafter going about like other soldiers pretending not to know the love of Jesus Christ.

After one particularly sanguinary campaign in which he distinguished himself on the battlefield, Theodore knelt to offer prayers of thanksgiving for having been spared from the death suffered by so many of his comrades in arms. This was noted by those nearby, all of whom were his friends and who held him in such high regard, not one would dare reveal him in betrayal. This did not prevent them from cautioning him, however, to be more careful lest he be seen by someone envious of his popularity.

On the return from this particular campaign, the Terian Legion was cited for its extreme bravery and given a well-deserved rest, which for Theodore meant a pause to make up for the services he had missed while in the field of battle. He was further warned by friends, however, that the Emperor Maximian had stepped up his persecutions of Christians, sparing no one who would not accept him as a god to be worshiped along with the other gods of paganism. Theodore thanked his friends for their concern and said nothing else, but he was even more determined not to hide his faith in shame when he could scarely suppress a yearning to go to the public forum and speak out for the Savior.

The emperor had ordered the commander of the Terian Legion to bring his bravest officers to the temple of the god Rheas where each could offer a sacrifice to the god as well as the emperor, thereafter to be honored for his heroism. Theodore used the torch with which he was to march before Rheas to set the temple afire. Later he passionately poured out his heart for the love of the Messiah. For this act, he was ordered to be burned to death, as he had burned the temple. Though he died in a fire, his body remained intact. He gave his life for Christ on 17 February 306 and was buried in a chapel in the province of Pontos, Turkey. When interred his body showed not the slightest scar, not even a singed hair, proving to all he was favored of God.

February 17

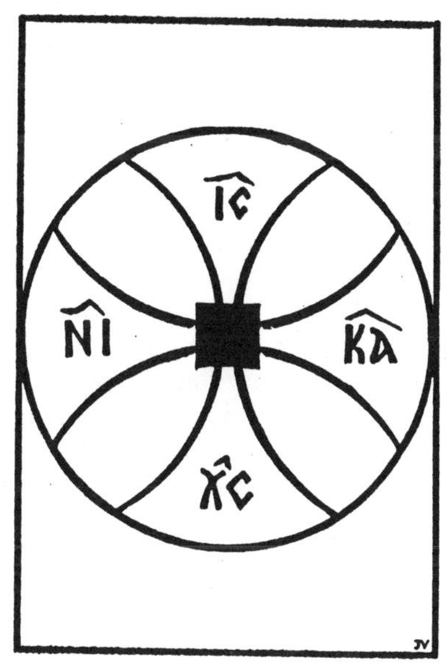

Saint Auxibios of Soli, Cyprus

The island of Cyprus is unique among the islands of the world in that it has seen more history than some continents, and has come under the rule of conqueror, invader, and opportunistic warrior without losing its identity. Lost in this maze of Cypriot history is the little known fact that Cyprus also served as one of the cradles of Christianity. Nevertheless, its primary religious leader, St. Auxibios of Soli, came from another land.

Auxibios was as unique in ecclesiastical history as was the island of Cyprus. He was born of noble parents in ancient Rome. As a son of prominent aristocrats, he seemed an unlikely candidate for sainthood. The first seventeen years of his life were spent in the social graces of the period and in the pursuit of the pleasures of affluence in an unquestioning pagan society. Once he had received the best education and training, the young Auxibios forsook the ways of his parents. He chose to seek out the Holy Land in order to learn about the Christian faith he had heard about and thereafter to find his raison d'etre.

The ship he boarded sailed to Cyprus, marking the beginning of one of the greatest labors for Christ in the first century. St. Mark, who was to spend considerable time on the island of Cyprus, was responsible for Auxibios' conversion to Christianity. It did not take long for St. Mark to realize the genius and sincerity of his convert, and in due course he placed him under his personal care, teaching him the wisdom of the Master. Years of service to Christ passed and Auxibios was rewarded by being appointed bishop of Soli. Shortly afterwards, St. Mark left for Antioch with the full knowledge that the Christian community in Cyprus was in the capable hands of his protege.

The people of Soli were for the most part pagans. Once his arrival in that city, Auxibios made it his first order of business to seek out the high priest of the temple of Zeus. He gained the confidence of this pagan priest with no difficulty. With consummate tact he brought about the conversion of the pagan priest, thereby obtaining a partner to assist him in bringing the message of Jesus Christ to the entire populace.

In a whirlwind of spellbinding oratory, Auxibios converted all of Soli. Soon a magnificent church was built where all could worship as Christ had ordained. Years passed and the entire island was dotted with beautiful churches. Christianity flourished as no other place so isolated. Bishop Auxibios died in A.D. 105 and was laid to rest in honored glory in a crypt beneath the first church he had built so many years before.

Very soon after he had been entombed, there issued from the crypt of St. Auxibios a spring whose water was discovered to the power of miraculous healing. According to church history, many lepers anointed themselves with the water of Auxibios' tomb and walked away cleansed. These miraculous cures continued for many years until suddenly the water ceased to flow from the crypt. It would not be wrong to point out here that since the birth of Christ, the checkered history of Cyprus has varied with the pennants that flew from the masts that touched upon its shores, but as steadfast as its hills and its inherent Christian religion is the reverence accorded St. Auxibios. The miracles that stemmed from the site of his martyrdom have ceased but there is a miracle, not attributed to Auxibios but certainly aligned with him, especially on his feast day. That miracle is the retention of the thoroughly Greek character of the islanders, the Turkish invasion notwithstanding. It is the observance of such days as the feast day of St. Auxibios which binds the Greek populace in the love of Jesus Christ. Without days such as these the island might well have lost its identity long before the Turkish troops overran the island in violation of international law. St. Auxibios and others like him assure the permanence of Orthodoxy on Cyprus.

The feast day of St. Auxibios is celebrated on Cyprus with great ceremony and solemn splendor each year on February 17.

February 18

Bishop Leo of Rome

A man of considerable influence while still a deacon, St. Leo had advanced to archdeacon when he was the unanimous choice to become bishop of Rome, oddly enough in absentia since he was at the time of his elevation, somewhere in Gaul settling a dispute between a pair of squabbling generals. The unity of the Christian Church had been tenuous at best for the first thousand years of its existence, since the western sector insisted on the primacy of the Bishop of Rome, while the eastern sector, never asserted its bishop's primacy but deferred to the extent that it conceded that the bishop of Rome was the first among equals.

Born in Rome, or as some historians claim, in Volterra, Tuscany, Leo came in 429, with his outstanding defense of the faith against the heresies, especially those of Nestorians and Eutychians who flaunted the Orthodox concept of the dual nature of Jesus Christ. Leo had already shown his superior ability in 431, nine years before becoming bishop of Rome when he joined with Cyril of Alexandria in suppressing the far fetched scheming of Juvenal of Jerusalem, who grasped for power in the Church.

When in 448 Euthyches, an archimandrite of Constantinople, wrote to Leo about a growing concern about the revival of Nestorian heresy in that eastern city, he made that heresy number one in his priorities for the sake of all Christianity. Euthyches meanwhile had been deposed and the emperor convened a council to settle the issue. Although Leo was not in attendance, he did send three representatives, one of whom read Leo's eloquent letter addressed to the council in defense of the Orthodox doctrine of the two natures of Christ. For some reason the letter was never read and somehow the opposition, in the person of Dioskoros, bishop of Alexandria, removed from office both Flavian and

Eusebios, bishop of Dorylaion, both opposed to Euthyches. When the news reached Leo of this shabby affair, he lost no time in asking the emperor for a new council.

Although Leo would have preferred that the council be held in Italy, the emperor opted for Chalcedon where in 451, the historic Fourth Ecumenical Synod took place. Leo's theological stance was upheld, but when the council reasserted an earlier canon establishing the equality of the sees of Rome and Constantinople, Leo refused to accept it. He could never accept the fact that the capital of the empire was Constantinople, clinging to the traditional concept that Rome was the center of the civilized world which was a political ideology that spilled over onto theological ground.

The textbooks of history, as well as those of the Church, record an event in which Leo is established for all time as a heroic figure, an event for which he is best remembered. The barbarians of western Europe, led by Attila the Hun had ravaged much of the countryside to the north of Italy and in 452 they began their descent on Rome, looting and pillaging villages along the way until they had reached the town of Peshiera. The barbaric horde was poised to strike the Eternal City, pausing in camp by the Mincio River before gathering for their greatest assault. Emperor Valentinian III saw that the only hope to save the beautiful city, virtually defenseless against insurmountable odds, lay in the hand of Bishop Leo who did not hesitate to comply with the royal request to save his beloved Rome.

Armed only by a small contingent of churchmen, with civic authorities in the persons of Avienus and Trigetius, consul and governor of Rome respectively, Bishop Leo met the barbarians at the outskirt of the city. Leo not only persuaded the feared Attila to spare the city but induced him to turn back as well. Attila was convinced that there was nothing to be gained by reducing magnificent buildings to rubble and butchering women and children but it is generally conceded that for going away in peace some tribute had to be paid to the barbarian. Some three years later Leo was less fortunate in saving Rome completely from the barbaric hordes of Gaeseric, the Vandal king. Meeting with Leo outside the city walls, the Vandal asked the bishop to step aside, entering the city for booty alone but sparing it from total destruction.

Pope Leo died in A.D. 461, and his feast day is observed by Orthodoxy on February 18.

February 18

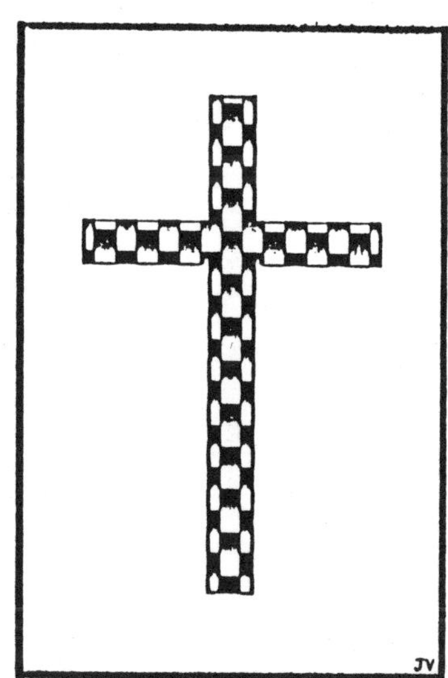

Saint Agapetos

Since the dawn of Christianity there has been such a profusion of spurious, self-appointed faith-healers who have defiled the image of Jesus Christ in opportunistic panaceas for profit that except for those few who have been enshrined in various parts of the globe, all others in history who have been divinely blessed are generally overlooked. Because there has been such a mockery of the divine will over a period of two centuries of countless deceptions in a ritualistic laying on of hands, the image of those who were true instruments of the Holy Spirit have been somewhat clouded and, in too many instances, lumped in with the charlatans of Christianity.

One such true instrument of God was a man named Agapetos of Sinai, whose quiet service in the name of the Savior was of a nature whose brilliance not only adds to the glory of God but serves to discredit all the imposters.

Agapetos was not a faith-healer in the accepted understanding of the phrase, but a man whose extreme piety imparted an aura of the Divine which coincidentally served to perform that which has to be called miracles. It was the will of God, not this holy man, that was expressed through a chosen human form to the benefit of men of faith about him and to the glorification of Christianity throughout the world.

Agapetos was born in the late third century and came of age just prior to the ascension of Constantine the Great who is revered as a saint in the Orthodox Church and remembered in all history by all as the emperor who declared personally for Christianity and extended toleration to all Christians in his momentous 'Edict of Milan' in A.D. 313. This served to swell the visible ranks of Christianity because of the simple fact that those who had been "closet

Christians" could now let themselves be counted without fear.

Like so many of the early saints before him, Agapetos embarked on a career in his youth which hardly suggested what he was ultimately to become. He had lived for a time in Cappadocia, one of the many cultural centers that were to usher in the Golden Age of Christendom.

The name Agapetos stands for "loveable one," a name that was never more deservedly given to a man who so endeared himself to his fellowman that he is one of the rare ones accorded saint-hood while yet living, a practice long since abandoned by the Church Fathers, but which would be resumed had he been born in the present generation. His popularity increased and his fame spread throughout the land when, as a humble monk, he was found to have the power of healing. The solitude he sought was denied him and he was ultimately received by the emperor, as a result of which he was prevailed upon by the hierarchy to serve publicly for the common good and was ordained a priest, at which time he carried out his duties while yet observing the asceticism and self-denial of the monastic. Agapetos was the unanimous choice as bishop in Bythinia, in a course of which he firmly established himself as a man who walked with God. He denied no one who came to him for help and although there is no doubt that many of the afflicted who sought his hand went away without cure, no one left his company without hope or at least a reaffirmation of their faith in Jesus Christ. He is said by church accounts to have achieved over 100 miracles, but the greatest miracle is that he was chosen of God.

Popes have no great difficulty in proving themselves equal to the task to which they have been elevated, but St. Agapetos was a rare pope indeed. In an era when modes of travel were slow, painful, and boring, he made one unified church out of the divided groups in the only way left to him. He took it upon himself to seek out every church and to chant the sacred hymns within its walls, bringing about the unity that had eluded his predecessors because he would allow no section of the church, however remote, to elude him. A doctor of the Church in every sense of the word, he brought about more healing of the Church's self-inflicted wounds during his tenure than in any of the tenures that were to follow, otherwise the great schism splitting east and west might not have occurred. Thus, in two short years, he was to bring hope to thousands who yearned for peaceful unity and it is only after five centuries that the dashed hope raised by Agapetos have been once again reasserted. St. Agapetos died in old age on February 18.

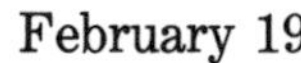

February 19

Saint Philothei

The time-honored country of Greece occupies an ill-defined peninsula of the Mediterranean which yields very little in the way of natural resources except perhaps its people, who have been resourceful enough down through the ages to yield to civilization some of the world's greatest figures in science, culture, politics, and religion. At the center of this glorious land is its capital city of Athens, which has been hailed throughout the world for centuries for its great minds, among which is a sixteenth-century woman whose stand for Christ parried the thrust of the Turkish invader and helped assure the permanence of Christianity not only in Greece but in other lands as well. Her name was Philothei, who translated piety into action for God and man in the face of overwhelming odds.

Philothei was born in Athens into a affluent family in the fateful year of 1550, when Christianity was being put to its severest test by a malevolence from Islam holding hostage all of Greece. Reared in an atomosphere of love and forbearance, she was given in marriage to a young man whose early death made her a widow before she was sixteen. Returning to her parents, she took up an active role in family as well as civic and church affairs, finding contentment only when she was doing something for the oppressed and the poor, a peace of mind which drew her closer to the Church. The family wealth afforded her the pleasure of charitable work, and while still a young woman she had gained the respect and love of the community not only for her charity but for her sincerity as well.

When her family died, Philothei found herself the owner of extensive holdings, the direction of which she assigned to others while she became a nun in the Orthodox Church. Meanwhile, her considerable wealth was put to use not only to help the poor, but in the glorification of the Lord with the erection of several churches and nunneries in and around the city of Athens. At her direction, the nuns transferred from passive to active interests, learning to supplement their devotions with practical crafts and arts for the good of the Church as a whole. Her useful works set the pattern for handiwork that has been the hallmark of nunneries for many years.

There was little trace of the glory of the Byzantine Empire but the glory of Christianity was present everywhere, much to the annoyance of the Turks, who had fondly hoped that Muslim pressure would result in the gradual replacement of Christianity by their own Muslim faith. This Turkish effort met with absolutely no success, but the pressure was constantly being applied to the hapless Greeks, nevertheless, and the unrelenting Muslims sought every means of discrediting the leaders of the Christian community. But leaders like Philothei did not give ground and were made even more resolute in their service to Jesus Christ.

When it was evident that Islam could not take root in Athens, a Christian stronghold since the days of the apostles, the Turks lashed out at those in the vanguard of Christianity. They deliberately selected Philothei as their principal target, not only because everything she did was in open defiance of the Muslims, but they considered her femininity a weakness that would more readily acquiesce. They were unaware that Christian defiance knows no sex. They might as well have assailed the rugged mountains that surround the city, and in their frustrated anger they set themselves on a brutal course of terrorism.

Philothei had built a beautiful church dedicated to St. Andrew which still stands today, and it was in this house of God that the Turks set upon her and her friends during a service. The defenseless women were clubbed and stoned, then dragged out into the street to be brutally murdered in full view of outraged Athenians. Philothei was carried from the scene of this carnage but succumbed to her wounds, 19 February 1589, at the age of thirty-nine.

A number of miracles have been attributed to Philothei since her death, particularly at the cathedral in Athens and at the Church of St. Andrew, in which her relics are enshrined. The street on which the archdiocese is located is named after her and the cathedral contains one of the most beautiful Byzantine icons of St. Philothei. Her churches and nunneries are still in evidence, and numerous women's organizations carry her name to honor one of the finest daughters of the city of Athens.

February 19

Saint Rabulas

In the sixth century, the full Hellenic nature of the Byzantine Empire was only beginning to emerge and the nations with ill-defined borders overlapping each other were more readily identified by the language they spoke. The ethnic background of St. Rabulas was unmistakably Syrian in the polyglot countries that made up the empire, but as a devout Christian he managed to retain his identity while assuming a cosmopolitan posture as a citizen of the civilized world.

What the renowned tutor Gamaliel was to St. Paul, a man named Barysabas, the greatest tutor of his age, was to Rabulas, an extremely apt pupil who, like the great St. Paul before him, was to exceed his mentor, eventually to be elevated to sainthood. An eminent scholar, historian and educator, Barysabas had every reason to believe that Rabulas was the brightest pupil he had ever taught, one who mastered the Syrian language and was fluent in others, particularly Greek, the language of the realm as well as the Bible. Rabulas coupled his intense study with a disciplined austerity patterned after monasticism.

It was inevitable that Rabulas would seek out a monastery, there to not only hone his scholastic aptitude but to engage in the isolated self denial of fasting which together with prayer and meditation, go to make the complete monk. In a few short years his renown as monastic scholar, theologian and holy man went beyond the walls of the monastery, as a result of which had no difficulty in getting financial assistance from the Emperor Zenon, as well as Archbishop John of Beirut, both of whom formed a lifetime attachment to the scholarly monk. Amply funded, Rabulas built an admirable monastery on a select hill which seemed to serve as a beacon for miles around. Its spiritual brilliance not only served to light the way for the religious residents of the area, but it attracted men of God in such numbers that there was always a full complement in the monastery devoted to serving Jesus Christ.

One of Rabulas' most monumental achievements was the conversion to Christianity of the rock ribbed pagan area of Phoenecia. Many a Christian missionary had abandoned these idolaters in disgust after barely winning a convert here and there, almost as if to say that they were not worth saving. Into this obdurate nest of agnostics, Rabulas seemed to have set himself a thankless task but with the resolve and convincing manner that had stood him in good stead in prior years, he swept aside the cobwebs of centuries of spiritual ignorance and within a short time Christianity had taken a firm hold in Phoenecia.

Rabulas had scarcely rested from his labors in Phoenecia when he was called to Constantinople by Emperor Anastasios I, who had succeeded Zenon. Anastasios had been dubbed Dikoros, because of the fact that his eyes were of two different colors. He seemed to have accepted this sobriquet in good humor, but Rabulas discouraged the use of the name Dikoros, for which he won an even greater respect from the emperor. A democratic and deeply religious man, the emperor was more than cooperative with his spiritual advisor, giving as much attention church affairs as he did to those of the state.

It was the emperor's idea that a monastery be built within the confines of the city. When the edifice had been completed, he was humbly grateful to the emperor who insisted on naming the new cloister "Rabulas," in honor of this faithful servant of God. The walled monastery seemed to escape the clamor of the city as its immediate neighbors observed a hushed silence. Within walking distance for the capital residents, the city monastery proved an immense success and a better understanding of monasticism was brought about for the thousands who for one reason or another were never able to reach the far flung spiritual bastions that lay in remoteness or inaccessibility.

In the course of the erection of this and other monasteries, Rabulas performed the amazing feat of committing to memory every word of the seventy-six books of the Old Testament, from which he could quote frequently for whatever occasion. Shortly after he had entered his eightieth year of earthly life he responded to Christ's call to come to him "and I will give you rest." He spent his last days in Constantinople, where he died in the year A.D. 530.

February 20

Bessarion of Egypt

The forbidding desert areas of ancient Egypt have beckoned holy men from all parts of the civilized world for a number of reasons, not the least of which is the bleak solitude that can be found in a land shunned by all, save the scorpion and the reptile. Unfit for human habitation, the desert has nevertheless sustained many a monk or eremite, one of whom was a fourth-century monk named Bessarion. His incredibly long endurance in a trackless waste makes him a standout in human endurance, if not holiness, among others who have acquired fame or sainthood in much the same manner, but who have not subjected themselves quite so much to the punishment on which he seemed to thrive.

In his quest for spiritual perfection, Bessarion literally wandered in the desert for a period of forty years, taking root in no particular spot and availing himself of no comfort of a hearth or home. He wanted to prove that his temporal life was of no consequence to him while he sought out every spiritual avenue he could find to prove himself worthy of the kingdom of the Savior to whom he was completely given over. His long deprivation staggers the imagination, but offers convincing proof that he had to have divine assistance to survive four decades in a test of fitness that would fell an ordinary man in a matter of days.

The self-denial of Bessarion exceeded that of his teacher and spiritual mentor, no less a person than the great St. Anthony, one of the first and undoubtedly the most famous desert monks to be sainted by the Church as a reward for their spiritual attainment through the exclusion of the practices of ordinary human beings. In addition to St. Anthony, the durable Bessarion had the good fortune to acquire a considerable knowledge of theology and dogma from another Christian luminary, the pious St. Makarios, who saw in his pupil that spark of divine grace that enabled him to withstand the rigors of the desert and reach the spiritual perfection so often sought and so seldom found. When some of the details of the life of Bessarion are known, even the most cynical of skeptics accept his purity.

Like a maverick that has strayed from the herd (except that it was by choice that he wandered), Bessarion never sought any kind of shelter. He endured the heat of the day with the same indifference he assumed as he sat or stood in the chill of night, sleeping in either position for all of his years. Not once did he allow himself the comfort of stretching out to lie down on the ground, to say nothing of never taking to a bed in sickness or health. The rigors that sap human life he found invigorating, allowing him to spend his every waking moment not concerned with his physical well-being, but with prayer, fasting, and meditation.

On the rare occasions when Bessarion found himself in the company of men, he exhibited that rare gift of healing that comes from proximity to God. From that it can be assumed that he is not known to have had an illness in his lifetime (inasmuch as he was capable of healing himself or was immune to diseases that ravage civilization). Oddly enough, in avoiding civilization he became all the more civilized in the sense that he was what every civilized man should be in his attitude towards his fellow man and to the Savior.

In an incident that cannot be doubted when it is considered that bears hibernate for a period of months in winter, Bessarion, for a period of forty days, propped himself against a tree in a thicket of the desert and remained in that fixed position without food and water. For the bear this is accomplished by nature's slowing down of the life process, but for Bessarion it was accomplished through a divine process.

Bessarion became a living legend with his extraordinary lifestyle, so much so that children were named in his honor. Apropos of which it is not generally known that a Russian named Bessarion had a son called Joseph Stalin whom he hoped would become a priest. Instead, the boy chose a course exactly opposite that of his father's namesake. Not many, if any, children bear the name of Bessarion today, but his name is perpetuated with an annual feast day on February 20th.

February 20

Saint Leo of Catania

While sorcery and witchcraft until recent centuries were not dismissed by God fearing Christians, they represented forces of evil which account for the wretchedness of today that cannot be denied for the simple reason that evil exists in many forms, most of which are dismissed as accidents. Even the tragedies of tornadoes or other destructive forces of nature are listed by insurance agencies as acts of God. They are more, the acts of demonic power to which only Christianity is the answer. Answers to evil have been demonstrated by men such as St. Leo, bishop of Catania, when overt acts of evil were witnessed but which today come in disguises that are passed off as bad luck, tragic coincidence, or that word "accident" which covers a multitude of evils. Even in this century, holocausts and genocide cannot be called accidents. They are the demonic forces of yesteryear and the only hope lies in the Christian love as demonstrated by men such as St. Leo of Catania.

Born in Ravenna, Italy, which to this day bears the traces of Byzantine glory in some of its architecture, St. Leo stemmed from nobility, which he chose to set aside in order to serve Jesus Christ. Like the newsboy who rises to become the editor, he rose from acolyte to bishop of Catania. He chose to serve Christ who embraced him for all his charmed life on earth and beyond. From youth he had evinced that spark of the divine rarely endowed on man but when he had reached the post of bishop his proximity to God was beyond question, needing not even a halo to convince the most skeptical and cynical who could not fail to see the divine aura about this man or feel a divine presence wherever he chanced to be.

That the power of the Lord was with him followed his missionary efforts in Sicily where pagan holdouts, including a great number of Hellenes, continued to plague Christianity even in the eighth century. It was Leo's tremendous success in converting pagans into devout Christians that placed him a cut above and earned him a renown as a man of God to be reckoned with by any who dared assail the faith in Jesus Christ. On one occasion he was challenged to demonstrate the power of his Lord, whereupon he went to one of the remaining Hellenic pagan temples and after praying briefly the temple was not only reduced to rubble but out of its remains there sprouted the Cross of Jesus Christ.

St. Leo, was challenged by a man named Heliodoris who had made a pact with Satan in order to gain power over his fellow man. An apostate who had denied Christ, Heliodoris challenged Leo to a show of strength between them to be held in public. At first inclined to scoff at this ridiculous proposition, Leo prayed for guidance and to be worthy of this challenge and affront to God.

Leo agreed to the test which was to walk through a roaring fire in an open furnace built especially for the occasion. A huge crowd gathered, including the emperor who was most anxious along with other Christians, to witness the power of the Lord and to pray for the man chosen to display this power. When all was in readiness and after some fanfare, Leo took Heliodoris and led him into the fire, emerging from the flames alone and unscathed. All that remained of Heliodoris could have been put in a small urn. The point had been clearly made. God has power over the devil.

This spectacular turn of events catapulted Leo into a prominence even the most faithful of his followers had not anticipated, as a result of which he was asked by Emperor Constantine VI to come to Constantinople where he could be greeted by the entire city and given a hero's welcome usually reserved for a conquering general. The accolades were humbly received by this servant of the Lord who remained in the city by popular request, serving as religious adivser to the emperor.

Leo was finally permitted to return to Catania. His first act upon returning was to erect a chapel, thanks to the generosity of the emperor, which was dedicated to St. Lucia, a martyred saint of Sicily, a church which still stands in Catania. The remainder of Leo's life was anticlimatic, choosing to roam about the island as the spirit moved him and winning even more converts. He finally passed away in 875 and was buried beneath the Church of St. Lucia, which is a shrine of Christianity to this day.

February 21

Eustathios of Antioch

The early church of Jesus Christ was composed of five episcopal sees, each supreme in its own sphere of influence and collectively answerable to the Kings of Kings. The five centers of Christianity were in the cities of Alexandria, Antioch, Constantinople, Jerusalem, and Rome, the last of which, because it was the political center of the empire, had a bishop, as did all the others, who was honored with the title of "first among equals." If America had one religion and each of its large cities had a bishopric see, it is doubtful that Washington, D.C. would be the first among equals, let alone preside over the entire country spiritually. If there were a power struggle among bishops such as there is among politicians, then the large metropolitan centers would have much more to say about who was supreme.

It is strongly felt by Orthodoxy that religion need not have followed the patterns of politics and that if each see acted in concert in guiding the destinies of Christians, the Church would never have splintered. This is brought out to emphasize the eminence of St. Eustathios of Antioch who is a little-known saint, not because of his small contribution, but because his stature has diminished over the years because Antioch is scarcely more than a memory. The assertiveness of Rome in 1054 split the East and West in a 900-year rift which both sides hope one day will be resolved in the interest not only of Christianity but of all humanity.

In the early fourth century, events were already taking place in which churchmen shamefully committed misdeeds with no thought given to the Savior's turning of the other cheek. Victimized in this religious upheaval was the bishop and Patriarch Eustathios, who alone could not stem the tide of heresy and intolerance, rising within the Christian community and threatening to engulf tradition and church law. One of the menaces was the heretical dogma of Arianism, but on its heels were other heresies being pursued by various segments of the church which were not far above the squabbling of soothsayers and cultists. This lamentable situation meanwhile was being looked upon with glee by pagans whose leaders anticipated the self destruction of a religion they had sought to destroy in vain for centuries.

A council was finally called by the Emperor Constantine in 325 to put an end to this internal strife. Among the champions of traditon called upon to discredit Arianism was the venerable Patriarch Eustathios, who joined other clerics of distinction in a condemnation of the wily Arius, excommunicated in a document with such a conciliatory tone that allowed his followers in the Middle East to continue to influence thought after the council had adjourned. Each of the dignitaries returned to his respective community convinced that peace and order had been restored, but that was hardly the case. The Arians were stubborn fanatics, as subsequent events were to prove.

While yet discredited they sought to fight back by bringing about a denunciation by devious means of those who had been in the ban at the council which had been so nobly conducted, only to be attached later on. The prime target for the malcontents who refused to concede to the truth was Bishop Eustathios, whose downfall was carefully plotted and relentlessly pursued. Conspirators to the man, they set false rumors into circulation, nursing these vile innuendos until they assumed serious proportions which they were clever enough to make appear credible.

With mounting howls of protests for the bishop of Antioch to step down, the detractors of Eustathios sent a delegation to the emperor with documents tailored to their claims of the holy man's guilt, the clamor being capped by a sworn statement of a bribed prostitute that the aging bishop had fathered her illegitimate child. When Constantine hesitated to act even with this contrived evidence, Eustathios was then falsely accused of having deliberately insulted the sister of the emperor. With ever mounting criticism assuming the proportions of a storm of protest never before to reach the royal household, Constantine finally gave in to the Arians in Thrace.

The woman's confession on her deathbed that she had lied after accepting a bribe to falsely accuse the bishop came late. Eustathios died in exile on February 21, but his earthly remains were brought back to Antioch for an apologetic funeral service at which he was eulogized by the greatest orator of all time, John Chrysostom.

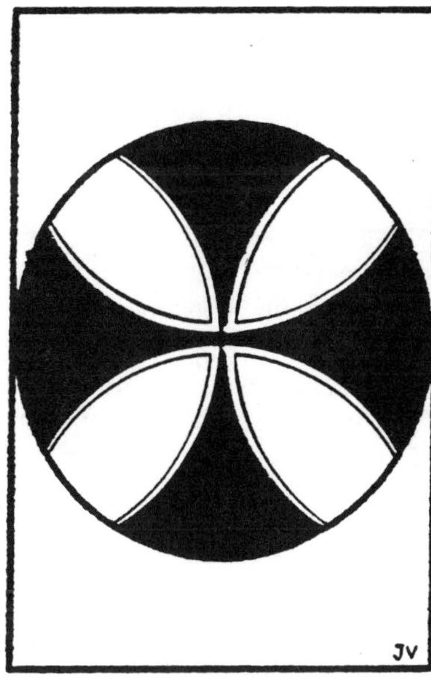

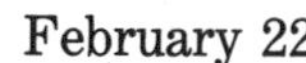

February 22

Saint Baradatos

Except for regions where irrigation techniques have altered the once bleak countryside, the barren desert areas of Egypt are much the same as they were in the fifth century when a man named Baradatos made such a name for himself as to be sainted. But for those who consider that the Church has been quite lenient in making saints out of monks who simply pledged themselves to self-denial and to the Savior, it can be noted that there is no rush of men into that same desert area today in total commitment to the Savior, the tensions of the Middle East notwithstanding. Modern man is inclined to look upon such an existence as that chosen by a fanatic or an escapist, but there were fanatics and escapists in abundance fifteen centuries ago, none of whom came to be saints, not even by accident.

There were much more than tensions in the area when Baradatos chose to walk away from comfort to the discomfort of the desert, facing something far more tangible than tensions which abounded in the form of roving bands of undisciplined cutthroats, land pirates and thieves. The monk of Baradatos' day faced more than deprivation and had to call on all his resourcefulness to avoid being murdered by a thief made angry when he found nothing to rob. Whenever he encountered another human being in the sparse desert, it was monk greeting monk or a holy man making the best of an encounter with a felon. If there are more saints to be found in the first thousand years of Christianity than in the second thousand, it might just be that extreme devotion decreased as comfort and safety increased.

The life and times of Baradatos are outlined in a work entitled "Philotheos," written by Bishop Theodore of Kyrros, Syria, a highly respected clergyman who chose to write about his fellow

Syrian, whom he reveals to have been formally educated and more than qualified to serve as a cleric. However, inspired by examples set by monks of the desert, Baradatos eventually withdrew to the solitude of the desert himself, but not until after having made a solid reputation for himself as a complete theologian whose counsel was sought by hierarchs and statesmen alike.

Although Baradatos was never allowed the complete solitude he would have preferred, he did manage to find considerable time to pray and meditate in a rude hut he occupied when he was able to get away from the clamor of the city. He never achieved the self-denial of his predecessor, Bessarion (whose phenomenal endurance was still fresh in the minds of monks after a hundred years); but he did display an asceticism through extreme deprivation in the wilds of the desert and in prolonged periods of spiritual attainment through prayerful vigil and fasting. These periods of penitent meditation were interrupted by calls back to civilization which he could not ignore.

The Emperor Leo summoned Baradatos to review and assess the synod that had been convened in Chalcedon in A.D. 451 at the behest of Marcian, the consort of the Empress Pulcheria, to be used as guidelines for any future clerical assemblies. The sight of the monk and a monarch was rather incongruous, but it only indicated that Leo had the perceptiveness to select the man best qualified to brief him on church issues that were constantly posing problems the hierarchy could not resolve.

On more than one occasion he was called to the side of the patriarch of Antioch, Syria, who respected the judgment of Baradatos more than he did any of his hierarchs, all of whom were quite capable theologians, but somehow not in the mold of Baradatos who was a man apart. The years of solitude in the desert which he so cherished gave added dimension to Baradatos, and his image was one which projected a piety he might otherwise never have evinced.

At a time when Rome was more a political than a religious center, the city of Antioch ranked with Constantinople and Alexandria as the principal bastions of Christianity. These cities attracted the finest minds in Christendom which rose to prominence in these centers when the faith of Jesus Christ was in its most critical stage of development. It was in these cities in these times that Christianity was set on its course for all time under the leadership of some of the greatest theologians of all time, among whom was Baradatos who served with honor until his death on 22 February A.D. 460.

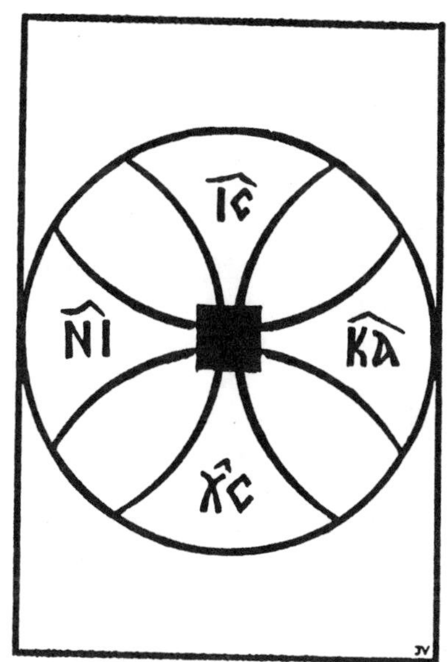

February 22

Ss. Thallasios and Limnaios

Many of the saints of Christianity who are known but to God would still be unknown except for manuscripts of the Church which have been uncovered to reveal their identity. Sts. Thallasios and Limnaios would have gone undiscovered had their lives not been recounted by a fifth century hagiographer who was also the Bishop of Kyrros, Syria, and who went by the name of Theodoret. Except for Bishop Theodoret's well preserved account, based on first hand knowledge, the names of Thallasios and Limnaios live only in anonymity.

Although Thallasios precedes Limnaios, the latter's life seems to have been outlined in greater detail by the bishop, in spite of the fact that they are revered together. Of the great eremites and monks of that period, Thallasios emerged to prominence in the city of Kyrros. His preaching was of such convincing eloquence that he was required by popular demand to remain for longer periods of time so that no one would miss an opportunity to hear him speak.

When he managed to get away from the city, he found peace and solitude in a cave where he was content to pray, meditate, and fast. The virtually inaccessible cave assured him the privacy he preferred until one day a young man named Limnaios, who had been searching for him for a long time, came upon the holy man's hideout. Ordinarily the uninvited guest would have been treated with cordiality and then be asked to leave with the holy man's blessing, but Limnaios so impressed the ascetic that he was asked to remain. This proved to be of mutual benefit because Limnaios was such an apt pupil that he and his mentor found inspiration in each other and thereby assured themselves a spiritual attainment that was to lead to greatness for both.

When Thallasios sensed that Limnaios needed a change after years in the same place, he recommended him to another holy man by the name of Maron, as ascetic whose sainthood is observed on February 14. A Syrian like himself, Maron had achieved a popularity on the level of Thallasios and the arrival of Limnaios seemed to spur him to even greater effort.

Having been identified with two of the greatest and holiest ascetics of his time, it came time for Limnaios to strike out on his own. With the blessing of Maron he sought out a high mountain peak atop which he decided to build a crude hut, omitting a roof that obscured an upward look to Heaven. One of the many visitors to this roofless home was none other than Bishop Theodoret, who came to pray with this devout monk.

One of the charities dearest to the heart of Limnaios was assistance to the blind. Realizing that he had not the omnipotence of the divine with which to cure those unfortunate souls who were forced to live in eternal darkness, he went forth from his homeless dwelling and raised money from his sighted brothers to help the sightless. He succeeded in erecting two homes for the blind, especially constructed with appropriate railings and rooms arranged in an orderly fashion so that the blind could move about without tripping over furniture and bumping into an object. His ingenuity and resourcefulness made life a great deal easier for the occupants.

In addition to making their lives useful and giving them the pride of independence, Limnaios brought to those who dwelled in darkness the light of Jesus Christ. A portion of their time was given over to arts and crafts which volunteers had taught them. Church services and vespers were held regularly and the holidays and feast days observed. Instead of cursing their fate, these devout Christians praised the Lord and in all probability envisioned the Savior more clearly than those who could see. To hundreds Limnaios brought hope and happiness to those who would otherwise have known despair and misery.

While traveling to his mountain top retreat with a pair of his closest associates, Limnaios was bitten by a snake whose venom was deadly. The alarmed companions marvelled when Limnaios simply said a prayer and continued walking as though nothing had happened. For thirty-eight years this holy man toiled in the service of God and man. Following his death, he was sainted together with his Thallasios, both of whom are commemorated by the Orthodox Church on February 22.

February 23

St. Polycarp of Smyrna

A spiritual song of lamentation equates the depths of misery with the lot of a motherless child, but such a child was St. Polycarp, who rose above the humble circumstances of his birth to glorify the name of Jesus Christ in the first century of Christianity and share honors with men of the magnitude of St. John the Apostle. He was privileged to know all of the apostles of Christ and because of this close association with the Savior's inner circle, he was designated as an Apostolic Father, of whom there were seven and among whom he was most probably the youngest.

St. Polycarp's beginnings were ignominious. He was born to a woman named Theodora, who had been imprisoned for her Christian belief and who knew her son for only a few weeks before being led off to be executed. Friends of the condemned Theodora took the child with the promise that he would be raised a Christian, a faith for which her husband had preceded her in death and to which the son would dedicate his life as well.

Polycarp was twenty-two years old when he met St. John as he preached in Ephesos. He had already been raised as a devout follower of Christ, but this encounter with St. John instilled in him a strong urge to serve with the Apostle in his missionary work, a purpose which was encouraged and which he pursued with such zeal that he, within a few months, was ordained a priest. He remained with John, the only apostle of Christ to die of natural causes, until John was exiled by the Roman Emperor Domitian to the island of Patmos, where he wrote the last book of the New Testament (Revelation).

In the first weeks of John's exile Polycarp was appointed assistant to the archbishop of Smyrna, now Izmir, Turkey, and in that capacity served with distinction, taking care not to upstage the archbishop. Nevertheless, when a crisis arose, it was to Polycarp and not the archbishop that the people turned for help. During his first years a severe drought brought great suffering to the people of Smyrna and the pagans had exhausted all their gods in a vain attempt to induce the heavens to yield rain so desperately needed. Finally, Christians were allowed to call upon their leaders to alleviate a worsening condition.

St. Polycarp promised the people nothing but an earnest appeal to God for His divine intervention in their hour of trial and went to seclusion for a period of three days, during which time he fasted and prayed for the Lord's help. At the end of the three days the clouds appeared, the heavens rumbled, and the rains came in answer to his prayers. The valleys once again became green and the trees brought forth their fruit, whereupon the name Polycarp, meaning "bearer of many fruits," was applied to the orphan who had been called Pankratios by his foster mother, and the name Polycarp stuck with the holy man all the years of his life.

Among his many talents Polycarp had a gift for writing, and after the rain episode he wrote his powerful Epistle to the Philippians, considered a gem in ecclesiastical literature, one that set a standard for the many gifted writers who were to follow. He divided his time between writing and preaching, waging a constant battle against spiritual ignorance and bringing countless converts into the ever increasing numbers of Christianity. With increasing converts came increasing issues, particularly in dogma, issues which had to be resolved by the Church Fathers, of whom he was one, forming the guidelines that were to be laid down for the generations of Christians yet to be born to follow in their worship of Jesus Christ.

During the reign of Marcus Aurelius the persecution of Christians was intensified, bringing about the arrest and imprisonment of St. Polycarp, who ran the gantlet in the tradition of the persecuted Christian. During this time he had a vision of his mother, Theodora, who bolstered his courage, and he calmly met a martyr's death. He died for Christ in the arena at the hands of an enraged procurator.

February 23

Saint Gorgonia

Never in the history of mankind has there arisen a family of five, each of whom reached the highest attainable spiritual plateau, in this instance that of a Christian saint—in a family tableau which would be second to Da Vinci's Last Supper had any artist immortalized on a mural this illustrious family. Theirs was not a joint venture in spiritual quid pro quos but an individual devotion to Jesus Christ, although there is no doubt that mutual influence had much to do with their contribution to the Christian Church, unparalleled by any other single family in the world.

The patriarch of this noble family was St. Gregory the Elder, bishop of Nazianzos, whose wife, St. Nonna, bore three children, the greatest of whom was St. Gregory, the Theologian, one of the "Three Hierarchs," as well as another son, Kaisarios whose feast day is observed on March 29, and last but not least St. Gorgonia who had to content herself with dwelling in the shadows cast by her spiritually giant brothers.

As though to prove her mettle, the gentle Gorgonia led an active life but was plagued by illnesses which taxed her considerably but never interrupted her ceaseless efforts on behalf of the Savior. Because she was never robust, it is to her everlasting credit that she was able to keep pace with her stronger brothers and parents through sheer grit and determination, that belied her physical weakness. Encouraged by a family she loved, she became a devout Christian who applied herself diligently to charitable work.

Gorgonia was all the more remarkable since she did not abandon society for an eremite's life. On the contrary, she became a wife and mother, raising three children while still serving Christ. Her purity of heart and depth of devotion were to be seen in everything she did, while her charitable activities earned her several names, including "Mother of Orphans," "Eyes of the Blind," and "Keeper of a Refuge of the Poor." Known as the house with the open door, her home was a haven and beacon for those in need for whom she somehow found the means to help.

In keeping with the Lord's admonition to "let not thy left hand know what thy right hand doeth," she sacrificed for others but in so doing sought to seek no credit, although such unselfish largesse very soon becomes an open secret. A legend in her own time, she loomed larger than life to those about her who watched with loving eye as she saw to her many ministrations. There were witnesses enough, as well as recipients of her sweet charity, to attest to her genuine humility in doing God's work with such tender benevolence that she could have been sainted at any time.

There were many instances when Gorgonia was favored of God as few women are. On one occasion when she was driving her not too sturdy cart in her rounds for the poor, her horse suddenly bolted and she was thrown to the ground, but as witnesses came running to help, certain that she had been fatally injured, she got to her feet none the worse for the experience for the several bruises on her frail body. She was given more reliable transportation and continued making her calls as though nothing had happened, despite the fact that she was in need of care as those for whom she was caring. After returning home she simply knelt in prayer and thanked God for her deliverance.

On another occasion, while attending people suffering from a highly contagious fever which had reached epidemic proportions, Gorgonia was herself stricken and for several days lay near death. With scarcely more than water, she wavered between life and death, praying only that God's will be done, when she began to recover. When the fever had gone, she found the strength to go out again among those desperately ill and to the amazement of all, the mysterious malady ran its course and the epidemic was over. The hand that had spared her, also spared the community.

Unable because of her sex to ascend the pulpit and preach, Gorgonia was content to address informal groups, forming ladies auxiliaries which are today the very heart of the Greek Orthodox Church. She literally spent her time in carrying out the mission of the Church: spreading the love of the Savior through her acts of charity. But her health began to fail rapidly and after having a vision in which heaven was beckoning, she called her family around her and after offering them her blessing, she died on February 23.

February 24

Discoveries of the Head of St. John the Baptist

It is not enough that the commemoration of St. John the Baptist be observed annually with his feast day because earthbound man, aware that the soul is intact, clings to a terrestrial relic of a revered saint of the magnitude of St. John as a Christian treasure so valued that the relic itself merits veneration on the occasion of its discovery. Grisly as it may sound, it is altogether fitting that a separate day be set aside for veneration of the head of the great Baptist, the noble head that was separated from the body of a most holy man at the whim of a most debased ruler.

Of the thousands of heads that have rolled in execution in the grim history of capital punishment, only that of St. John the Baptist is as much a part of Christian heritage as it was a part of his human form. The result is that a Christian can put out of his mind the brutality of a severed head and look upon it as a symbol of the Christian spirit that is constantly brought to mind by the crucified Christ. February 24 marks the commemorative date of the lost-and-found relic known as the "kara," or head of St. John, in two incidents. A third recovery is recounted on yet another feast day, May 25.

The gruesome details of the death of St. John the Baptist form a dark chapter in history known to countless numbers other than those who worship Jesus Christ. It is too often forgotten, however, that St. John was not only a prefiguration of the Messiah, but his cousin as well, a fire and brimstone preacher whose exhortations anticipated the mission of the Savior. When he was dragged from the prison cell of Machaerus, it was at the bidding of the infamous Herod—not to still his stout heart, but to make a present of the head of this spiritual giant to a heartless girl whose mother shared in the guilt of the most senseless killing in history.

According to Eastern historians of the Church, the body of St. John was allowed to be taken for burial in Sebaste, Samaria. But the head, which had been taken to the dance hall for the most depraved of pagan orgies, was subsequently cast aside only to be discovered some time later, as if by divine edict, by two pilgrims enroute to the tomb of Christ. The treasured relic was thereafter passed on to a potter who took it with him to the city of Emesa where it remained in his family until it came into possession of a monk named Eustachios. Because he subscribed to the Arian doctrine, this monk was not in the mainstream of Orthodoxy. He chose to hide the relic in a cave, and he died in the reign of Valentinian (A.D. 431) without revealing the whereabouts of the priceless relic of antiquity.

The relic was lost again, but was regained for posterity when it was discovered shortly after the monk's death by no less a figure than Bishop Uranios. Uranios was a prominent clergyman of that era who might have been led to the relic by a divine hand, but who more than likely came upon it by accident when he sought out the cave for one of his many periods of solitude which he observed in monk-like fashion. He was in the habit of withdrawing into the recesses of a cave for prayer and fasting when he entered the cave of the Arian monk.

Bishop Uranios knew that the cave had been inhabited when he found a large pitcher in which water was usually stored, but which now contained the holy relic which he instantly recognized to be that of St. John the Baptist. When he knelt in reverence before this water pitcher, he felt a serenity and a divine presence which convinced him that it was the precious relic of St. John. Not one to retain this keepsake for his own as the monk had, he removed it to his church where it became a veritable shrine for all to visit.

Second in sanctity only to the tomb of the Savior, the relic of St. John the Baptist attracted a steady stream of pilgrims, many of whose afflictions were cured with prayer at this now holy site. It would have remained there in Cappadocia perhaps for all time, but by order of the Emperor Valentinian it was transferred to Constantinople. Not even royalty could assure the full protection of this relic which vanished only to reappear a third time, an account of which can be found in the May 25th commemoration.

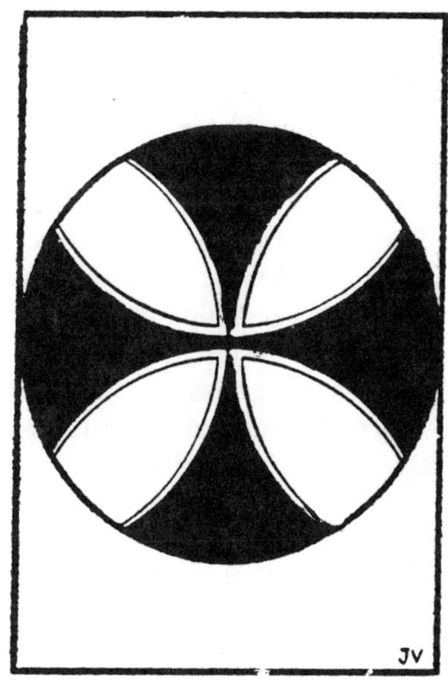

February 25

Tarasios, Patriarch of Constantinople

The temporal leadership of the mighty Byzantine Empire was assumed by a succession of monarchs whose authority emanated from power politics which finally vanished with the last Greek emperor. But the spiritual leadership of Orthodoxy, which commenced with St. Andrew, has extended to the present day in an unbroken line of patriarchs, one of whom was a man named Tarasios, an eighth-century man of God who proved himself to be one of the strongest links in the chain of church stewards that has assured the permanence of the faith of Jesus Christ. His uncompromising stance in an era of political upheavel and theological dispute marked him for the greatness that led to sainthood.

Tarasios was one of the most popular figures of his time, admired as much for his devotion to the Savior as for his devotion to duty to the empire in his capacity of chief secretary to the Empress Irene who ruled as regent for her ten-year-old son. An established statesman, his religious learnings led to close ties with the Patriarchate (within whose walls he was a familiar figure). He evinced a sensitivity to religious matters and a profound knowledge of theology which placed him on a level with ranking prelates as a servant of God, as well as man. Despite the fact that—for all his piety—he was still a layman, he was looked to for spiritual leadership by church and state alike when the Patriarch Paul VI, weary of the turbulence of the times, decided to step down.

With a mandate from the people and the hierarchy, Tarasios was the logical choice to succeed the outgoing patriarch, and within a week the one-time statesman was made a reader, ordained a priest and then bishop. Finally, on Christmas Day in the year A.D. 784, the Empress Irene made her friend and confidant patriarch of Constantinople. In the ensuing years no one, including the royal authority which he was to defy, regretted the selection of Tarasios. A divine will had placed him among the Christians he was to lead out of the confusion and doubts that obscured, even defiled, the Cross. From the moment he took office, he made it evident he was a vicar of Christ.

A precondition for his acceptance to the post of patriarch was the empress' promise to Tarasios that she would immediately invite all the hierarchs from all the corners of the empire to resolve once and for all the problem of Iconoclasm, an issue which had been tearing at the fiber of the Church for several generations. Thus convened, the Ecumenical Synod of Nicaea of 787 was attended by over 300 bishops and presided over by a patriarch who set the mood for harmony with such convincing fashion that the assembly was soon in unanimous agreement that the iconoclastic movement had no part in the Orthodox concept of Christian worship. The icons have ever since adorned church interiors as reminders that the Son of God lives in the hearts of men through the devotion and sacrifices of men and women, but for whom the image of the Savior might have been obscured altogether by the forces of evil which have assailed the Church.

Tarasios maintained the dignity of his office while showing great humility through his preference for simplicity in all personal matters, avoiding any semblance of pomp in his affairs and retiring to a small room as time allowed for meditation and prayer. He exhibited a rare administrative excellence in meeting the challenges that arose and in preserving a harmony among clergy and laity which had been lacking for years.

When the son of the Empress Irene came of age, he assumed the throne in place of his regent mother as Emperor Constantine VI, a ruler who was a far cry from his namesake as events were to prove. Tiring of his wife, Mary, the emperor sought to divorce her in order to marry a handmaiden named Theodote with whom he had fallen in love. When refused a divorce, the emperor declared his marriage annulled and proceeded to marry Theodote. Tarasios thereupon excommunicated not only the emperor, but the clergyman who had performed the ceremony, and followed this with such a denuciation of the royal action that the ruler was eventually forced to abandon the throne in favor of his mother. After his death on 25 February 806, Patriarch Tarasios, who had led the simple life, was given a funeral with pomp reserved for royalty.

February 26

Saint Porphyrios of Gaza

Associated with the sightless Sampson, Gaza is the name of a city in which a mighty bishop of Orthodoxy in the fifth century advanced the cause of Christianity seldom matched by hierarchs of the early Christian era. This crossroads city in southwest Palestine was a vital link for caravans between Syria and Egypt, best remembered for the biblical account of Sampson's bringing down the pagan temple on his captors and himself. The Orthodox Church remembers this town as the see of Bishop Porphyrios who managed, among other things, to destroy not only pagan temples but paganism itself.

Born in Thessalonike into a family of means, his was an uneventful life until, at the age of twenty-five, he emerged as a man pledged to serve Jesus Christ. To this end he made his way to the Holy Land where he became a monk. He had been in Jerusalem for about ten years when his health began to fail rapidly, whereupon he painstakingly set out for Calvary. Along the route a monk named Mark, who had assumed a vigil at the base of the hill, offered to assist the agonized Porphyrios who insisted on continuing on his own.

This same monk who had looked upon the weak traveler with compassion, very soon thereafter saw a robust Prophyrios as he approached after having been healed by the power of the Lord. Mark joined his fellow monk in giving thanks to the Almighty. The two monks entered a monastery for the ascetic life when word came that Porphyrios had inherited a considerable estate. His reaction was to send back word to the authorities in Thessalonike that the holdings be disposed of and that all proceeds be given to the poor. He gave it no more thought and resumed his austere life.

It was not until he was forty years old that Porphyrios was ordained a priest, by Patriarch Parilos of Jerusalem, who had observed the monk's quiet service to Christ and had admired him for his humility and reticence. The newly appointed priest fairly leaped into prominence, emerging into public view after years of isolation to dazzle his Christian listeners with his message of all consuming love of the Savior. No one was more surprised than he when, with no advance notice, he was appointed by Archbishop John of Caesaria to serve as bishop of Gaza.

The reputation of Porphyrios proceeded him to Gaza, a city in whose midst were numbers of pagans and atheists. Undaunted, the new bishop, with his friend Mark, ignored the jeers and taunts which greeted them and proceeded to the Christian sector without serious incident. He had been in Gaza for a few weeks and in all that time, by coincidence there had been a total lack of rainfall. While periods of drought were nothing new to this area, this latest prolonged dry spell became serious and the atheistic malcontentents, making note that the rains had failed to come since the arrival of the Christian bishop, attempted to make him the scapegoat, blaming him for their parched land.

Porphyrios walked out of the city to the cries of derision of the pagans who locked the gates behind him, determined to bar his reentry. The bishop walked into the Chapel of St. Timothy where he prayed for divine assistance. As dawn approached, clouds formed overhead and a steady downpour ensued. The bishop then returned to a grateful Christian flock.

This display of the power of God, served only to intensify the age-long hatred of the pagans who stepped up their anti-Christian campaigning which sought the life of the bishop. At the insistence of his communicants, Porphyrios slipped out of the city and went directly to the Byzantine Emperor Arkadios to ask help in putting down the mounting insurrection. The emperor sent troops and peace was restored.

On his return to Palestine, Porphyrios chanced to pass the infamous temple of Venus, pausing to stare at its affront to God. Within moments the temple came crashing down in ruins. A glance of the Lord, through the eyes of a noble bishop, had brought down a bastion of iniquity, just as Sampson had brought down a temple at the cost of his life centuries before. Thereafter, it was much better for the bishop who slowly converted pagan after pagan until all but a few of the most intransigent remained. Where once temples stood, churches were erected and Christianity advanced. Bishop Porphyrios, died on 26 February A.D. 420.

February 26

St. Photini
The Samaritan Woman

The incredible saga of the Samaritan woman rivals any other in fact or fiction. The story of her life is also the story of her remarkable family that lived during the early development of Christianity. In its scope and grandeur, her story reads like a passage from Homer; in fact, no amazon or superwoman of classical Greek literature could match the skill, courage, and spirit of this religious heroine.

The New Testament gives the familiar account of the "woman at the well," who was exiled from her native Samaria and was thus known as the Samaritan woman. According to the book of John (4.5-42), her life to that point had been anything but exemplary. However, she responded to Christ's stern admonition with genuine repentance, was forgiven her sinful ways, and became a convert to the Christian faith. Tradition has it that the apostles of Christ baptized her and gave her the name of Photini which literally means "the enlightened one."

Without further ado, she set about bringing the word of Christ to others. She journeyed as far as Carthage on the African continent with the message of salvation, but not until she brought her sizeable family into active participation in the Christian cause. Photini had five daughters: Anatoli, Photo, Photes, Paraskevi, and Kyriaki. She also bore two sons: Victor (later given the name Photinos) and Joseph.

Following the deaths of Sts. Peter and Paul at the hands of the tyrant Nero, Photini and her family traveled extensively, converting countless pagans to Christianity through her zealous faith in Christ. During the difficult days of Nero's persecution of the Christians, Photini and her family contributed to Christianity beyond measure. Her son Victor became an officer in the Roman army even though he was a Christian. At first he managed not to incur the displeasure of his superiors because of his faith. Soon enough, however, his duties as an officer came into direct conflict with his Christian principles. He was put in charge of a detail whose mission it was to seek out Roman citizens who dared to acknowledge Christ. Refusing to obey such an order, Victor was brought to swift military justice not only for insubordination and treason, but also for his own admission of belief in Christ. His subsequent imprisonment and torture were brutally inflicted by his former comrades.

Hearing the tragic news of her son's imprisonment, Photini straightaway demanded and received an audience with Emperor Nero himself. In an impassioned plea for her son's life, she bodly spoke for the cause of Christianity. She told the disbelieving tyrant how the gentle Jesus is worshiped by the world as the Messiah and the Son of God. The astounded Nero could not but admire her quiet courage, but his seething hatred for Christians could not be subdued and he sentenced her and her family to prison. There they languished for two years enduring endless suffering. But Photini not only lived when Jesus Christ walked the earth, she was also privileged to look upon his countenance, even if it was an encounter which evoked rebuke from the Savior, an admonition she never forgot and which placed her on a course of early Christianity from which she never wavered. She epitomizes the love to be found in the Lord and in the family—the very core of Christianity. The apostles have given her the name by which she is remembered. But it is of no consequence what she first was called, being remembered by the incident at the well. A mother's impassioned plea for her son's life can be expected but St. Photini may as well have been addressing herself to Satan because she was pleading her son's case before Nero. With a gesture of his vile hand the cruel emperor snuffed out the lives of Photini and her seven children, but he was helpless to snuff out rising Christianity, for which Photini and her children stood.

Finally, when Photini and her family of five daughters and two sons were at last put to death, it was the end of an unsurpassed labor for Christ and the beginning of immortality for the Samaritan woman who came to the well for water and was transformed into a wellspring of Christian faith.

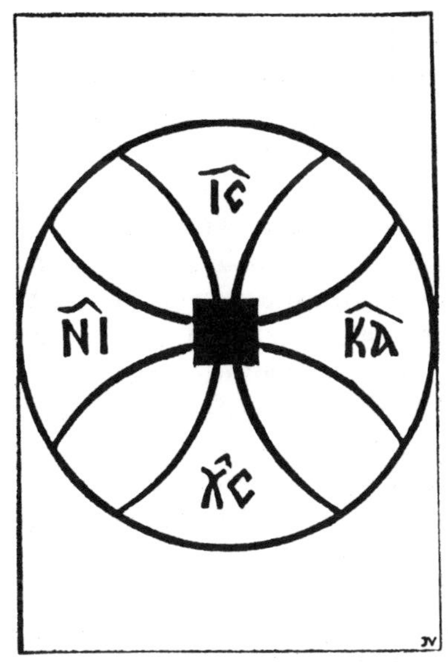

February 27

St. Prokopios of Decapolis

An indomitable monk named Prokopios earned his niche in Christianity's "Hall of Fame" for his staunch defense of the use of icons in the tradition established by earlier Church Fathers. The disaffection for the icons brought about a clamor for their removal by disidents whose numbers formed the iconoclastic movement, a movement which surged, ebbed, flowed, and brought disharmony within the Christian community for the prolonged period of 150 years. It vacillated from ruler to ruler and prelate to prelate, pitting priest against priest and brother against brother over an agonizing century and a half of strife that brought utter misery to some and discomfort to all. But for men with the resolve of Prokopios, the damage to the structure of the Church might well have been irreparable and all mankind could have suffered as a result.

The story of Prokopios is little more than a study of the iconoclasm that projected him into prominence. Influenced by the Jewish and Muslim traditions banning the use of images of any kind in their houses of worship, the Emperor Leo III issued a decree forbidding the use of icons in the Christian Church in the mistaken belief that they represented the graven image outlawed by God in his commandments to Moses. It was against such formidable opposition that Prokopios dared to raise his voice in an impassioned plea for the iconophiles. Drawing a distinction between veneration and worship, he argued that icons merely represented those largely responsible for bringing people together to worship Jesus Christ. Despite his divinity, Prokopios argued, Christ relied on flesh and blood humans to establish his Church for all mankind, and without the help of these select few there would be no Church at all. They, therefore, merit representation, to be observed and remembered, whereas Christ is adored.

Oddly enough, the clergy offered little resistance to the edict, some even choosing to venerate the icons in secret, but the monks almost to a man were vociferous in their objections and proclaimed an open defiance of the law of the land, vowing never to abandon the icons.

Prokopios was so outraged by the iconoclasts that he left the confines of his cloister to preach out in the open, to any who cared to listen, against the evils of the iconoclastic movement, which he protested would lead to a namelessness and eventually to oblivion. He spearheaded an exodus from the monasteries of a great number of monks who ventured abroad to preach, as Prokopios before them, in open defiance of the emperor, the supreme authority of the church and state. This brought on the swift enforcement of the emperor's law and many well-meaning monks were not only prosecuted but persecuted as well for taking their rightful stand on this burning issue.

Prokopios commanded such respect from the general populace that not even the emperor would risk meting out too harsh a judgment on the crusading monk, but, nevertheless, Prokopios was apprehended and imprisoned for more than a year. When his voice carried out from his cell, he was exiled and could return only after the death of the Emperor Leo III. He preferred the serenity of his monastic retreat but remained in Constantinople to carry on his personal war against the iconoclasts.

The iconophiles were a long way from restoring the icons to all churches in the land after the many years of strife and Prokopios carried the restoration to every corner of the land, exhorting priests to openly avow their adherence to traditionalism and rallying the faithful to a renewal of the faith of their fathers, with no interference from state authority. He brought the full influence of the respected monks of the land to bear on the timid, who in some cases simply wanted to remain within the law, even though the law was an unpopular one.

The progress of restoration was painfully slow but Prokopios never slackened his pace in his crusade, which he carried on relentlessly until at last he was satisfied that the tide of battle had turned in his favor. He returned to his beloved monastery outside the walls of the city and led a comparatively peaceful and full life. He died on February 27th, leaving a legacy of courage and faith that has enhanced monasticism for all time.

February 28

Patriarch Proterios of Alexandria

The Christian Church was begun by men of good will who formed an original church for the purpose of worshiping Jesus Christ, but in the years to follow history has witnessed a fragmentation of the one and undivided Church by clerics of equally good will but of human frailties, a good number of which came forward with radical ideas in the early going which would have all but ruined the structure of the Church had they not been challenged by men such as Proterios, a fifth century patriarch of Alexandria. Long before the Reformation and its resultant welter of denominations, self serving members of the clergy spread the venom of heresy throughout Christendom that lingered for years in the Christian body and might even have brought about its demise save for the antidotes of Proterios and others like him.

Feelings were running high when Proterios had become a priest in A.D. 570 in Alexandria, Egypt. The controversy over the heretic Euthyches, questioning the dual nature of Christ, had reached alarming proportions. It was into this tempestuous state of affairs that Proterios stepped forth, throwing the full weight of his support in opposition to the heretics. An orator and debator of high caliber, he projected himself into the fray with such vigor and sound defensive reasoning that he came to be feared by the heretics more than any others.

The issue was being heatedly argued in every corner of the Byzantine Empire, threatening not only the Church but the state itself since both were so strongly interdependent. Because the gathering storm, the Fourth Ecumenical Synod was convened to settle the issue but its decision in favor of tradition provoked the dissent of the defeated whose continuing assault on accepted Church dogma seemed to make the Fourth Ecumenical Synod, superfluous.

When Patriarch Cyril of Alexandria, an ally and friend of Proterios since the latter's ordination, passed away, Proterios not only lost a devoted friend and fellow protagonist but found himself in deeper trouble since the successor to Cyril proved to be an intransigent Monophysite. The new Patriarch, Dioskoros, was no match for Proterios and after the deliberations of the Fourth Synod was deposed. Proterios was chosen to serve as patriarch of Alexandria, but in spite of the unanimous vote in his favor, endorsed by the patriarch of Constantinople and the emperor, the fanatics lingered in defiance, spurred on by a pair determined opponents named Timothy and Eluros, both unyielding supporters of the deposed Dioskoros.

Patriarch Proterios found himself in a house of God divided against itself. It is to his everlasting credit that under these disquieting circumstances the loyal patriarch stood his ground, even in the face of withering blasts from some of his own hierarchs. However twisted their reason, his enemies were aware that he was the lawful head of the Alexandrian Church and could not be deposed. This very legality was to lead to his undoing, ironically enough.

The heretic champion Eluros had a personal ambition to displace Porterios as patriarch and found Monophysitism as the vehicle to project him into the public image. Strangely enough there were enough in his camp to intimidate the patriarch but no amount of pressure could move this uncompromising head of the church.

Meanwhile, a blight struck the area, bringing with it a famine that suited the enemies of Proterios who saw a chance to cause considerable unrest, envisioning a rabble stirred to enough wrath to take matters into their own hands and the patriarch and put him to flight. That bubble burst when it was announced that the emperor was shipping food supplies to the beleagured city for distribution throughout the famine stricken area. The envious Eluros went so far as to propose to his followers that a means be found of preventing the supply ship from reaching port. Unable to carry out this deed, Eluros and his henchmen became desperate. There was only one way to rid themselves of this great patriarch whom they failed to discredit.

Proterios was kneeling in prayer in his cathedral when assassins entered the house of God and stabbed the patriarch to death. He died on February 28.

February 28

Kyranna of Thessalonike

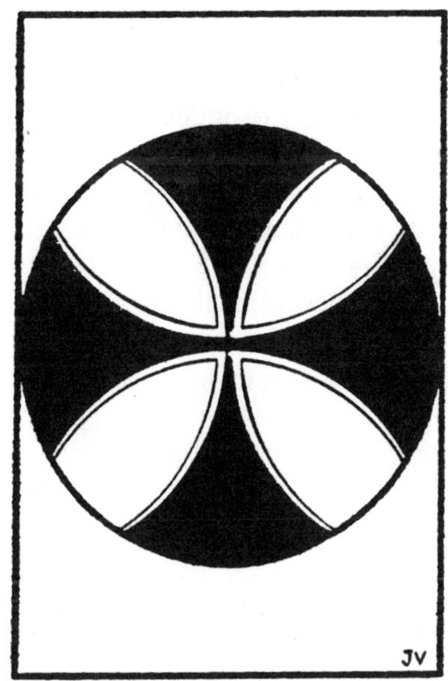

The age-old concept that might makes right was disproved for nearly four centuries by a courageous Greek people who suffered the tyranny of Muslim Turks with no discernible weakening of their Christian faith. The might of the invader was pitted against a smaller Christian band, but the right of the Savior prevailed for nearly four hundred years against overwhelming odds. The rest of the Christian world looked on helplessly but felt a debt of gratitude to those hardy Greeks who withstood the withering onslaught that most certainly would have annihilated a lesser faith.

While it is true that the atrocities committed in the name of Allah were primarily localized and that many Greeks actually prospered and gained a degree of progress under Turkish rule, it is equally true that the struggle was as much Islam against Christianty as it was Turk against Greek. Islam not only frowned on any religion not their own but treated other religions, especially Christianity, with a cruel disrespect as evidenced in their defilement of Christian churches and debasement of the Greek populace. After having seen the recent motion picture about prison life for a convicted American in the 1970s, a film unsurpassed for sheer horror, it does not leave much to the imagination to picture what it must have been like for hapless Greeks in like circumstances going back to the fifteenth century and lasting until the nineteenth.

This, the darkest chapter in Greek history, which both sides like to put behind them, had a brighter side in that it provided a proving ground for Christianity out of which emerged heroes and heroines, some of whom have been sainted and not the least of which was a girl name Kyranna of Thessalonike, a city which was under complete domination of Turkey when Kyranna was born in 1731. Many isolated areas, particularly the inner mountain regions and a few lesser islands, managed to escape the yoke, but Thessalonike was the focal point of the conqueror.

A practice of the conquerors was to seize a boy from his Christian family and take him with others to a spiritual and military training area where they would be brainwashed and raised as Muslims. The youngsters grew up to be known as Janissaries, as pitiless and cruel as their mentors, all sworn to die for Allah in what they considered a holy cause. An encounter with one of the Janissaries was to prove the undoing of Kyranna and lead to her ultimate sacrifice for Jesus Christ.

Reared in a devout Christian family of Thessalonike, Kyranna attained womanhood with a reputation for piety which was belied by her extreme beauty. It did not seem to the casual onlooker that a woman of such breathtaking beauty could be such a devout church-goer, more concerned for how she looked to God than how she appeared to those about her. Her hand was sought by a good number of young Greek males, but she was also the choice of a young Janissary who made his intentions known after meeting her while carrying out his duties as a tax collector.

The youthful tax collector had the appealing good looks and bearing of his ancestry, but Kyranna rejected the suitor with the flat statement that she would never love a Muslim, let alone marry one. Thus denied, the spurned lover vowed she would be his or no one else's and in a jealous rage brought charges against Kyranna, who was promptly hauled before the magistrate in a mockery of what passed for justice in those days.

Kyranna was accused of having accepted a proposal of marriage, together with a promise to become a Muslim convert, and then having withdrawn her solemn vow. The denial of these trumped-up charges was of no avail, and the presiding official condemned her to prison, there to reflect on her affront and perhaps change her mind. A week of horror in a squalid jail could not force Kyranna to recant, and she was then subjected to tortures too inhuman to describe. The suitor visited her in jail to find her hanging on the torture rack and observed a heavenly light shining on her bruised and battered body. She died on February 1751 at the age of twenty, and the site of her burial place has since been the scene of many miracles.

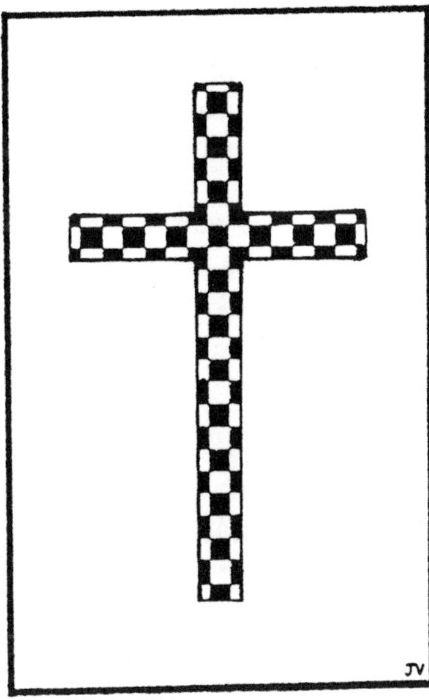

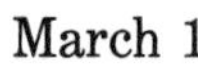

March 1

Saint Agapios

The rugged promontory jutting off the Macedonian coast features Mt. Athos, offering nothing but stark barrenness in a setting which nature seems to have formed for the express purpose of isolating on its craggy zone men who could never abide there for anything except spiritual attainment. This uninviting stretch of mountainous stone was an ideal locale for the monasteries of Mt. Athos which for 1000 years have beckoned men from all parts of the eastern world. The cloisters, run by the many monks, formed a thriving community which invited invaders who scaled the rugged terrain in infamous forays on the unarmed fortress of God.

One of the victims of these raids was St. Agapios, who literally lived up to his name, stemming from the Greek word for "love," in a most remarkable stint of making sweet the uses of adversity. This thirteenth-century monk was a member of a community numbering at times as many as 50,000 ascetics since it was founded in 961, with a single monastery built to house 4,000 men, to be followed in ensuing years by nineteen more buildings. An independent spiritual principality, it bowed only to the King of Kings; although there was a liaison with the state, and it presently relies on the Greek state for police and fire protection.

Agapios was but one of thousands of Mt. Athos monks whose commitment to Jesus Christ was total. His origins, like so many of his fellow monks, remain unknown, and he would have been another face in the crowd of holy men who have lived and died on Mt. Athos had it not been for an attack on Mt. Athos. Life passed without serious incident for the most part. A look at this citadel makes it seem impenetrable and invulnerable, but it has been raided more than once in its long history.

Agapios was distinguishing himself while a member of the

monastery known as Vatopedi when the peace of Mt. Athos was shattered by a Saracen horde who succeeded in scaling the sacred walls and pillaging whatever treasures they could lay hands on. One of the treasures was St. Agapios himself who was taken captive and enslaved. The holy man was made a servant in a Saracen household where he remained for several years, serving not the Savior, but an avowed enemy of Christianity. In all the years he was enslaved, he was denied the purpose for which he had become a monk, and although he was not treated harshly, it was this denial more than anything else which made him determined to escape. He had earned the respect even of the irreligious family who gradually looked upon him with trust, and finally, as he was tilling a garden, he dropped his hoe and walked away. When he was out of sight of the village, he took to his heels in a burst of speed which carried him into the wilderness where he paused to catch his breath and eventually made his way back to his beloved Mt. Athos.

Warmly received by his brethren, who had presumed him dead, he recounted his years among the Saracens after offering prayers of thanksgiving for his deliverance. After a few days, he visited the office of an abbot who, in the course of a discussion of his life among the Saracens, asked Agapios if he had spoken to his captors about Jesus Christ. When the abbot learned that Agapios had not even mentioned the Savior, he reminded him that a prisoner of war was duty bound to attempt his escape, but a man of God had a Christian duty to attempt not an escape but a conversion of the people who held him captive, eventually to win a release and not risk an escape.

Agapios returned to his cell to bow in prayer for not having done what he clearly saw as his Christian duty, a duty which he had subordinated to his self-preservation. It was not enough for him to ask for forgiveness, and with the courage that comes from spiritual inspiration, he went back to where he had been held captive. He was pleasantly surprised when he got nearly as warm a reception as when he had returned to Mt. Athos. The entire family was delighted to have him back, so much so that as much as they wanted him to stay, he was free to go. Agapios then sat down with them and after a number of sessions won the entire family over to Christianity. Not only did he convert them, but induced them as well to return with him to the Holy Mountain. All became monks and were still at Vatopedi when Agapios died peacefully on 1 March 1265.

March 1

Saint Eudokia

It is generally considered that a woman blessed not only with great beauty but with immense wealth as well would be voted the least likely to become a candidate for sainthood, but, without so many improbabilities, by human standards, little could be expected in the way of divine miracles. A faithful Christian lives in hope, knowing that the unexpected can and does happen to those who keep the faith. St. Eudokia was, by any standard, unique in so many ways that had she not found the Savior, she would have crowded the glamorous Cleopatra in the pages of history. She chose the less spectacular course of following Jesus Christ, as a result of which she is not found among the empresses and queens but in the more elite company of the saints of Christianity.

Eudokia was a woman of Samaria who lived her life for Christ during the reign of Emperor Trajan (98-117). She seems to have led a charmed life from the outset, enjoying every advantage and achieving an enormous popularity not only among Samaritans but among other people of the Middle East as well. While there is no likeness of her extant, since portraiture of that day was primitive, it is generally acknowledged that she was in all probability the world's most beautiful woman. This cannot be denied, any more than it can be denied that Franz Liszt was the world's foremost pianist, despite the fact that there is no stereo recording to substantiate this. In addition to her exquisite comeliness, she had a talent for making money to the extent that by the time she was twenty-four years old she had amassed a considerable fortune.

Born in Baalbeck, Syria, Eudokia used her good looks to her advantage in winning over the financial support of men of influence, all of whom she had outstripped while still a young lady in a meteoric ascent to the pinnacle of economic success. The entire Roman Empire seemed to be at her feet and she was beset by suitors and others seeking her favor, some of whom lavished expensive gifts on her, which was like carrying coals to Newcastle. She did nothing to discourage this adulation and took delight in unabated revelry with a retinue of fawning sycophants.

Suitors and swains streamed to the palace of Eudokia, but not one could win her over and they were dismissed unceremoniously. One day, however, a man came to see her who was neither suitor nor swain who, unlike the others before him, was not brushed aside. He was allowed to see Eudokia, and it was not long before he had conquered her heart. This man was a monk whose name was Gerasimos, a holy man who offered her the wealth of the love of Jesus Christ, a treasure she clasped not too long after Gerasimos came to her. She induced Gerasimos to remain in a large hall next to the palace which had heretofore been the scene of orgies, but which was now converted to a chapel in which the monk held services and where Eudokia was consumed by the Holy Spirit, eventually becoming an instrument of good.

Eudokia was thirty years old when she gave herself over completely to the service of Jesus Christ. Her first act was to build a monastery near the city of Baalbeck, where she administered the disposition of her vast wealth to projects for charity. She sold her extensive real estate holdings, including her fabulous palace, and poured the money into a fund for the needs of the Church and for the underprivileged. In a short time her monastery became a beacon which attracted thousands of spiritually as well as physically starved people, and Eudokia became famous for the beauty of her soul as well as her face, acquiring in the process of her noble work a proximity to God no treasure could buy.

The stream of suitors to the palace became a river of pilgrims to her monastery, but there was one suitor named Philostratos who was persistent enough to seek her out in the hope of securing favor before her fortune had been dissipated. Eudokia refused to help him, and, when in his anger he seemed struck dead by the Lord, she prayed to God for his recovery. Brought back to his senses, he was easily converted to Christianity.

The continual conversion of so many pagans by Eudokia brought down upon her the full wrath of the Syrian officials, who had her beheaded on 1 March 107.

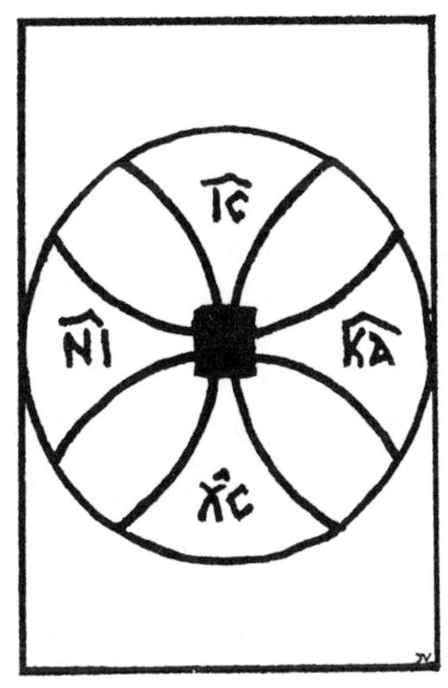

Saint Hesychios

Prior to the turn of the fourth century, Christians were sustained in their firm belief that the Messiah was to reappear and that his second coming was virtually at hand each dawn. Among those whose faith was rock ribbed, but who were pragmatic enough to know that in the timeless infinity of God there a different timetable, was a man who has come down to us as St. Hesychios, a man who let it be known to his Christian friends that the lack of the Lord's company did not mean that he was not among them at all times. To spend an hour with this devoted servant of God was enough to allow one to feel the spiritual euphoria of Christ's love and to retain that feeling for the rest of one's days.

Never a man of the cloth nor even in close association with hierarch or primate, Hesychios was nevertheless an overpowering personality when the subject of faith in Christ was discussed. A far cry from what his saintliness proclaimed him to be, he was actually a civil servant in his temporal life, rising in the ranks of state government to become a magistrate in the court of Emperor Maximilian.

Forced to keep his true Christian identity masked behind a veil of unmistakable benevolence which his associates could not see as deriving from the love of Jesus Christ, he became a trusted friend and confidant of the emperor who assigned to him delicate matters that called for tact, diplomacy, and astuteness. The beguiling, insincere and shrewd politicians were no match for the astuteness and intellect of a man who had the light of Jesus Christ probing the darkness of pagan minds. Whenever meetings were convened, those calling for the most serious of discussions were invariably chaired by Hesychios whose judgment even in most crucial matters was never questioned.

At the time of Hesychios no Christian was allowed to hold high office, but he had convinced the emperor that among Christians were to be found some of the finest minds in the land who could serve the state with the same loyalty they applied to their religion. This resulted in the employment of many Christians in the lower echelons of the state. The pagan superiors, aware of the influence of Hesychios but unaware of his Christianity, countenanced their Christian underlings towards whom they would otherwise have been hostile.

One day, Hesychios intervened in behalf of a Christian who was being abused by a scornful pagan superior. The pagan's wrath turned to Hesychios and in the ensuing argument, the saintly man, wearying of his burdensome secret, unmasked himself and flatly declared for all to hear that he was a Christian. At that moment, he was by law no longer a magistrate and in the absence of the emperor, he was demoted to the ignominious post of overseer of the city brothels, and he was stripped of the trappings of his office. He endured the accompanying indignities with Christian forbearance, happy at last to shed the mantle which had disguised him for so long and content to be on the same level with other followers of Jesus Christ.

When the emperor returned from his extended tour, the gleeful pagans hastened to tell him about his now discredited friend Hesychios who had betrayed his trust for so many years. The emperor's disbelief on hearing this news soon gave way to an embittered anger as he listened to more and more accusations. When he had regained his composure, he ordered his former friend to be brought before him so that he might hear from the accused man's own lips of his alleged treachery.

When confronted by the emperor, Hesychios declared his loyalty to the king, but also his higher loyalty to the King of Kings. When asked how he could endure the humility of the degrading office, the condemned man said he accepted it as the will of God as any Christian would. He then attempted to draw on his past record, and those of his fellow Christians, to prove that the empire itself was better off by the presence of Christians whose increasing numbers were a help and not a hindrance to the state. This drew a rebuttal from the prosecution whose revilement provoked the king to even greater anger. In a seething rage he ordered Hesychios to be put to death immediately. Hesychios was latched to a huge millstone which was rolled into a river, thus drowning him. He died for Christ on 2 March 303.

March 2

Theodotos of Kyrenia

The island of Cyprus is no stranger to oppressive hordes which have invaded this citadel of Christianity under many banners, the latest of which was as recent as 1974 when, under the Turkish flag, regiments numbering into upwards of 40,000 swarmed over Greek soil in what is laughingly referred to as a protective measure in the interest of the fifteen percent of the population which are of Turkish nationality. Those who consulted maps to see just where Cyprus lay and sympathized with Turkey because it is a scant sixty miles from its shores have to be reminded that the entire area was once the Byzantine Empire and the peaceful Greeks who live there are the descendants of the Byzantine era and beyond, who pose no threat to the much larger Turkey.

Theodotos, a native of Kyrenia, lived on this often beleaguered island during the fourth century at a time when the decline of the Roman Empire was several years down the road. The subjugation of the island by Rome had long since been complete and Theodotos had to live in the midst of hostility centuries before there was anything called a Muslim faith. To islanders today it matters little because an enemy of the Christian faith by any name is an enemy to the Prince of Peace whom they worship.

The hardy Christian stock of Cyprus represent the legacy of men such as Theodotos who, in turn, inherited the Christian legacy implanted on Cyprus for eternity by Barnabas, the saint sent to the island by the great St. Paul. St. Barnabas was finally to return after many missions to become a bishop of Cyprus and eventually die for Christ there. In that respect the life of Theodotos bears close resemblance to that of Barnabas, and it is to these great saints that Christianity is indebted for having so firmly planted the Christian religion. That Christianity has survived there after so many centuries of foreign invasion is a credit to the people themselves, every one of whom is Greek in thought, action, and tongue. The Greek majority there does not speak Turkish as the Greek minority does in Turkey simply because the island does not belong to Turkey, and if it did, its language would be that of the Turks.

A native islander has a feeling of belonging, so much so that people from the mainland are looked upon as visitors or intruders. It takes more than one or two generations to get that feeling of belonging, and Theodotos had roots on the island stemming from so many generations back that not only did he really belong there, but the islanders extended themselves in the spirit of brotherhood he might otherwise not have known.

Long before he became a priest, Theodotos was known for his seriousness as a boy and in his youth for his devotion to the Church as well as to those with whom he worshiped. After his ordination, he became a highly respected cleric known for his quiet dedication, eventually to become one of the youngest prelates of the realm when he was appointed bishop of Kyrenia. It was as bishop that the entire island came to know him as a spiritual leader who spoke for Christ, not only for the people of Kyrenia, but for the entire island as well.

The Christian-hating Emperor Licinius, realizing that this isolated island might slip from the Roman grasp in total embrace of Christianity, dispatched his most callous official to serve as governor of Cyprus. The name of this tyrannical governor was Savinos, who made his presence felt as soon as he had arrived by issuing orders that every known Christian be brought to justice. The best known Christian on the island was Theodotos, who found himself facing the new governor in a tribunal set up for the dispensing of harsh justice without ceremony.

Asked if he were a Christian, Bishop Theodotos replied with a firm yes and stated that no power on earth could make him change his mind. His firmness helped to shorten the trial but prolonged the agony that was to follow. Suspended from a beam, he was slashed with razor sharp knives and beaten severely before being returned to prison. Savinos was replaced by a merciful governor after the emperor died and Theodotos was released from prison. The torture had taken its toll, however, and he lived only two more years. He died on March 2, on which day he is commemorated in the small Chapel of the blessed Virgin Mary in the village of Armatios.

March 3

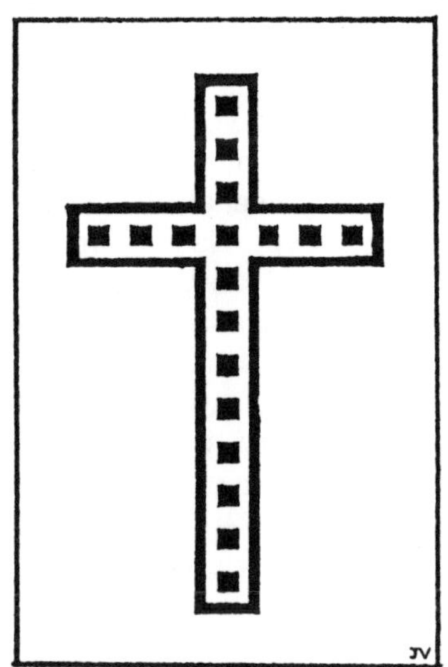

Piamun of Egypt

There are many instances in history in which divine intervention has come to the aid of a threatened people, the most notable of which is outlined in the Old Testament and further immortalized in an epic poem concerning the event by Lord Byron, entitled, "The Destruction of Sennaccherib," wherein is described the awesome power of God in destroying the Assyrian King and his armies in their assault upon Jerusalem. A little known such intercession of the divine in quite another setting but under similar circumstances is that which took place in early years of Christendom in a remote corner of Egypt as a result of the pious plea of a devout Christian maiden named Piamun, whose saintliness is found only in church archives and remains unmentioned in either the Bible or any inspirational poem.

Had Byron, an Hellenophile of first rank, ever read about Piamun, it is reasonable to assume he may have written about this sweet saint as a companion piece to his well-known and often quoted poem about Sennaccherib. Piamun has remained an obscure figure down through the ages like some "flower born to blush unseen and waste its sweetness on the desert air"(Thomas Gray). But, fortunately for the Christians in a small village of Egypt, that flower of Christianity named Piamun did not waste her sweetness with a fragrance born of Heaven which acted on the community like some holy incense during her lifetime as one of God's own servants.

Nothing is known of the early family life of the young maiden now known to us as St. Piamun of Egypt, except that while still a young maiden she evinced a piety which made it quite evident that while a close member of the community, she was at the same time apart from them, somehow enjoying the company of the Lord when she was not in the company of others. While still very young she won the admiration and respect of her fellow Christians as much as she would have had she been the highest member of the hierarchy.

Piamun lived in one of two villages which remained hostile to one another because of their geographic proximity and their common access to the sacred river Nile, which then, as now, was the life's blood of the arid lower regions of Egypt. Each village vied with the other for obtaining water from a strategic spot on the Nile, as a result of which the contention burst into open conflict. Because of their dependence on the waters at hand, they were two armed camps, constantly at each other's throats to the extent that although they were of the same blood, the struggle for supremacy over the Nile became a sustained campaign of war in which sporadic fights threatened the extinction of both.

At one point in this mutual harrassment, it became clear that the enemies of the village where Piamun lived were planning an all-out assault aimed at annihilating the river camp and having the waters of the Nile all to themselves. The numbers of the attackers had been increased by a horde of mercenaries and the outnumbered village where the pious Piamun huddled with her friends now seemed doomed. The stage was set for a one-sided confrontation similar to that when the Assyrians of many years before set to destroy Jerusalem.

Perhaps with this in mind, Piamun knelt in prayer and beseeched God for help in her hour of peril. Her prayer was heard and answered. She had no sooner finished praying than the hordes of the rival village swooped down on her village, but their charge was suddenly halted at the outskirts by an unseen hand. They found themselves powerless to advance upon their neighbors and became transfixed at the sight of a young girl gazing skywards in thanks to God. Unlike the Assyrians of old, these invaders were not destroyed, but through the divine intervention in an answer to a girl's plea, they realized that the solution lay not in the power of arms but in peaceful negotiation. Peace was achieved and Piamun lived a long life in the Lord until she died on March 3.

March 4

Gerasimos of Jordan

The credibility of the story of a pious monk named Gerasimos and his attachment to no less an animal than a lion, the acknowledged king of beasts, suffers somewhat through fictional accounts such as that of Androkles, which was expanded upon by George Bernard Shaw in his entertaining play about the Greek slave. When the true story about Gerasimos and his encounter with a lion unfolds, the reader's brow is liable to furrow in disbelief unless he calls to mind that the power of the Lord Jesus Chrsit is extended to all of his creatures. More recent evidence of the tractability of lions outside of the circus arena is clearly demonstrated in the highly successful account of the friendship of a lioness in the book and documentary entitled, "Born Free."

Much more implausible occurrences than that of Gerasimos are sprinkled throughout history and are accepted without question. He was born in the seventh century in the province of Lycia in Asia Minor, a time when lions roamed that particular region much as they did when Sampson slew one with his bare hands, as told in the Old Testament. What seemed implausible was that Gerasimos, who came from a family of leisure class wealth, would one day walk away from the abundant life for the austere self-denial of monasticism. Yet this is precisely what happened when Gerasimos felt the call to the service of Jesus Christ and turned his back on comfort to stride willingly into the bleak confines of a cloister of the desert in order to come nearer to God and dedicate himself totally to the Savior.

He was tonsured a monk by an abbot who saw in him the true piety many sought but few acquired, and went to live in complete asceticism in the valley of the Jordan not too far from the fabled

Jordan River. Eventually, he set up his own monastery and through an active service to the community as well as to God he attracted several dedicated monks who developed a highly respected cloister that was a spiritual oasis in the desert. A student of the eminent St. Euthymios, he evinced a remarkable knowledge of dogmatic theology, which he imparted to his fellow monks, as well as a wisdom for which he won wide acclaim.

He often went to the banks of the Jordan River to meditate and pray by the stream, which is celebrated in Scripture and in which he found an aura of tranquility which was conducive to the inner peace that nourishes the soul. While in this state of meditation, he heard the roar of a lion and turned to see an animal licking its paw furiously in obvious pain. The calmness he had achieved while seated at the river bank remained with Gerasimos as he approached the lion and discovered that its huge paw was swollen from a large sliver which had become imbedded in its flesh. Quite possibly, instinct told the beast the man meant him no harm and it remained still while the monk withdrew the fragment.

This done, Gerasimos simply turned and started walking back to his monastery and was quite pleasantly surprised to see the lion following him like a pet dog. He stopped to stroke the beast and then and there was formed a friendship with the animal, which was as tame as a cat by this time, as they strode together to the cloister. The monks were frozen in terror when Gerasimos walked into their midst in the company of his new-found pet, and it was quite some time before they could find themselves at ease with a lion lolling about. But the nameless beast soon became a household pet which never posed a threat to the monks and which preferred to remain at the side of his benefactor.

The rare sight of a lion sprawled at the side of a busily engaged monk was as much an attraction, if not more so, than the renowned wisdom of its master. But pilgrims, monks and students alike, came to realize that they were beholding a manifestation of the mysterious and unexplainable workings of the Lord.

Archbishop Sophronios of Jerusalem, admirer and biographer of Gerasimos, relates that the presence of the lion seemed to enhance the image projected by Gerasimos as a man of rare power, as a result of which the venerable monk is depicted in icons with a lion at his side. It is further related that when Gerasimos died, the faithful lion seemed to lament his passing and he was found dead at the foot of the grave of St. Gerasimos.

March 4

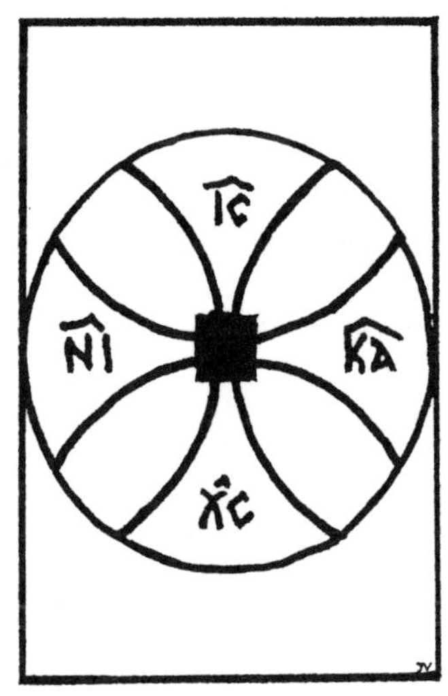

Gregory of Assos

The turbulent era of the Crusades underscored the surge of Christianity, demonstrated by the many marches across Europe by primarily French and English pilgrims, whose goals were never attained but who came to know at first hand a glorious Greek Orthodox hierarchy, among whom was Gregory of Assos, a towering figure during the ill-fated second and third campaigns.

Born on the island of Lesbos during the reign of the Byzantine Emperor Manuel Komnenos (1140-1180) to parents named George and Maria, both devout Christians and well-to-do landowners. He fulfilled the traditional studies on the island, and in keeping with the custom of generations of his wealthy family, he was sent to Constantinople at the age of fourteen for a secondary education which then required three years. As a seventeen-year old honor graduate, he had acquired a knowledge of the classics together with a love of the social life of the city, where he might have lingered had it not been for the formation of a strong friendship with a monk named Agathon, whose influence was such that the young man saw a finer purpose in the service of Jesus Christ than in any of the many alternatives available to him.

As a dutiful son, however, Gregory turned his back on the glamorous city and returned to Lesbos to join his father in helping to run the family business. It soon became obvious that his heart was not in it and that he was repressing a desire to serve Jesus Christ out of a sense of obligation to the father who had seen to his every need. When the father saw that the influence of Agathon had made a thorough Christian out of his son, he took his son aside, assuring him that his duty to Jesus Christ exceeded that of his loyalty to his father. He then invited Agathon to Lesbos to discuss his son's future.

Agathon had been a guest in George's home for but a short time, during which he brought out the true Christian spirit of Gregory for all to see. After a brief visit, Gregory left the comfort of his father's home and went to the monastery where Agathon had become abbot. The austerity of monasticism suited young Gregory and under the tutelage of Agathon, he became the most promising novice of the monastery where, after a period of three years, he was tonsured a monk.

Following a year in which he demonstrated a true sense of purpose through prayer, meditation, fasting, and a mastery of theology, Gregory was given permission to visit the Holy Land. The customary tour of a monk in the Holy Land was extended by Gregory who remained in the Holy Land for a period of fifteen years. Inspired by the knowledge that he was treading on the very sacred ground where Jesus Christ had trod, he took to preaching as well as praying. He was so immersed in his service to the Savior that it was only when letters from Agathon finally caught up with him that he returned to the monastery.

Reunited with Agathon, the now erudite Gregory anticipated that he would live out his days in the cloister, but circumstances dictated otherwise. He was somewhat taken aback when the patriarch, on the recommendation of Agathon, appointed him to the post of bishop of Assos, a prestigious diocese under the jurisdiction of the metropolitan of Ephesos. Appropriately enough, he was ordained on Christmas Day in the Cathedral of Assos, with a beaming Agathon, bearing witness to this elevation.

A new side of Gregory appeared when he took office. This side, was an administrative excellence which he applied gently but firmly in a bringing order in what he discovered to be a near chaotic state of church affairs. Demanding no more of others than he would of himself, he weeded out the driftwood and molded the undisciplined staff into an efficient group. Before long his dedication to Christ had passed on to those under him, who in turn had instilled it to communicants of every church in the diocese.

There was a need for intelligent and dedicated priests, and to that end Gregory screened his applicants carefully, selecting the best minds. He ran a tight ship, denying even those he deemed inadequate in spite of recommendations or letters of reference from hierarchs themselves. Seeking to favor God and not to favor undeserving applicants, he was assailed by a few who demanded his removal. But his position was secure and he continued to serve with distinction until he died on 4 March 1190.

March 5

Mark the Athenian

When St. Paul spoke from Mars Hill, he opened his remarks not with a polite "Gentlemen" or "My Friends," but commenced with the words spoken in respect as well as greeting: "Ye men of Athens." When this magnificent saint spoke, he was addressing polytheists, but as he faced the Acropolis, which was already 500 years old, at that time, he already knew that Athens was the cradle of democracy and would be receptive to the humble carpenter in whose eyes all men were equal. That Mark should come down to us as St. Mark the Athenian is not just to distinguish him from other Marks, but to have us know he was one of the "men of Athens" four centuries after St. Paul.

Mark was born in Athens into a family of intellectuals to whom he was indebted for his intelligence but whose highly successful commercial enterprises he valued little, preferring to devote himself not to the business of making money but to the deadly serious and much more rewarding business of purusing a career in religion. He could thank his family for the very best education that money could buy but thereafter the achievements were strictly his own. He also owed a debt of gratitude to a loving family who never interfered in his choice of career and never discouraged him in any way to depart from the merchant tradition which had amassed a family fortune in which he was assured his share.

Mark dismissed the money matters from his mind and concentrated on his preparation for service to Jesus Christ, attaining a scholastic stature that drew the attention of no less a person than the eminent St. John Chrysostom who took a personal interest in him and closely followed his remarkable mastery of every phase of ecclesiastical lore. Mark is said to have committed to memory the entire Bible from which he could quote passages at any length from the twenty-seven books of the New Testament. This was not an ostentatious display of his cerebral prowess but the full use of a tremendous intellect dedicated to the word of God, aiming at spiritual perfection with all the mental processes he could muster, leaving no stone unturned that lie in the path of the approach to Heaven.

After receiving the utmost in religious tutoring from St. John Chrysostom, Mark sailed to Africa and traveled deep into the interior of what is now Ethiopia, settling at last atop a mountain to enter a life of asceticism far removed from the clamor of the city. Assured a quiet solitude, he commenced a life of meditation, prayer and fasting, interspersed with religious writings. He had left word with his family that, should he not return, his share of the wealth be given to various charities. He was to remain long after the family wealth had been divided after the death of his parents because he remained in his bleak retreat for an incredible sixty years.

It is said that the prolonged spiritual vigil of Mark resulted not only in his awareness of the Holy Spirit about him, blotting out the mundane completely, but he came to actually witness a physical manifestation of the Spirit. On the occasions following a fast, he is said to have received Holy Communion from a heaven-sent hand which he looked upon with his own eyes and was sanctified in life as saints are after death. The miraculous appearance of the hand, which placed the sacred spoon to his mouth, was perfectly formed and when he looked for the rest of this angel, the arm was only visible to the elbow.

Some distance from his mountain retreat was another holy man of the desert of Egypt who is known as St. Serapion and who in a vision was instructed to go to St. Mark's mountain where he would be told by Mark himself the nature of his visit. Serapion made the arduous journey not without a great deal of pain and discomfort, arriving finally at the mountain peak exhausted.

After he had rested, Serapion was told by Mark that he had been sent to see Mark's funeral and interment. By now 120 years old, the venerable Mark had been told by his unseen visitor that his time was at hand and since there was no other living soul to attend him, Serapion would be sent to bury him. Soon afterwards, Mark died at the age of 121 and was given a Christian burial by Serapion who, like everyone else who knew about St. Mark the Athenian, never ceased to be amazed by the wondrous life of a man of the city of Athens who left family and friends to find the kinship of the Holy Spirit.

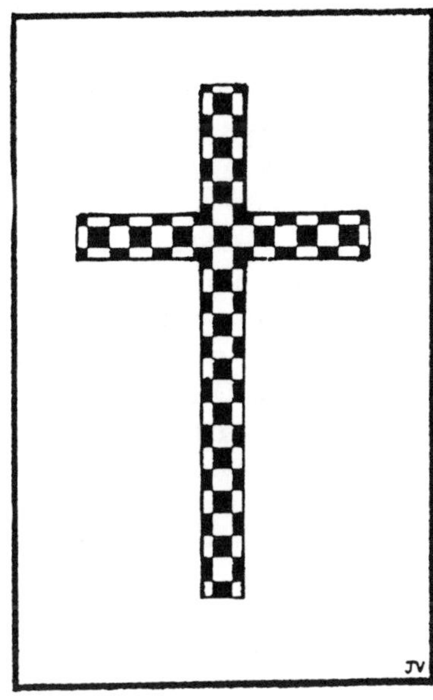

March 5

John the Bulgarian

Much has been made of Turkish brutality and the old enmity between Turks and Greeks, to the point where some of the younger generations consider the ill feeling an overreaction on the part of their elders, but the life story of John the Bulgarian who lived until nearly the twentieth century is recent enough in memory to dispel this notion.

Nothing is known of the early background of John, who was one of the carefree young who grew up in the shadows of the minarets and who numbered among his friends boys of the Muslim faith. He had been born and baptized a Christian but did not seem to take his Christian religion seriously. He was not known to have been what one might call a churchgoer and in spite of the fact that he was of decent character, was not known to have a childish faith in Christ. Religious training was not a part of his childhood, but later he proved himself more a Christian than most.

At some point in his early teens John the Bulgarian's relaxed religious attitude was such that he allowed himself to turn to Islam, which at first appeared to be no more than crossing the border into another country. It soon became apparent as he approached adulthood that it was a much more serious matter and that his carelessness could prove costly since he failed to realize that in turning his back on Christianity, he had become an apostate who denied Christ. When he was eighteen years old he faced the harsh reality of what he had done and the latent spirit that had been within him since his baptism asserted itself.

It was not fear, but abject contrition that drove John the Bulgarian from the one extreme of indifference to a gnawing desire to repent. Not content to rejoin his Christian friends and simply embrace Christ again with a parish priest to hear his confession, he made his way to the monasteries of Mt. Athos, where he was admitted with no credentials except one; that one, a desire to atone for his ill-considered apostasy, was enough to gain him entrance in the company of men who could help him cleanse himself completely in the eyes of God.

John the Bulgarian was assigned to the Monastery of St. Athanasios, where he spent four years in meditation, prayer, and fasting. He led the life of the most ascetic of monks, not in preparation for monkhood but to attain forgiveness. One of his duties was the care of a monk who had lost an arm in an accident, but not his faith in spite of his misfortune. The monk assured John that he would love Jesus Christ with all his heart even had he been rendered limbless. John was reminded that all he had lost in his past years was his reason, which was easily restored, and in showing his true contrition he was showing a great love of Jesus Christ. John found considerable comfort in the old monk's counsel, particularly when he insisted that John's incident was not so much as apostasy as it was an aberration.

John the Bulgarian felt that his forgiveness would be complete only after kneeling in prayer in the Church of Hagia Sophia, in defiance of Turkish law. This display would serve a dual purpose, since it would allow an overt declaration of Christianity in what once had been the mightiest citadel in Christendom.

Despite warnings that his action was needless and that his debt had been paid, John the Bulgarian made his way to Constantinople and prior to entering the cathedral, donned his Turkish garb over his street clothes. He then entered the huge cathedral, scarcely noticed until he went before what was once the altar, and casting his Turkish garb onto the floor, knelt in prayer, constantly making the sign of the cross in true Orthodox fashion as bewildered guards looked on. He continued to pray out loud, declaring Christ as his deliverer and denouncing Islam as only one who had experienced it could. It was some time before he was subdued by guards and ordered to pick up his Turkish clothes.

John's answer was to step on the garments and grind them into the floor. He was a man possessed, doing what no Christian had dared to do since the Turks had forbidden Christian prayer in Hagia Sophia. In complete disregard of the consequences, he shouted out that the Turks should be ashamed of themselves for having defiled this House of God, just as he was ashamed of himself. Shouting the praises of the Lord, he was dragged out into the street where police pounced on him, slashing him to death. Without trial, he spilled his blood for Christ on 5 March 1889.

March 6

Hesychios the Miracle-worker

A person who has climbed a mountain of moderate height reaches the pinnacle and then takes in the breath-taking view below. An ascetic who has scaled the mountain may glance for a moment below but then looks upward to the breath-giving view of that which lies beyond. It is this difference in perspective as well as purpose that distinguishes a tourist from a man of God although nothing says a person cannot be both. Hesychios was no roaming tourist, but he was a man of God who did climb a mountain to be closer to God in the physical sense and to attain that perfection of the spirit that places one quite close to God in the spiritual sense.

Of humble origin, Hesychios was born in the eighth century in the area of Galatia, Asia Minor, an area which has seen an outpouring of saints but which in the days of Hesychios was a zone where angels feared to tread because of the lawlessness and violence. Whether driven out of poverty or sloth or immorality or a combination of all three, reckless bands of thieves and highwaymen roamed around the outskirts of the city, ever ready to pounce on an unsuspecting and unwary traveler, leaving him either stripped to the skin or beaten out of sheer cruelty. The law had its hands full within the city walls in coping with criminals, as a result of which none but the most foolhardy or heavily armed groups would venture beyond the city limits after dark.

Hesychios was a man of peace who preached against sin with little success but never ceased to remind the innocent that the blight of violence would end in God's good time and they would be free to walk abroad, day or night, without being in fear of their lives. His cheerful optimism made the cares lighter for those good Christians whose forebears had seen persecution enough for all the generations to come.

Hesychios had suppressed a desire for many years to go to the nearby mountain of Maionos in order to be among his fellow Christians but when at last he could no longer suppress the urge to seek the isolation of a hilltop he made preparations for the journey. His alarmed friends reminded him that he would not last beyond a day or two in the open and lest great harm come to him urged him to remain. He reassured them that he had placed his faith in God, who would see to it that he would arrive safely at his destination, which was the summit of that foreboding mountain. Kneeling in earnest prayer, he placed himself in God's hands and walked out of the city.

Hesychios walked leisurely all through the day, camping at night at the base of the mountain before beginning its ascent that would surely be the most likely time to encounter a bandit.

He had neither seen nor heard another soul and the fact that he got to the summit without incident was in itself proof that here was a man favored of God. He remained for several days at the summit in meditation and prayer before deciding to return for a brief period to assure his friends that he was in no danger.

Any doubt as to the miraculous power that he had been granted was soon dispelled when a woman came forward with an epileptic child, asking Hesychios to pray for her cure. He laid his hands on the child and prayed for her, after which she went home with her mother forever cured of the dread disease. Besieged by a host of villagers, he remained to bless them and to preach the word of God as they had never heard it spoken, after which he returned to the hilltop to be alone with the Holy Spirit.

He was sought out by the woman whose child he had healed and was told she had the financial backing required for whatever manner of residence he would like, but he said he would prefer that the money be applied to a better purpose, as a result of which there was erected at the base of the mountain a nunnery which soon housed a good number of nuns. Miraculously, the vermin that had preyed on innocent travelers had taken themselves elsewhere and the people were free to come and go as they pleased.

With this freedom of action, most of the people for miles around came to visit Hesychios the Miracle Worker, as he came to be known, not only in this community but through Asia Minor as well. Hesychios worked for the good of the people to the end. After he died his remains were brought to the basilica of the capital by Bishop Theophylaktos at the request of Emperor Constantine and his mother Irene in the year 781.

March 7

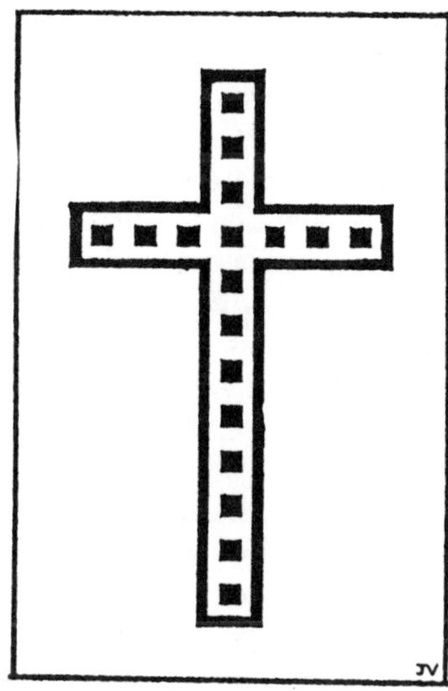

Saint Paul the Simple

The best known saint bearing the name of Paul was, of course, St. Paul the Apostle of Christ, credited with having written more than half of the New Testament. In the fourth century, however, another Paul came forth. This Paul was to become a saint in his own right. Although he had no part in the writings of the Bible, he patterned his life after its teachings. The man was Paul the Simple, so called because of the simplicity of his life, not his intellect, and certainly not his dedication of Christ.

The original great St. Paul would be the first to agree that history should carry down to us a man inappropriately named St. Paul the Simple. The implication in this sobriquet is more apt to apply to one's mind than to one's tastes, but nevertheless anyone who looks beyond his name can readily see the power of the mind of St. Paul the Simple. Very often an adjective will be added to a man's name to avoid confusion in identities, especially among those with popular names. It is much easier to associate guilt than it is innocence, hence the use of the term guilty by association. But by association with such great men of the church as St. Anthony, greatest of all eremites, St. Paul the Simple captured the mood of self denial through which so many of our saints have come to that pinnacle of the soul which we choose to call spiritual attainment, or fullment, as the case may be. Unlike the fire and brimstone preachers who carry the message sometimes too strongly to suit their enemies, St. Paul the Simple was spared an early death and lived to carry on God's work for an extended span of years.

Paul the Simple was a farmer whose first full fifty years of life were lived in complete obscurity with no indication that he would ultimately attain prominence in Christian thought and deed.

His sincerity in Christian endeavor was that of the average devout believer in Jesus Christ. He followed a quiet pattern of church attendance and prayer. Outwardly he was a pious but unobstrusive, somewhat inconspicuous tiller of the soil who would scarcely have been expected to actively promote Christianity.

What stood in the way of his complete devotion to Christianity was his marriage to a girl several years his junior, whose ultimate infidelity left him a sadder but wiser man. Having done his best to preserve the marriage, and rewarded for his patience by his wife's leaving for other companionship, Paul the Simple found a noble purpose for his life. With high expectations he left for the desert and his true destiny.

His travels brought him into Egypt. There he sought out the greatest monastic figure of the day, St. Anthony, who was unimpressed by the farmer and suggested that he seek out some other approach to the throne of heaven. Now sixty years of age, Paul the Simple saw no reason to move. Therefore, for three days and nights he camped outside the cave of St. Anthony. The latter was thereby convinced of Paul's complete sincerity and welcomed him into monasticism. Thus at the age of sixty, at a time when most men look to a life of ease in retirement from life's daily struggles, Paul set about laying the foundation of his work for Christ that brought him due recognition.

He settled in a cave not far from that of St. Anthony. After a period of fasting, meditation, and prayer, he plunged into the work of God which he had so earnestly sought. Soon his tiny cave was a haven for those who sought the truth of Jesus and not long afterwards his reputation became as great at St. Anthony's, who then smiled whenever he remembered the way he had first slighted his strong friend Paul.

Paul the Simple acquired great intellectual power in his work for Christ and was said to have commanded a great power of exorcism. For this reason he was constantly consulted by troubled souls who found comfort in his gentle wisdom.

Paul's first fifty years of life were spent in obscurity. His next forty years were those of comparative glory, for he lived to the ripe age of ninety. He died on 7 March 340.

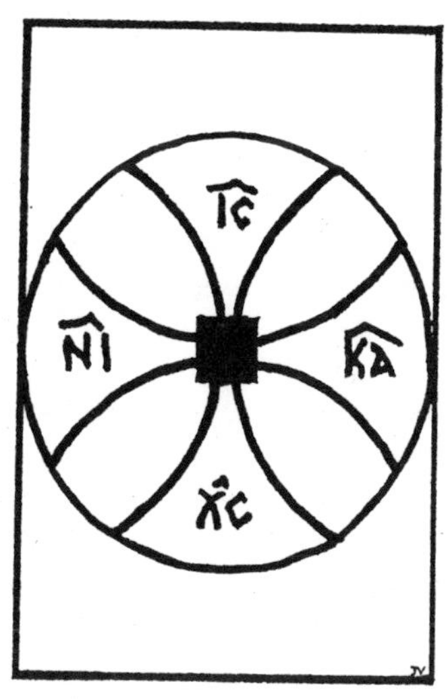

Saint Lavrentios

In an extension of fourth century monasticism, the eighteenth-century St. Lavrentios continued an unbroken line of ascetics whose lives have been given over exclusively to Jesus Christ to the degree that some, as in this case, have been made saints of the Church. Like St. Anthony, who lived to be 105 despite his self denial, Lavrentios took upon himself "the whole yoke of the Lord," joining an exclusive society of men who have substituted asceticism for martyrdom.

Born with the given name of Lambros to parents named Demetrios and Kyriake in the village of Megara, Greece, he was to assume the name Lavrentios in honor of the monk under whom he was to become a novice and subsequently tonsured. In the years that passed, he led a fruitful and eventful live as a man who married young and became the father of two children named John and Demetrios. A well-educated and highly intelligent person, he became a successful farmer, mason, and businessman, displaying an acumen and resourcefulness that made him a leading figure. His image was enhanced by his extreme devotion to the Church, assuming lay responsibilities for its progress.

The sons of Lavrentios had become adults and had married when he crowned his business accomplishments with the acquisition of a considerable tract of land in Liantros, Corinth. Approaching middle age his design was to settle in this area, content to be a country squire of means, a good portion of which he was to continue donating to the church and other worthy charities.

One summer evening, he had a vision of the Virgin Mary in which he was told his destiny lay not in Corinth but on a remote island in the service of her Son. He was asked to go to the island of Salamina and to erect a church in her name. The vision was dismissed by Lavrentios as a product of the summer heat but the vision was repeated the following evening, but this time with such clarity that there was no mistaking the reality of the vision. With humility and soaring spirit, he told his wife of this pnenomenon and after selling what he had, he was joined by her. She was equally convinced he had been given a holy mission.

The devout couple made their way to the island and upon traversing the north end, they came upon the ruins of a church which, as they were told later by native islanders, had been the Church of St. Mary. In the excavation on the site in preparation for the erection of a new church, an icon of the Virgin Mary was unearthed and taken to a run-down monastery, a short distance away, to be shown to the abbot. Admitted to the monastery, he and his wife were presented to the abbot. All three knelt in veneration of this holy relic. When the couple made known their intentions, the abbot identified himself as Lavrentios, the name which Lambros was to later call himself in honor of this man.

Lavrentios not only built a new Church of St. Mary but remodeled the monastery as well, entering it to be tonsured a monk and assuming the name of his mentor shortly before the latter passed away. Meanwhile his wife, Vasilike, had matched her husband's stride in the service of the Savior, becoming a nun and assuming the name of Vassiane.

The cloister of St. Mary on the island of Salamina, not far off the mainland, was soon filled to capacity with dedicated monks performing communal work with dedication. The same talents that Lavrentios had applied in the material world now stood him in good stead in the spiritual.

Lavrentios was an instrument of the Lord to those who really came to know him but to a covetous Muslim who envied his popularity and eminent success, he was an anthema to be discredited. This enemy, through devious means, brought about the confiscation of monastic property on spurious grounds but soon came to regret his action. The wife of the wretch who loathed the righteous monk was forced to turn to him for help when his wife fell victim to an illness that physicians failed to cure. Lavrentios went to the side of the ailing woman and after kneeling and praying, the stricken wife was cured. This done, the repentant husband admitted his wrongdoing and the improperly seized property was restored to the monks.

Even after his death on 7 March 1770, many other miracles were attributed to Lavrentios.

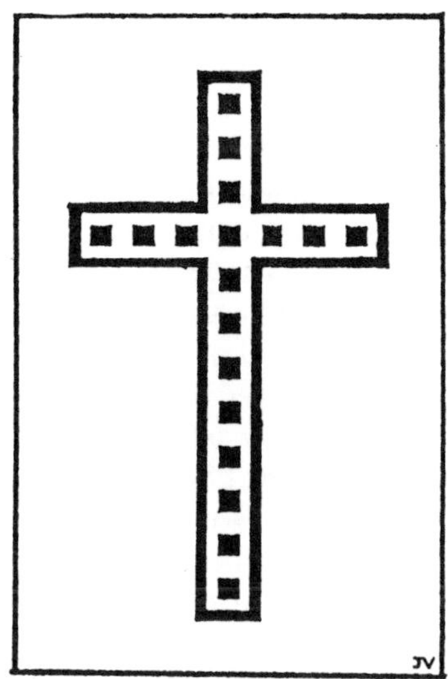

Saint Theophylaktos

The power of emperors in the Byzantine Empire was a guarantee against any serious political differences because his authority was never challenged in this area. But in matters of religion, in which he was also supreme, voices were raised against him by Church leaders who stood their ground in defense of the faith regardless of consequences. One whose voice was never muffled by the awesome utterance of royalty was Theophylaktos, the bishop of Nikomedia, whose quiet mien belied the fierce determination with which he would have taken a stand against all odds like an eighth century David whose sling contained the rock of truth against any Goliath, royalty or commoner.

At the center of the burning issues which were ravaging the Church in the days of the peace-loving but determined Theophylaktos, was the Inconoclastic movement which he deplored but which the unknowledgeable Emperor Leo the Armenian supported, on the side of the short-sighted who looked upon the icons of the Church as paganistic menaces. It was the contention of Theophylaktos and other brighter churchmen that the icons were symbols of veneration, representing a holy group without whom there might very well not have been a church in which to worship Jesus Christ.

The iconoclasts were a stubborn lot, particularly since they were able to win over the supreme civil authority, as a result of which the controversy raged more than 150 years, during which time there was a serious erosion of the Christian spirit. Men like Theophylaktos tried to reason with the dissenters to no avail in what grew to be a bloodless religious war not much different from a civil war that puts brother against brother in a bitter dispute that demeans all concerned. The real sufferer in this shameful strife was the Savior who must have looked down with anguish at this sorry scene, where men of good will had become combatants.

The dedicated administrative skill of Theophylaktos as bishop of Nikomedia was diverted from the worthly causes in which he was constantly improving the spiritual and general welfare of his see, to take up the defense of the holy wallpaper. It was little wonder then that this exalted prelate was called upon by Patriarch Nikephoros, who had succeeded the compromising Patriarch Tarasios, to lead a contingent of other selected prelates with a view to convincing the emperor he had been misled by iconoclasts.

Theophylaktos, together with Bishop Michael of Synada, Bishop Emilianos of Kyzikos, Bishop Euthymios of Sardes, Bishop Joseph of Thessalonike, and Bishop Eudoxios of Amorion formed as holy a squad as ever marched together for the Savior. They were received in the palace at Constantinople in a cool greeting by Emperor Leo who barely acknowledged their presence, let alone recognized his indebtedness to men who had made the wearisome journey, right or wrong, in the interests of the Church of Jesus Christ. After a strained exchange of pleasantries, the bishops took up the matter of their purpose and as respectfully and delicately as possible presented their case, taking care not to offend the volatile Leo.

There was no appeasing or convincing the obstinate Leo who construed their presentation to be an affront to the royal sensitivities, and whenever one of the bishops would try to reason more, the cleric would be shouted down by the emperor, who declared that icons would be removed from every church and monastery and even every private home in the realm. It was then that Theophylaktos raised his voice, stunning Leo with a verbal blast that blistered his royal ears, saying that the uninformed Leo, the greatest heretic of them all, would one day feel the wrath of God and that his chosen path would lead to his destruction.

Bishop Theophylaktos was ordered to be exiled by the enraged Leo who then turned and offered him clemency if he would reverse his stand. The bishop said he preferred banishment and found himself an outcast in a bleak area of Strovylon, a pariah in an isolated strand from which he was never to return. After thirty years in disfavor he died, but on the assassination of Leo, the body of the bishop was returned for burial by order of the Empress Theodora. He is commemorated on the day of his death, March 8.

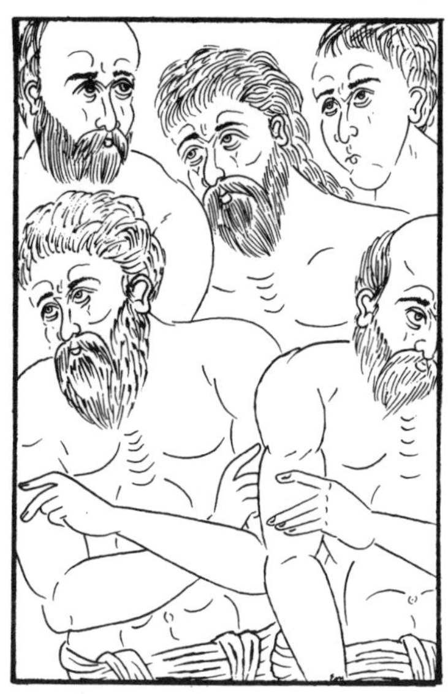

March 9

The Forty Martyrs of Sebaste

A blissful couple standing before a priest as he intones the beautiful prayers contained in the sacrament of marriage of the Orthodox Church are aware of the solemnity of the words they hear, but cannot grasp the real significance of one of the prayers offered unless they know the story of the Forty Martyrs of Sebaste. In the 1500 years since the prayers were introduced by the Holy Fathers in the marriage ceremony, those who have taken the trouble to ask why the Forty Martyrs are invoked in this sacrament hear a sacred story which is both tragic and beautiful and gives added meaning to the occasion.

The prayer reads, "Remember them [the bride and groom], O Lord, as thou didst thy Forty Holy Martyrs, sending down upon them crowns from Heaven . . ." The symbolic crowns, with which many a nervous man has fumbled in the wedding ceremony, stem from the traditional crowns sent from Heaven for the holy martyrs, and thereon hangs one of the most poignant tales in church history.

The story begins in the fourth century during the reign of the cruel Emperor Licinius (A.D. 320) when a group of forty young soldiers of the Roman army garrisoned in the city of Sebaste, Armenia, were deeply committed to the service of Jesus Christ while yet finding it possible to serve the emperor in the devout country of Armenia, the first nation to proclaim Christianity as the religion of the realm. They were as courageous and as fiercely proud of their garrison as any in the armies of Rome, but unlike most others had found the truth of the word of Jesus Christ. They were prime examples of men who could bear arms for their country and still worship the Prince of Peace, not at all difficult to conceive today when chaplains are in evidence not only in the armed services but in law enforcement bodies as well. There was no chaplain to see to the spiritual needs of the forty young men, the lack of which only serves to underscore the fact that they acted in the service of the Lord completely on their own.

Not only did these forty young men accept Christ as their Savior on their own initiative, but they did so with the full knowledge that in so doing they ran a considerable risk to their personal safety. It was only a matter of time, therefore, until the word of their allegiance to Christ became known to Licinius, a tyrant of less than noble character who forthwith issued an edict that those who failed to worship the pagan gods would face punishment that could include torture or death.

A contingent was sent from Rome to Sebaste for the express purpose of bringing to justice the forty soldiers of this Armenian garrison, all of whom refused to disavow Christ. On orders from Licinius they were given the choice of recanting or dying, but not a single soldier among the forty stepped forward to be counted as a pagan and thereby save his life. It was bitterly cold at this particular time and this led to the idea to strip the soldiers naked and stand them out by a lake where the frigid winds would eventually and painfully freeze them to death.

The forty young soldiers stood shivering in the cold, looking across to the warm fires of the pagans to which they could go if they would only deny Christ, but the forty preferred death to that kind of dishonor and stood their ground. There was one in this holy group that finally weakened and, expressing his defection, he started for the warmth of the glowing fires but died before he could reach them.

As death approached, a band of angels descended from Heaven and placed crowns on the heads of the dying soldiers, a spectacle which so overcame one of the pagan guards that he stripped himself and rushed to die at the side of these who had been made the bridegrooms of Heaven. The late arrival's death brought to forty the number who died for Christ on that somber day, replacing the solitary defector who died in vain.

It is for this reason that a prayer invoking the forty young members of the Roman garrison is included in the wedding rite as a symbol of the blessing of Heaven for those who keep their faith in Jesus Christ.

March 10

Saint Anastasia

As a lady in waiting in the court of the great Emperor Justinian, the extremely attractive Anastasia very often heard her name called out by the Empress Theodora. This call heard by no one, but felt within this gifted girl, was a loud and clear call of the spirit which came from the highest of authority, the answer to which was made in a fashion that could lead only to sainthood. The entrancing beauty of this noble maiden assured her a place in the royal household which, had she so chosen, could have made her a courtesan whose name might very well have been as commonly known as that of Jezebel or Delilah. Instead she chose to heed the call from above with such resolve that her place is not in the history books where she might have been recorded as an empress who could have helped rule the world. Her place is on the sacred roster of saints, one of the many known to so few people but very well known to God.

The story of Anastasia's life is a reversal of the conventional rags to riches theme which makes for interesting reading in the minds of some, but a riches to rags story, by design rather than misfortune, affords far more rewarding reading in the discriminating minds of those who place greater value on a stirring of the spirit than a tickling of the mind. Anastasia was endowed not only with outstanding beauty but with considerable wealth as well, the combination of which made her a coveted prize in her lofty social circle. Her deep Christian faith placed her on a level even higher than that of Emperor Justinian and Empress Theodora, the royal pair responsible for the erection of the awesome Church of Hagia Sophia in Constantinople, as well as the Monastery of St. Catherine at the foot of Mount Sinai.

Anastasia's social position grew to be less a concern for her as her love for Jesus Christ deepened, reaching a point where her absence was noticed at state functions. She abandoned the posturing required at these affairs to kneel in a chapel, therefore secluding herself to study the holy Scriptures in preparation for the calling which subordinated the activities that swirled in her meaningless social circle.

Eager to serve the Messiah, Anastasia fled the clamor and intrigue of the royal court, and after converting her assets into cash, she left the city unnoticed and went directly to Alexandria where she was unrecognized. She lost no time in putting her money to good use and built a nunnery second to none in the empire, in which she herself spent many years in becoming a full-time servant of the Lord. When she was not sewing garments for the needy, as well as church materials, she sought seclusion in which she could pray and meditate. She became a highly respected figure in this citadel of Christianity which is still in existence and bears the name of St. Anastiasia of Alexandria, Egypt.

Following the death of the Empress Theodora, the Emperor Justinian decided to remarry and he made it known he wanted as his new bride the girl named Anastasia, who had not escaped his eyes at court and whose memory had not escaped him in the intervening years. Unaware of her actual presence, he sent out representatives to find her, confident that wherever she was and whatever she was doing, she would drop everything for the opportunity to become the empress of the mighty Byzantine Empire.

News of the emperor's search preceded his agents and a distraught Anastasia, long since pledged in chastity to serve the Lord, decided to vanish as she had years before in Constantinople. Bidding a reluctant farewell to her sister nuns, she fled to the desert. She had no wish to be empress, nor could she anticipate Justinian's reaction had she refused his bidding, but taking no risks, she traveled in the disguise of a monk for fear of recognition, accompanied by Abbot Daniel of Alexandria until she was safely secluded in a spot well off the beaten paths.

Alone in this bleak spiritual haven, Anastasia was never to reappear in public, but to the occasional straggler who chanced upon her spiritual retreat, she identified herself as a monk named Anastasios the Eunuch, concealing her lovely features with a false beard when anyone came near. For the next twenty years she lived thus until her final hour was approaching, at which time the Abbot Daniel was summoned to give her final communion and to identify her as the once lovely Anastasia who forsook the Byzantine throne for Jesus Christ. She died on March 10.

March 11

Sophronios, Patriarch of Jerusalem

One of the lesser known heresies that cropped up to pose a mild yet ominous threat to accepted Church dogma was the theory of Monotheletism, and the Church's suppression of this heresy was the handiwork primarily of a man known as Sophronios, a patriarch of Jerusalem in the seventh century, against whose eloquent logic no voice of Monotheletism was any match. It may seem trivial by comparison with the iconoclastic movement which ravaged the Church for 150 years, but its theory, nevertheless, was an affront to God that could have had disastrous consequences without the forceful opposition of such as Sophronios.

Quite simply, the doctrine of Monotheletism held that Christ had one will, not two, which was in contrast to the traditional concept of the Lord's having two wills, one divine and the other human, inasmuch as He was both human and divine. Surprisingly, a number of well-respected theologians were swayed to this view and their short-sightedness may have spread except for the compelling reasoning of the Jerusalem prelate.

Sophronios was born to a Christian couple named Plythas and Mary, whose circumstances were such that they provided more than adequately for the educational and spiritual needs of their son. More fortunate than most, the boy grew to maturity with the gnawing feeling that there was something lacking in his life, and he felt that the void could only be filled by an approach to God through the medium of asceticism, and to that end he gave up all social and economic ties to take up monasticism.

Sophronios was enrolled in a monastery in Egypt, there to encounter a monk named John for whom he developed a deep personal attachment in acquiring from him the benefit of his prolonged experience as a monk and tutor. An authority on dogmatic theology, John imparted to Sophronios the wisdom which was to stand him in good stead in his service to Jesus Christ, and in due course the student was to excel the teacher. The extent of the knowledge of both these pious monks was encyclopedic and they delighted in testing each other, with John usually yielding to his superior friend.

After Sophronios had taken up his successful stand against Monotheletism, a posture which brought him wide recognition, he was given the post of archbishop of Jerusalem, a prestigious office in which he gave full expression to his piety and wisdom. In 638 the Persian hordes of King Uram overran the Holy Land, terrorizing the people and removing all authority except one—that of Patriarch Sophronios, who refused to be intimidated by the infidels. Not wishing to stir up an insurrection, they retreated from the holy ground of the Patriarchate.

The invaders did surround the city, however, forbidding travel in or out of the limits, but when Sophronios heard news of the death of John the Merciful, Patriarch of Alexandria, he went through the guardpost without incident and continued to Alexandria where he delivered a stirring eulogy for his longtime friend, John. He returned to the Holy City, again passing through the barricades without incident because not even the wretched Persians dared to approach this holy and resolute man of God.

In the ensuing months of seige, Sophronios ventured out into the crowded city daily, offering his blessing to those who were needlessly oppressed and bolstering the flagging spirits of those whose hopes were growing faint. Even the enemy came to respect this awesome prelate as he exhorted the populace to continue their work as though the enemies of Christianity did not exist, and his inspirational leadership brought heart to the long suffering people, who found within themselves the capacity to bear burdens they had never anticipated. For as long as he remained patriarch, the spiritual business of the entire community went on uninterrupted and the social order remained intact.

While all this was going on Sophronios found time to express himself in writing, thereby creating some of the finest works in ecclesiastical history, particularly the books that touched on exegetics. He also produced the quite marvelous biography, "Mary of Egypt," among his many outstanding writings. He died peacefully in Jerusalem on 11 March 669.

St. Symeon the New Theologian

The superlatives applied to the wondrous gifts of men such as St. John Chrysostom and St. Gregory the Theologian allow no comparison with either of these church greats, each of whom compares with the other but invites no comparison with any other saint. They were considered incomparable until there appeared in the tenth century a man now known to us as St. Symeon the New Theologian, a churchman of such intellect that neither St. John Chrysostom nor St. Gregory the Theologian suffers the least by the recognition of Symeon as their intellectual equal.

Symeon was born with the given name of George in 957, the son of Basil and Eugenia who were devout Christians and of high social standing in the city of Galatine, Paphlagonia. After completing his elementary studies, he was sent at the age of fourteen to Constantinople in the care of an uncle of considerable influence in the capital city. Despite a high intellect which had been amply demonstrated, he was disinterested in the study program offered, and to relieve the boredom he sought a change by paying a visit to the famous Monastery of Studios in Constantinople. It proved to be a visit that was to alter the course of his life, much to the benefit of Christendom.

At the Studios Monastery, George spent many hours in conversation with a remarkable and quite pious monk who had earned the name of Symeon the Devout, who so inspired the young student that he asked permission to remain as a novice. Because of his youth and relative lack of study, the request was denied, and George returned to his uncle with a determination to be the brightest scholar of his day. Returning after some years of intense study, he was again denied admission to Studios because his learning had been misdirected, and he was advised to apply himself to the study of the fathers and Scriptures. The resolute George took this course of religious preparation, and at long last he was admitted to the monastery in 984 when he was twenty-seven years old.

No man has ever entered a cloister better prepared for the service of the Savior than the eager George, but again he was denied permission to be at the side of the elder monk Symeon because it was in violation of monastic rules to allow such privilege to a novice, and he was, therefore, sent to the monastery of St. Mamas where he was finally ordained a priest at the age of thirty by Patriarch Nicholas Chrysoberges. At his ordination he assumed the name of his spiritual father, Symeon, with whom he remained close until the latter's death.

Appointed by the patriarch to be abbot of the Monastery of St. Mamas, the younger Symeon brought about sweeping reforms within the monastery which called for a strict adherence to the rules concerning self-denial and fasting, reforms which brought protest from the monks. An appeal to the patriarch availed the monks little because he knew Symeon's sterling character and supported him in his disciplinary action. A former metropolitan of Nikomedia named Stephanos, now chancellor at the Patriarchate, sided with the insurgent monks and for reasons best known to himself sought to discredit Symeon with a series of harrassments that after six years finally influenced the patriarch to the point where Symeon was exiled and sent out to fend for himself.

After some wandering, Symeon came upon a private chapel owned by one Christopher Faguras, a man of deep religious faith, who welcomed the pariah and allowed him to establish a monastery of his own. It was at his private chapel that Symeon composed sacred hymns of great beauty as well as masterful writings which encompassed all phases of theology, including catechisms. His prolific writing was of such calibre that it was recognized throughout Christendom and acknowledged by the patriarch to be the works of a man divinely inspired.

Vindicated at last, Symeon was asked to return to Constantinople, but he preferred to remain at the chapel to continue his literary efforts which form an integral part of church reading. He died on 12 March 1022.

March 13

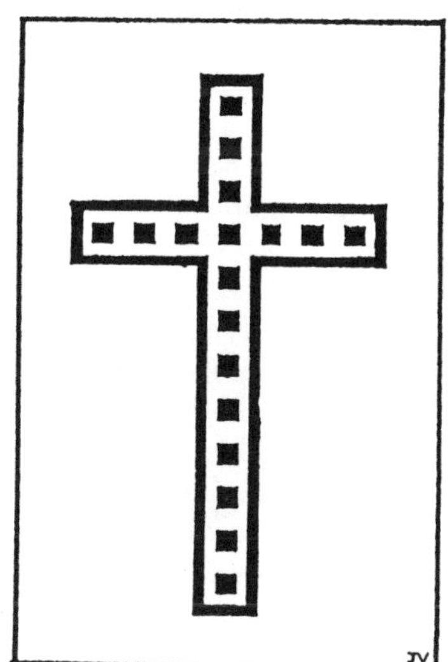

Puplios, Bishop of Athens

Launched by a missionary zeal for the Savior, which was spearheaded by the magnificent St. Paul, Christianity was sustained after the departure of the apostles and disciples by a series of resolute bishops of the first and second centuries who kept a very fragile Christian faith from withering in the face of oppression and persecution. The urban centers of antiquity (after centuries of a sophisticated culture that embraced all branches of the arts, sciences, philosophy and democracy) still had a stubborn adherence to polytheism which placed Christians into a minority group made formidable by the truth of Jesus Christ whose bishop spokesmen slowly but surely advanced the Christian cause.

The cultural center of the world was Athens, the home of true servant of God who bore the rather odd-sounding name of Puplios. He was an accomplished thinker and philosopher, fourth in an illustrious line of the bishops of Athens, a city which has never lacked for a spiritual leader, commencing with the very first named Ierotheos and followed by Dionysios and Narkissos. Puplios assumed the post of bishop of Athens with the knowledge that his two predecessors had met cruel deaths. But he was no stranger to the hazards involved and evinced a courage which earned the respect even of those who were most bitterly opposed to his Christian faith.

Puplios served as bishop of Athens during the reign of Marcus Arurelius (A.D. 161-180) at a time when paganism was as entrenched in Athens as it was in Rome, requiring a bishop to be as resourceful and diplomatic as he was courageous. Because they were forced to worship in secrecy, the lives of Christians were so unobtrusive as to make them unknowns until they assumed positions of leadership in the Christian community; even then altogether too many have melted into oblivion for lack of record.

Thanks to an ecclesiastical historian of renown named Eusebios, who was also bishop of Caesaria (A.D. 280-340) and who painstakingly searched out ancient documents and manuscripts, some of the extraordinary life of Puplios, have been handed down. The noted historian found considerable material concerning Puplios in the letter of a contemporary theologian named Dionysius of Corinth addressed to the second-century Athenians.

The Corinthian displays a familiarity not only with Puplios the person, but also with his outstanding achievements in missionary work that met the challenges of the era, challenges which were met head on with amazing intelligence and resolve. To begin with, Athens was the home of some of the finest minds of the empire, minds that had been honed to a fine edge in the tradition of savants and scholars that could be traced back to many centuries before Christ appeared on earth. If some of these philosophers and others refused to accept polytheism, and even went so far as to accept the concept of an omnipotent being, they were nevertheless proud skeptics who took a dim view of the carpenter from Nazareth.

Much had been made by this time of the Old Testament, and a factor aiding Puplios in calling for the worship of Jesus Christ as the Son of God was the fact that the New Testament had been written in Greek. Armed with the power of their own language, he assailed profound thinkers with their own brand of interpretation; those who did not capitulate retired in confusion. His preaching took on the form of public debate in which he won converts from the listeners, particularly since they not only heard the word of the Messiah, but witnessed an awesome interpreter of that word.

It is clear that the Christian Church grew in strength under Puplios in an electrifying fashion unsurpassed by any other bishop, despite the fact that statistics to support this do not exist (if any figures were kept to begin with). The glorious temples of Athens were emptied of the idols and transformed into cathedrals to an extent that eventually alarmed the obstinate pagans. A petition was sent to the emperor for authority to rid Athens of the menance of Puplios; although Marcus Aurelius was quite the debater, he chose not to square off verbally against the eloquent bishop of Athens. Instead he methodically ordered the execution of the noble Puplios who died for the Savior on 13 March 175.

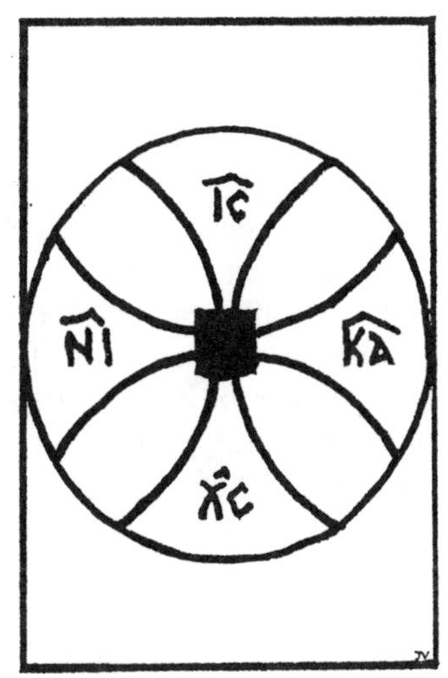

Saint Benedict of Nursia, Italy

Although monastic retreats were never intended for any other purpose other than prayer and meditation, because of their strategic sites and formidable walls, they were often used by invaders for military purposes. The monastery atop Mount Cassino was no exception; during World War II the Germans transformed the monastery into a fortress. The citadel of peace was sacrificed to the bombs of the Allied Forces so that it unwittingly became a factor in shortening a terrible war and in bringing peace to all the world. The World War II bastion that had been the handiwork of St. Benedict had originally been erected as a tribute to the Messiah as well as a haven for those who chose to give their lives over to God. Benedict himself could not have foreseen what lay in store for his stout cloister in a great war but its very durability is conclusive evidence that "except the Lord build the house, they labor in vain that build it." The unseen hand that went into making a holy place in the interest of liberty in the twentieth century gave it the added strength to withstand the assault against the hardy Christians who defended Christianity and oppression in a manner beyond Benedict's concept of man in God's image. But the principles for which he stood were gallantly upheld by young men not in monk's garb but in uniforms of a Christian country for which many gave their lives.

The monastery of Cassino was founded by St. Benedict and stood for centuries as one of the monuments to his Christian piety and dedication. That it was to be a battleground fifteen centuries later could not have been anticipated, but perhaps Benedict himself would have willed that the walls crumble under bombs so that peace might be restored. At any rate, the monastery has since been rebuilt and is as sacred now as it was before its demolition.

St. Benedict was born in the city of Nursia (Umbria) in A.D. 480 of the noble family known as Aniccii—a great family that was to Nursia what the Medici were to be in Florence. The influence of affluent merchants, who were very cultured, brought to young Benedict every known advantage, including an education in Rome. However, the decadence of Rome and its society disenchanted Benedict. For this reason he turned his back on all that his family stood for and took to the hills in search of a meaningful life.

Abiding in caves and grottoes, Benedict allowed himself the luxury of one friend, upon whom he depended for his sustenance. Otherwise he chose to seek the real truth, beauty, and closeness to God in the complete seclusion which allowed concentration without distraction. Over a span of three years as an eremite, Benedict discovered an approach to the service of God by isolation of not one, but groups of men. From this concept grew the monasteries that evolved into the order bearing his name.

Here was no martyr, no heroic gesture, no romantic journeying to foreign lands to propagate the faith. The quiet, humble ways of the monks of Benedict did God's work in obscurity, often with little recognition of their efforts toward peace on earth. It is said that they also serve who only stand and wait, but Benedict and his monks did more than stand and wait.

Young people from all walks of life were entrusted to the care of the monks, who saw to their spiritual needs together with their education. The ranks of the monks were swollen by those who had come to learn and had chosen to stay.

St. Benedict developed the rules of Western monasticism with such administrative and procedural perception that to this day there has been little or no change in the daily application of his concepts. With his two closest disciples, Maura and Placid, St. Benedict founded a monastery that became renown and was named after him, the Monastery of St. Benedict on Mount Cassino. This institution worked with the Church to the glory of God. His mission fulfilled, St. Benedict's life came to a peaceful end on 14 March 547.

March 15

Saint Aristobulos

The outermost region of the world at the time of Jesus was the British Isles; they were as remote to the early Christians of the eastern Mediterranean as the reaches of outer space are to us today. The moat of the English Channel kept many travelers, friends and foes alike, from setting foot on this isle, but it was no barrier to the apostle who dared to go that far from the land of the Savior.

After the crucifixion and resurrection of Jesus, a group of seventy men banded together who pledged to carry the message of salvation throughout the world. They were called the "Ebdomekonta," from the Greek word meaning seventy. The man who undertook the trek to the western edge of the then-known world was Aristobulos, as hardy and dedicated a Christian as ever took up the cause of Christ. But in retrospect the likelihood of a virtual non-entity becoming a saint in the first century to take his place in a select company numbering thousands all the way back to the time of Christ, was highly improbable. Nevertheless St. Aristobulos can number himself among men whose memories we hold most sacred, only a few of whom were of humble station and most of whom comprise some of the finest minds in all history, lay or ecclesiastical.

The reference made by St. Paul in no way diminished his prospects for sainthood but that was far from his goal when he ventured forth, all but lost in the host of missionaries with whom he shared a rare courage and a devout faith in perilous times. It is not unlikely that the original seventy, in whose ranks he was virtually obscured, swelled in numbers as converts joined this army of Christ in ever increasing numbers. The remarkable group that formed to leave not only the Holy Land but the continental limits of Europe as well, were introducing the New Faith to new frontiers, making them pioneers as well as missionaries.

When viewed in this light, St. Aristobulos deserves the highest regard for being foremost among men who were a breed apart in a joint effort which lesser men would have avoided irrespective of the depth of their faith. Today the name Aristobulos, for the most part, is a name on a church calendar, but in his day he was the symbol of the utmost in devotion to Jesus Christ.

Aristobulos was a favorite of St. Paul. What pleased St. Paul most was his tremendous missionary spirit and his willingness to journey to any area, friendly or hostile, just as long as he could take with him the word of God and the message of the Messiah. His unbridled enthusiasm made him the most likely candidate for the very difficult trek to the islands. In Romans 16.10, St. Paul's considerable respect for his friend is evidenced as he says: "Salute them which are of Aristobulos' household."

Wherever Aristobulos went in that uncharted land his encounters would have made lesser men retreat to more hospitable atmospheres. Nevertheless, with infinite patience and inspired persuasion his movement drew support.

With boundless energy and a cool detachment and disregard for adversity, Aristobulos' labors bore fruit; the Christian Church in this forsaken land became a reality. His mission, which many viewed as the least likely to succeed, was fulfilled beyond expectation with the steady growth of Christianity and the establishment of churches.

The British Isles became an integral part of the Christian world. The light of salvation glowed through the forest of the land that was to become a mighty empire, with no little thanks to its Christian character.

Aristobulos seems to have been spared persecution principally because the scattered array of opponents to his holy mission were put to rout by his oratory. Surviving many crises and dangers, he preached for many years until his voice was stilled by death on March 15.

St. Aristobulos' feast day is also observed together with the other members of the "Seventy" on October 31.

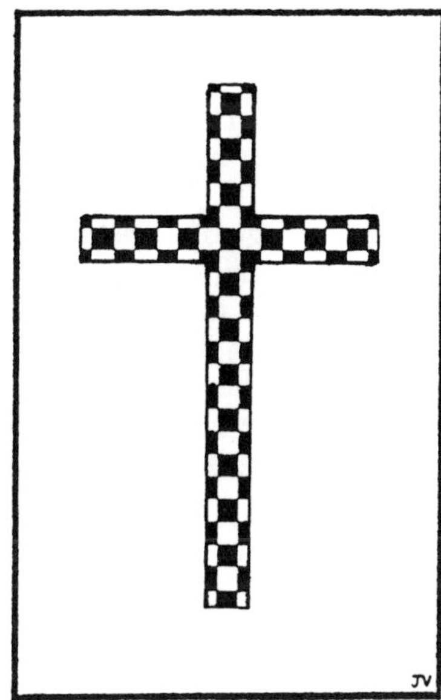

Saint Nikandros of Egypt

As if the bloodletting of persecuted Christians in the late third and early fourth century were not enough, the pagan officials carried their vengeful cruelty to the extreme by disallowing bodies to be removed for proper burial. Unnamed and unnumbered martyrs would have lain in the streets where they fell to become carrion by law had it not been for St. Nikandros of Egypt whose defiance of Roman law, with regard to the removal of fallen comrades in Christ, was to eventuate his own martyrdom.

In a holocaust of the third century, the blood of countless Christians was shed for Jesus Christ in a program inconceivable to the modern mind. The scenario for the heroics of St. Nikandros was set by the administrative policy of the Emperor Diocletian who ascended the throne of the Roman Empire in 293. Prior to his reign, the Christian Church had for years been allowed to carry out its own function. So long as a Christian did not interfere with the civilian masters of the empire they were countenanced, but Diocletian apparently saw the New Faith as a menace, and issued a decree whose aim was the total elimination of the Christian Church.

Nikandros and his fellow Christians were helpless to stem the tide of which was an unprecedented scale. Although Nikandros himself was to die before the full fury of the persecution had been spent, he was to take counter action in his own limited way to slow the brutal process down.

Diocletian's persecution was organized with military precision, unlike the sporadic assault on Christians by unruly pagan mobs whose bloody campaigns were guided only by a seething hatred and had no far-reaching effects. Nikandros and his friends therefore, were faced by trained soldiers for whom they were no match, and from whom they had to flee as their churches were destroyed. The fearless clergy who stood in the way to protect their houses of worship were dragged off, at first to be intimidated into recognizing paganism, and then being put to the sword for refusing. This led to the wholesale slaughter of not only priests but to any Christian, peasant, or aristocrat.

With carte blanche to wipe out every vestige of Christianity, the military needed no court orders to raze the churches of Christ, and abandoned the judicial process altogether in the execution of innocents without benefit of trial; there were no concentration camps to which prisoners were forced to march whether sick or healthy, old or young; there was only a confrontation, a denunciation and the sword in most cases, and whenever it suited the captors, there was the sport of the torture of the defenseless.

Agonized Christians who managed to escape the persecution remained in hiding, not daring to expose themselves, but under the cover of darkness Nikandros would dart to wherever a body lay and then snatch it up and make off with it. There was no body count, but it can be assumed that hundreds were recovered under the very noses of witless sentinels. It was not uncommon for Nikandros to recover, in the course of one night, not one but several Christian martyrs, each of whom had a Christian burial. Although there were mass murders, there were no mass burials. The very least that could be done for each fallen martyr was to give him his own private funeral service before being committed to the Lord and placed in an honored grave.

At one point, Nikandros had boldly recovered so many Christian bodies that there remained little time for individual services and interment. A proposal was made to depart from church requirement that the body be returned to earth intact and as a matter of urgency and expediency to cremate the bodies. Nikandros staunchly opposed this since the Church had forbidden cremation in accordance with St. Paul's admonition that the "body is the temple of the Lord." To burn that which housed the soul was the equivalent to burning churches, which was precisely what the pagan state was doing. In spite of the increasing risk of being caught in the act, the Christian burials continued. It was inevitable that Nikandros would take one risk too many. He was captured, tortured, and in a final act of infamy, beheaded. He gave his life for Christ on 15 March 284.

Saint Christodulos of Patmos

The city of Nicaea was not only the site of the First Ecumenical Synod, convened at the order of Constantine the Great, it was also the birthplace of St. Christodulos, one of the most energetic figures in Orthodoxy, whose unceasing efforts in many areas are a marvel of human endeavor. His peripatetic undertakings were monumental feats of holy action which spanned time and space at a pace that shortened both, so that he crowded into his lifetime the accomplishments of a dozen ordinary men. His energies were prodigious, as were his talents, all of which he applied seemingly without respite.

Christodulos was born to Theodore and Anna, a Nicene couple who baptized him John and held out a hope that their son would be anything but a monk. Like so many other parents, they considered becoming a monk to be like dropping out of society, but their son John was to prove to them that quite the opposite can happen. Proded by a deep devotion to Jesus Christ, he left his disapproving parents to go to Mt. Olympos in Prusa, there to remain for several years in the conventional manner of the ascetic, assuming the name of Christodulos after being tonsured a monk. He grew restive in this passive approach to the service of Jesus Christ and after the death of the abbot, he struck out for Rome, after having had a vision in which he saw the Apostles who had suffered martyrdom in the Eternal City.

Having paid his respects in Rome, he departed for Jerusalem where he became active in the monastery there, until he was forced to take to the hills by invading barbarians. He settled in the eastern province of Palatia, near the mountain of Latros, where he resumed his activities at an accelerated pace. His parents finally got in touch with him and wrote an appealing letter for him to return home, and his classic reply convinced them he had, indeed, found his place in the world. He remained in this region long enough to become convinced that certain heresies were eroding the moral fiber of monasticism, and, refusing an offer to become abbot of one of the larger monasteries, he again pulled up stakes and this time headed for the Byzantine capital city of Constantinople.

Once in Constantinople, Christodulos lost no time in going directly to Patriarch Nicholas II to warn him of the heresies that were going unnoticed, particularly in the remote areas of the empire, and the patriarch was impressed by his earnestness and interest that he made him an archimandrite of the church and put him in charge of all the monasteries in the area of Latmos Caria. In this capacity, he rooted out the small evils that were detrimental to spiritual advancement and was so intent in his helpfulness that he took no heed that some of his great work was being called miraculous. He acquired renown as a man of peace and a man who was in constant touch with the Holy Spirit. Not content to rest on his laurels in Latmos, he again sought to relocate and received permission to traverse the Greek Islands.

The first stop on the ambitious itinerary of Christodulos was the island of Patmos, where St. John the Divine had written the Book of Revelation, the last of the New Testament, which deals with things to come. The sorry condition of this sacred spot appalled this ebullient holy man and he wrote a stirring appeal to the Byzantine Emperor Alexios Komnenos at Constantinople for funds with which to restore the ruins to their original beauty. The money was not long in coming, for such was the convincing earnestness of this hard-working monk, and there was erected on the island the Monastery of St. John, a cloister whose breathtaking beauty is without equal anywhere in the world. With Christodulos in charge, this magnificent cloister beckoned Christians from all parts of the globe in such numbers that the emperor issued a citation of commendation to Christodulos and then provided a permanent fund for the perpetuation of the monastery.

This seems to have at long last satisfied Christodulos that he need look for no more fences to mend and he decided to remain on the island of Patmos for the rest of his days. Because of the emperor's decree, as well as for the sake of Christodulos, the island of Patmos to this day remains under the spiritual jurisdiction of the Church of Constantinople. The holy remains of Christodulos are enshrined on the island of Patmos.

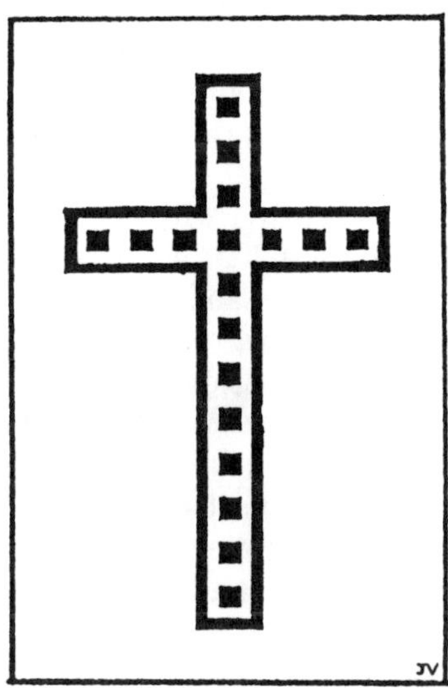

March 16

Saint Julian of Cicilia

The more widely known name of the Emperor Julian the Apostate lives in infamy, but the lesser known name of St. Julian of Cicilia lives in honored glory, a gallant martyr for Jesus Christ who might have gone unrecognized had it not been for St. John Chrysostom. The blood of the martyrs of the early centuries of Christianity nurtured the Church but too many of those who shed their blood for Christ are unknown to us, despite the fact that there appears to be an abundance of saints, especially in the formative years of the Church. Just as there can be no excess in charity, there can be no excess in the number of saints venerated by people of the Greek Orthodox faith. The veneration of little known saints extends beyond them to those who are, like the unknown soldier, known to God.

Julian was born in the province of Abazarbos, Cicilia in Asia Minor, the son of a pagan Greek and Christian mother. His father was a member of the senate, and therefore, a man of prominence who countenanced his wife's Christian belief and had no objection to his son being raised as a Christian. The father died when Julian was a child and the responsibility for his upbringing rested solely with his mother, who passed on to her son the strong faith in Christ that was to sustain him in his hours of ordeal. A gifted scholar, he was noted for his photographic memory which enabled him to commit to memory an entire page with scarcely more than a single reading. He applied this incredible talent to the Scriptures, to the classics, and to all forms of learning so that by the time he was eighteen he was an acknowledged authority on just about any topic.

Since the art of conversation, in the absence of technological distractions, was one in which the more enlightened took delight, Julian was a welcomed guest at any gathering. In these informal sessions he attained a prominence which by word of mouth carried to the public forums where the great debates between intellectuals provided the best entertainment to be found. These open forums also substituted for the classroom because they not only enlightened, but were open for question from the listeners who thus acquired learning. Radicals were greeted with scorn and heckling, but the words of men such as Julian were warmly received and he found himself in popular demand.

Where abstract philosophy was for the few, religion was for the many, and therefore, the subject of discussion most sought after was religion, a topic that summoned forth the greatest debates to be heard. Such was the caliber of Julian's oratory that he came to be recognized as Christianity's most powerful protagonist. With a mental alertness that dumbfounded his opposition, he was constantly emerging as winner in a battle of wits, so much so that challengers began to dwindle in number, leaving him oftentimes to occupy center stage alone.

The city magistrate, an overbearing man named Marcian, was the supreme authority whose word was law and who accordingly looked down at debaters, but when he heard of the eloquence of Julian, he decided to take him on with his own brand of pagan eloquence and humble the Christian upstart. So he issued a challenge for the two to meet in public debate on the subject of religion. What he did not know was that the power of the Lord was behind Julian, rendering his own power useless.

At the appointed hour, the two met and in very short order Julian had scrambled the wits of Marcian with the power and beauty of his Christian eloquence. The pagan's confidence gave way to frustration, which in turn developed into a seething rage. His screaming was in stark contrast to the calm composure of his Christian adversary. No longer able to cope with the scriptural truth being hurled at him, Marcian called for the arrest of Julian on charges of treason and stalked off in full retreat, all the while thinking how badly his prisoner could be mistreated.

Julian was then brutally tortured and then led out to be shown to the public as an example of what happens to those who speak treason against the pagan gods. Even Julian's mother had to witness the brutality inflicted upon her son, who was led through the streets time and again after torture enough to kill an ordinary human. He was then trussed up in a sack containing snakes and cast into the sea. His body was recovered and sent to Antioch for burial on 16 March 299.

March 17

Alexios, Man of God

The rare title, "Man of God," was bestowed on St. Alexios for the manner in which he gave himself over to Jesus Christ, forsaking a bride even at the altar in order to fulfill to the letter the admonition read to him while he was contemplating enlistment in the service of the Lord. He kept his true identity a secret for an entire lifetime rather than run the risk of betraying the Master through his own emotions and there is no telling how much mental anguish he suffered in silence for the sake of his commitment. When he felt the call he answered with a hesitation for which he judged himself too harshly and which he bore in mute secrecy.

Alexios was born in 380 in the eternal city of Rome during the reign of Theodosios the Great and was raised in a royal household by his parents, Ephemios and Aglaia, who discerned a predilection for the Church in their son, a religious fervor they could not share and which they sought to discourage for fear they would lose him. They lost no time in arranging for his marriage and in impressing upon him the debt he owed to his parents, for which he should respect their wishes in all things. He had reluctantly suppressed the call he felt to the Lord's service and had agreed to the marriage when he had a vision one day of St. Paul, who said he should answer the call to God at all costs, reading to him the passage in Matthew which says: "He that loveth father or mother more than me is not worthy of me."

The bewildered Alexios was torn between his sense of duty to his parents and that urging to serve the Lord, and swayed between both, at long last deciding to go through with what he had promised his family. The feeling that he should go the other way gnawed at him even as he stood at the altar, and when the ceremony had been completed he looked upon the Cross of Jesus and without a word walked away from bride, family and friends to do what he had to do.

He stepped into the anonymity of a Syrian monastery where for the next eighteen years he assumed another identity, and never looked back at Rome. Having made a choice they had opposed, he suspected his parents had disinherited him and that his bride had had the marriage annulled, but this was not the case. As a matter of fact, the bride had gone to live with his parents in the fond hope that Alexios would someday return, and the parents spared no expense in trying to locate their son, but after eighteen years with no word from him they presumed him to be dead.

In his eighteen years in the monastery, Alexios was transformed into a respected holy man whose solemn dedication to Jesus was the subject of many discussions among not only the monks but the community which he served. Unlike other monks, he was a man of few words and left the preaching and sermonizing to other brother monks while he concentrated on writing on many issues concerning the faith. The vision that he had had many years before of St. Paul still haunted him and he had a burning desire to go to Tarsus, Paul's birthplace.

He boarded a boat bound for the short trip up the coast, but while at sea a violent storm arose and blew the vessel miles off course also leaving her a derelict at the mercy of the wind and tides. They were finally picked up by a ship bound for Rome and Alexios found himself back in the city of his birth. Nostalgia seized him and he went to the family estate, primarily to get a glimpse of his folks, but when they failed to recognize him he felt compelled to remain and was given the task of spiritual counselor, not only to the estate, but to the neighboring families as well.

The abandoned bride was still living with the parents and she also failed to recognize him, for which he was grateful, for he found contentment in being able to serve the Lord while not revealing his true identity, which he considered would be a disservice to the Savior after all the years of anonymity. He went about his duties with grace acquired and enjoyed the respect of families for miles around.

When he felt death drawing near, Alexios wrote a letter to his family in which he expressed his love for them, which he could not do in life. The letter was read posthumously not only by his family but by the bishop of Rome, who had him interred in the chapel of St. Peter's. He died for Christ on 17 March 440, after thirty-four years of celibacy and anonymity.

March 18

Cyril of Jerusalem

The checkered career of Patriarch Cyril of Jerusalem in the fourth century is an involved and complex study of a man of God caught in a web of intrigue of great magnitude. In fact, he is to be admired if only for managing to keep his balance on the tightrope he was forced to walk in the whirlwinds of controversy that would have toppled a lesser man. It is to his everlasting credit that, in spite of falling in and out of favor in the political and religious ambivalence that prevailed during his tenure, he was able to inspire and administrate with an authority that never lessened, even when assailed from within the ranks of his own Christian faith.

Born in Jerusalem in 315, Cyril rose through the ranks to become patriarch in his native city. He succeeded Patriarch Maximos after firmly establishing himself as an illustrious theologian capable of assuming the spiritual leadership of any region of the civilized world, but particularly qualified to lead in the Holy City. He earned this honor through association with a society into which he was born and by dint of a thorough knowledge of church and state matters. The respect he won over the years came to be the envy of certain religious figures, particularly Metropolitan Akakios of Caesaria, who considered himself to be equal, if not superior, in his see to that of Cyril.

Using the artifice and guile usually attached to political, ambitious men, the wily Akakios (a close friend and confidant of Emperor Constantios, son of Constantine the Great) set in motion a program calculated to discredit the patriarch. Using the controversial Arianism as a weapon, he convinced the witless monarch that Cyril was a menace to stability in the Church, and thus brought about the exile of the patriarch who never gave ground in his stand against Arianism. Cyril spent the next several years in banishment, but not disgrace, in Tarsus (the city which had given to Christianity the mighty St. Paul). He put his time to good use writing on theological subjects, thanks largely to the hospitality of the local Bishop Silvanus who saw to the needs of the patriarch made pariah.

In a gesture never quite understood, the successor to Constantios, the infamous Julian the Apostate, restored Cyril to his patriarchal throne in a sweeping edict that reversed the Arian direction of his predecessor. It was probably a matter of expediency, because Julian acquired the name of "Apostate" by reverting to paganism; he even went so far as to order the conversion of the Temple of Jerusalem back to the practice of idolatry. The conversion never came about because an earthquake severely damaged the structure, and an even more disastrous fire reduced it to rubble. But the indestructible Cyril managed to survive the wave of persecution set in motion by Julian.

It was presumed that with the death of Julian, the new emperor Valens would secure the Patriarchate; but the royal whim dictated otherwise, and Cyril was again victimized and sent into exile. He returned, with the succession of Emperor Theodosios, to resume his tenure as patriarch which was highlighted by the miraculous appearance of the Cross of Jesus emblazoned against the sky. This occurrence is marked by a feast day on May 7, the first of which was proclaimed by Cyril who recorded the event as follows:

"On the nones of May, about the third hour, a great luminous cross appeared in the heavens just over Golgotha, reaching as far as the holy Mount of Olives and was seen not by one or two persons, but clearly and evidently by the whole city. This was not, as might be thought, a fancy-bred and transient appearance; it continued for several hours together, visible to our eyes and brighter than the sun. The whole city, penetrated alike with awe and with joy at the portent, ran immediately to the church, all with one voice giving praise to our Lord Jesus Christ, the only Son of God."

What ensued was anticlimactic, but in the course of his tenure there were other momentous occasions for Cyril. One was the great Second Ecumenical Synod of 381 where he sat in council with men such as St. Gregory to form the Nicene Creed and set forth other guidelines for Christian worship. His illustrious service ended with his death at the age of seventy in the year 386.

March 18

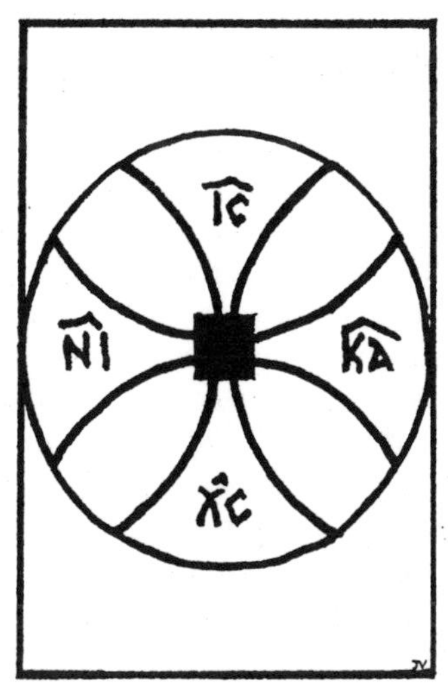

Saints Trophimos and Eukarpion

There are many saints whose lives parallel those of Sts. Trophimos and Eukarpion, but few are as theirs. A great number of saints, drawn from the military ranks in the service of an emperor, did an about face to serve the King of Kings, but the story of how the transformation came about with this duo is both fascinating and glorious, adding a brilliant chapter to Christian ecclesiastical history.

Officers of field rank in the army of the Roman Empire, Trophimos and Eukarpion were in command of troop detachments whose specialty was the ferreting out of Christians under orders from Emperor Maximian who, in A.D. 298, instituted a wave of persecution whose aim was to obliterate the Christian religion. These two officers, who were pagans as well as disciplined soldiers, scoured the countryside in search of Christians. While other search parties were being frustrated, time and again in their efforts to track down the elusive Christians, the wily twosome directed their search with cruel cunning, acquiring a reputation as masters of the hunt for their innocent prey.

The mere mention of the names of Trophimos and Eukarpion drove fear into the hearts of Christians, all of whom considered them the worst enemies of Christ. Concentrating their efforts in the area of Nikomedia, Asia Minor, the two officers snatched men, women, and children and hustled them off callously to suffer the fate of persecuted martyrs. Feared by those they hunted, they were rewarded with bonuses by the Roman general staff who looked upon them as heroes deserving of medals for their vile achievements.

Acting on information given them, Trophimos and Eukarpion were making their way to a suspected Christian hideout when they were suddenly halted in their tracks and brought to their knees by a clap of thunder and a flash of lightning. As the skies darkened behind the cloud that hovered over them, they heard a booming voice between the flashes of thunderbolts asking why they were persecuting Christians. The voice advised them to abandon their evil ways before it was too late and become servants of the Lord. This awesome experience transfixed the army officers who rose from their knees, bathed in the spirit and reversed the course of their lives.

In a manner akin to that of St. Paul, who embraced the Christ he had set out to discredit, Trophimos and Eukarpion embraced the Christianity that they were bent on destroying. The Christian camp, at first fearful of some diabolical plot by the mere presence of this fearsome tandem, accepted them with warmth and delight after hearing the story of the awesome display of the power of God. Before they were to doff their uniforms for simple Christian garments, they went about the arena, ordering the release of those whom they had only recently captured. They continued to act in this manner, emptying the jails with reckless abandon until a superior officer discovered their activity, at which time they took to their heels and settled among the Christians.

Now feeling a euphoria in serving Jesus Christ which they had not known in serving a Roman emperor, Trophimos and Eukarpion revealed the methods used, as well as the habits followed by the military in pursuit of Christians. This knowledge served them in good stead and the news of the elusiveness of the Christians, thanks to the converted officers well trained in military tactics, annoyed the high command in Rome.

Trophimos and Eukarpion were not in the least deterred in their efforts when it became known to them that they were the sought after by the Roman military. Anticipating every move of the soldiers eager to seize them, the two officers were always a step ahead of their pursuers. Combining the stealth with which the Christians had learned to move with the knowledge of the tactics of the Roman army, the Christians appeared to have vanished from the earth.

It was inevitable that treachery was the only answer to the problem of snaring Trophimos and Eukarpion. A Roman spy, posing as a convert, won the confidence of the Christians with patience and feigned piety. One night he slipped and brought back with him troops of the army who seized several Christians, the first of which were the two most sought. Special tortures awaited Trophimos and Eukarpion who suffered greatly before dying for Christ on 18 March 299.

Saint Pancharios

The joint reign of Diocletian and Maximian as co-rulers of the Roman Empire from A.D. 284 to 305 mark a twenty year period in history which for political intrigue remains unequalled in cunning and for the cruel persecution of Christians remains unparalleled in horror. The very name Diocletian struck terror into the hearts of even those pagans loyal to him because of the assassinations which were committed on mere suspicion as part of the routine power play of the day. To be a Christian in this period was to live in constant dread and to remain one was equivalent to being put to the test every moment with death as imminent as the sword of Damokles.

It is little wonder that the unrelenting persecution of Christians produced so many saints in this span of two decades, but greater wonder still that one of these saints should come from the inner circle of friends of the heartless Diocletian. This intimate companion destined for sainthood was a man named Pancharios, a complex person whose Christian beginnings had given way to a misdirected loyalty only to rise again in a declaration for Jesus Christ.

Pancharios was born in what is now Germany of extremely devout Christian parents whose love and devotion to their son was not enough to direct his restless spirit which was forever thrusting him toward the glory of Rome. While a mere youth, he obeyed the impulse to leave the land of his birth and made his way to Rome where he enlisted in the army. Able and intelligent, his rise through the ranks was meteoric, and only a few years after leaving his home, he found himself appointed captain of the Royal Guard. He soon found favor with the emperor Diocletian himself who looked kindly on members of the military because he had been an army commander prior to succeeding the murdered Numerian and had risen from humble station like his trusted captain of the guard. Their mutual admiration ripened into a strong friendship and, like one who cannot see the forest for the trees, Pancharios could not see the merciless persecution of Christians for his attachment to Diocletian, the emperor to whom he was loyal and who could do no wrong.

The true loyalty to Jesus Christ lay dormant in the heart of Pancharios until he received a letter from his sister in which he was admonished for clinging to a murderer who was annihilating Christians with a cruel vengeance. The sister quoted two passages from the Bible which read, "To what profit a man if he gain the whole world and lose his own soul" (Mark 8.36), and the quotation from Matthew 10.33 which reads, "Whosoever shall deny me before men, him will I also deny before my Father which is in heaven."

Pancharios read the letter of his sister, especially the passages from the Bible, over and over again until at last in full realization of his transgression, he wept in contrition and his lament was cried out aloud as he begged for the Lord's forgiveness. Other members of the guard looked on in disbelief and reported what they had heard to the emperor. Diocletian could scarcely believe what he heard and asked that Pancharios be brought to him at once. The emperor reminded Pancharios that he was one of his few trusted friends and asked him to deny Christ and reassert his loyalty to the emperor. When Pancharios adamantly refused to deny Christ, reminding one and all he had been born a Christian and was now willing to die one, the emperor even in his cruel heart could not condemn his captain and directed him to another tribunal for sentencing.

Pancharios was taken to Nikomedia to be tried before a prefect who was unaccustomed to seeing a military man of high rank accused of being a Christian but who, nevertheless, ordered the customary punishment for the offender. Pancharios, the man who had rubbed elbows with the mighty, now found himself in prison where he was tortured unmercifully and at last, with the name of the Lord on his lips, was put to death on 19 March 303.

March 19

Saints Chrysanthos and Daria

The term "marriage made in Heaven," could be applied to a third century couple whose marriage could be said to have been made "for heaven" because of a rare singular purpose, i.e., to serve Jesus Christ. Sts. Chrysanthos and Daria are among the lesser known martyrs of the early Christian Church, They joined the early martyrs in shedding their blood for Christ as he did for all of mankind.

Chrysanthos was born to a patrician named Polemios whose political stature in Alexandria was on a level of government lofty enough to require his presence in the imperial court of Numerian in Rome. It was in these two cities of the Roman empire that Chrysanthos was educated, mingling with aristocrats and nobility, the majority of whom were far removed from the new faith in Jesus Christ.

With education completed, Chrysanthos gave his full attention to the Savior, aided in his quest for spiritual attainment by a bishop by the name of Karpophoros who had taken refuge in a cave to avoid persecution. Remaining with the bishop for complete catechism, he was baptized, thereafter to go on to the glory of sainthood. His absence from pagan rites did not go unnoticed by his father who feared for his son's life, considering the dangers besetting Christianity at that time. Polemios could but admire his son's courageous choice, but nevertheless, thought it more prudent if he could be brought back to the safety of paganism.

As was the custom of the day, marriages were arranged by parents, and sons and daughters were bound by tradition to accept parental matchmaking. Polemios had a friend in Athens whose daughter was not only eligible but an attractive and intelligent girl as well, who went by the name of Daria. She also happened to be a priestess of Minerva, which Polemios anticipated would prove to convince his son the error of having strayed from the pagan fold. Unfortunately for Polemios, and happily for Christianity, it went the other way. Observing the usual procedure, there was a period of courtship, during which time Chrysanthos converted his bride-to-be to Christianity with such success that both gave themselves totally to Christ. By mutual agreement, the couple entered into a marriage that was never consummated, pledging their lives to the Savior in a celibacy expected only of monks. It was an arrangement known but to God, and only declared as they were about to die for Christ.

Realizing that their efforts should be aimed at those of higher station, Chrysanthos and Daria began by entertaining friends who soon found themselves accepting Jesus. With no formal theological training the couple attracted converts to secluded places of worship. It was no easy task to lure pagans to the faith of Jesus Christ.

It was inevitable that word of the Christian movement would spread and that its two luminaries would be found out. A somewhat incredulous Roman tribune named Claudius decided to look into the matter personally since the suspected Chrysanthos and Daria were of high station. The couple was confronted by Claudius in the privacy of their home but before the evening was out, Claudius himself was won over to Christianity. To assure the salvation of his family, Claudius brought his wife Hilaris and their sons into the Christian midst and they were converted as well.

Christianity had gone on unnoticed, by many, some of whom saw no harm in the new religion so long as it did not violate Roman law or preach treason. But when the activity of Claudius and his friends grew, suspicious Romans were stirred into action. In due course, the Christians were found out and Claudius, together with Chrysanthos and Daria, were brought to trial before the Emperor Numerian himself. Claudius was consigned to military justice to suffer an unknown fate. The couple remained to be questioned at length but their staunch defense of Christianity, construed as an affront to the pagan gods, brought them the sentence of death. It was decided that Chrysanthos and Daria be buried alive in a sandpit just outside of the city on March 294. Later a chapel, which no longer stands, was erected on the site and was the scene for centuries of miraculous occurrences.

March 20

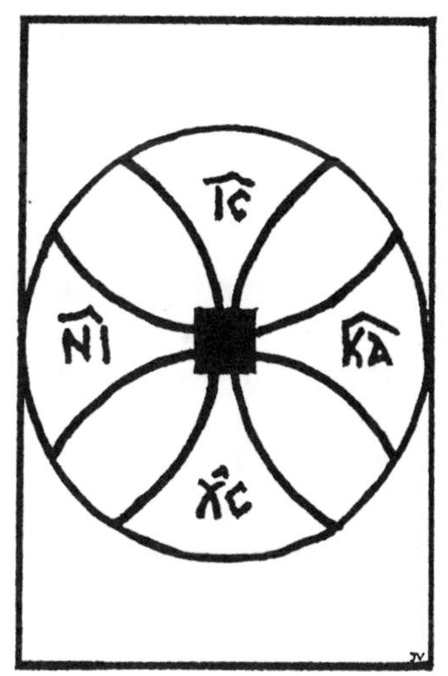

Myron of Crete

In the fateful year of 1775, when America was about to assume an identity of its own, the ancient land of Greece was several years away from its return to normalcy after more than three centuries of Turkish tyranny had failed to separate Greece from an identity with its ancient glory and its hallowed Greek Orthodox faith in Jesus Christ. Events leading to revolution are marked by the deaths of men who were complete patriots, but because of the religious overtones in the Greek cause men died not only for country but for Jesus Christ, as a result of which out of the many patriots have come saints of the Church.

It was in the year 1775 that the Neomartyr Myron was born in Crete and shared the misery of the rest of the islanders under the brutal conquest of the Turks, who seemed to have a special contempt for those living off the mainland. The remoteness of the island attracted the worst of the enemies of Christianity and democracy, bringing much more cruelty and religious persecution than could be found in the major cities under the best of a bad lot. Crete over the centuries had witnessed fleets of various countries spilling conquerors on its shores, but as inured as they were to hardships, the islanders felt the Turkish infestation more keenly than most realize.

Myron was born into a family who bore up under the oppression with no detectable loss of their Christian spirit and managed to compromise their political differences with the Turks without sacrificing one bit of their religion. Myron's family was an extremely devout group to begin with and their misfortune served only to rally them closer to Jesus Christ and to one another. Myron himself was an exceptionally devout Christian whose fervor stemmed from genuine love for his church and for Jesus Christ.

He served as cantor in his church and assisted the priest in this harrassed village, giving his free time willingly to relieve suffering.

Myron applied his trade meanwhile as a tailor, operating a small shop in the business district where he was constantly under the watchful eyes of the Turks, who detested his good looks and his very obvious Christian faith. A man of peace who posed no threat to the authorities, he was nevertheless, singled out by the vengeful Turks as a target for their special brand of harrassment by which they sought to demonstrate the power of Islam over Christianity not with reason but with the only weapon afforded them—brute force, coupled with guile.

Myron found himself being systematically heckled, badgered, and abused with insults, aimed at arousing his temper to the point of striking back, but he maintained his outward calm, mindful of the consequences if he did otherwise. When their taunts had failed to bring a response, the Turks then produced a twelve-year-old Turkish boy whom they bribed to accuse the peaceful tailor of having made improper advances. Formally charged with depravity, the innocent Christian was jailed to await trial.

In what passed for a trial, Myron protested his guilt to no avail, but in a gesture of what laughingly was called good will, the court offered to forgive him his lecherous behavior to come over to the side of Muslim decency. There was no mercy offered in the alternative, a prospect which might have weakened a lesser Christian than Myron who vigorously defended his faith in Jesus Christ for whom he was willing to die.

The court found him guilty, as expected, but unexpectedly sentenced him to be hanged the following day, rather than subject him to torture before finally executing him. The reasoning was that the sight of a limp body at the end of a rope in the town square would be enough to frighten the Christians into a more compliant frame of mind. On the day after the trial, Myron was led to the square and after refusing a last chance to recant was hanged. The remorseful twelve-year-old who had falsely condemned him came forward to admit his treachery but not until it was too late.

Myron was only twenty years old when he gave his life for the Savior but a manifestation that he was in God's favor brought him instant recognition after death. Hundreds stood in awe as they witnessed a ray of light descend from the sky onto the inert form of Myron, who was made a saint only a few months after he died.

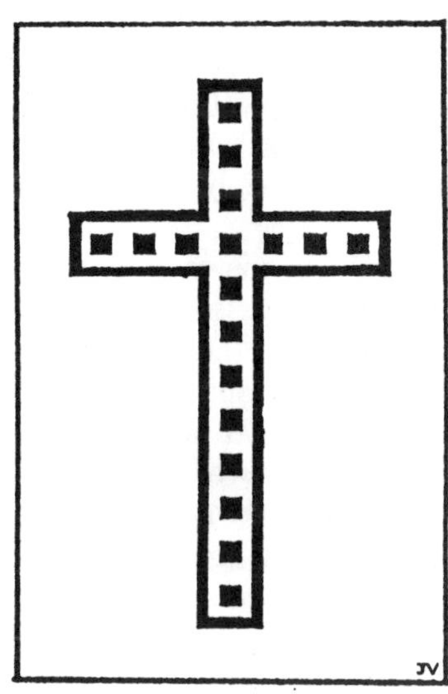

March 21

Iakovos (James), Monk and Confessor

There is no telling how many deserving Christians who took a stand against the iconoclastic movement lie buried in anonymity like unknown soldiers—known only to God. Fortunately, the ninth century ascetic known to us as Iakovos, monk and confessor, is more than an unidentified religious figure. Scraps of information gleaned from correspondence between prelates shed some light on the courageous life of one Christendom's staunchest iconophiles.

From the correspondence of St. Theodore and other epistles, we can piece together the picture of a man whose total dedication to the Savior commenced when he was scarcely out of childhood. He was a self-motivated crusader who was well-equipped to make his presence felt wherever there was a just cause. The many achievements of Iakovos are subordinate to his masterful defense of the icons, where he displayed a fiery resolve which parried the thrusts of some of the most powerful figures, up to the emperor himself, who had taken it upon themselves to draw up a parallel between the icons and images. They distorted the very real reasons for the veneration, not worship, of men and women, but of the Savior without whom there might very well have been no church in which to worship.

Iakovos' beginnings appear to have been auspicious enough since he was accepted at the very prestigious Monastery of Studios where he was privileged to meet the noted St. Gregory who was to chronicle the details of Iakovos' life and help perpetuate his memory. Iakovos distinguished himself in a brilliant society devoted to the Savior, an accomplished group who won international renown known as the Studite, with the very capable St. Gregory in the forefront for the preservation of unity and harmony in the Church. These people, in the name of the Church, were forever combating dissidents who were, for the most part, malcontents who would seize any occasion to sow discord, the most serious of which was the proliferation of Iconoclasm. Causes came and went, but the iconoclasts hovered menacingly for altogether too many years.

Together with Theodore the Studite, who is commemorated on November 11, Iakovos presented the case for the icons wherever and whenever possible, venturing to the royal house in Constantinople but without success. The reasons were twofold: first, the iconoclasts had the ears of the royal household; and secondly, a change in the royal position would have been construed as weakness and vacillation. With this in mind Iakovos was all the more persistent, so much so that he was unceremoniously ushered from the premises and thereafter set upon by ruffians—who by command would assail anyone like a pack of dogs. His persistence was branded as insolence, for which he paid dearly with bruises and lumps; but he was undismayed and simply licked his wounds and started all over again.

St. Gregory looked upon Iakovos with an affection that led him to call his associate "his amiable brother," but warned against further provocation in the capital, suggesting that both retire to the monastery for a time in order to refresh themselves with rest and prayer in preparation for yet another campaign. After some discussion Gregory returned to the monastery, while Iakovos went on a tour of the churches to preach and to continue his denouncement of the iconoclasts.

Iakovos soon enough realized that the friendly faces he saw in church were not the challenge that would see the end of the iconoclasts. Thus he decided to take to the public forums with the optimistic hope of unifying his brethren under no banner, but the symbol of the Cross and, of course, in the presence of his precious icons.

At one of these gatherings, where he saw that he was winning misguided Christians to his side, he was dared to present himself to a group of iconoclasts who were at the moment holding a rally in a nearby arena. Iakovos strode into the arena without fear and with his customary optimism and confidence launched into an oration that spelled out the folly of their view. His words fell on deaf ears, and a group of rowdies beat him mercilessly. He died of his wounds on March 21.

Virillos of Catania

Privileged to have lived at a time when Christ walked the earth but never known to have seen him, Virillos was nevertheless afforded the next greater privilege of having set eyes on the great Apostle Peter and of having heard his sacred voice. To have seen and heard any of the apostles was tantamount to seeing and hearing the Savior himself, but having heard any of these great men and thereafter becoming a Christian did not make anyone a saint. Those who went beyond the call of their Christian duty were established as saints, among whom was the valiant Virillos, who was one of the few men of the early era of Christianity to have become a saint without having to become a martyr.

Virillos gave everything to the Savior except his life and remains obscured in the shadows of the giants with whom he was associated, chief among whom was a man called Peter who is universally known. It is probable that there are more churches named after the great St. Peter than there are Christians who know who Virillos was.

All that is known of this man of little fame is that Virillos was a face in the crowd who stood transfixed as Peter spoke in ancient Antioch. Consumed by the spirit of the Savior, he stepped forth to be embraced by Peter and to accompany him in his travels, all the while becoming a devout missionary himself whom Peter must have held in high esteem. When Peter had become bishop of Antioch, he appointed his friend Virillos bishop of Catania, Sicily. It was more an outpost than a post inasmuch as Cantania was teeming with pagans of long standing, as opposed to only recently converted Christians.

Virillos changed the course of the island, directing it to Christianity. In a whirlwind of missionary zeal he converted pagans in large numbers so that in a short span of years the Christians comprised the vast majority. Ironically, those clinging to myths and idolatry were Greeks whose spokesman and chief protagonist bore the honorable name of Pericles.

Only a few years older than the Messiah himself, Virillos was still being menaced and challenged by the intransigent pagan minority. They interrupted him as he spoke and made nuisances of themselves in general, heckling the respected bishop.

Bishop Virillos prayed for the spiritual strength with which to demonstrate the truth and power of the Lord, and it was not long in forthcoming. His opportunity came when a sneering papan dared him to transform a contaminated water fountain into one which would yield potable water. For years this wellspring yielded a rancid, bitter water which even animals avoided and which was not fit even for laundering purposes. It had been considered for generations as having a source so vile as to suggest it sprang from a demonic subsurface and was as polluted as that which settled in the bilge of a ship.

Bishop Virillos went to the side of this putrid well and with arms upraised, called upon the Lord to purify the water and its source so as to yield sweet drinking water. In an instant the darkened water became clear, sparkling with the freshness of a mountain stream. To prove this was no trick, he cupped his hands and drank from the well, inviting others, including the amazed pagans, to do the same. With the transformation of this once brackish water into clear sweetness beyond belief, there was witnessed a miracle of the Lord which even the most intransigent pagan could not deny.

If there were any pagans about after this, they were invisible and so long as he remained bishop, Virillos preached his sermons to nothing but Christians. Even the once defiant Pericles came forward to become a Christian, calling upon all his cohorts to accept Christ. Thereafter Pericles sought permission to go into the surrounding hills to carry word of the miracle to those who had not witnessed it. Many who had known of the contaminated well became Christians. It is estimated that the tenure of Bishop Virillos lasted for sixty glorious years. This bright and early chapter in ecclesiastical history was closed when Bishop Virillos died of natural causes on 21 March 98.

March 22

Saint Euthymios

The rugged mountains of central Greece, the Peloponnesos area, has produced illustrious sons who have added lustre to the history of Greece already crowded with heroic figures of both Church and nation. Distinguished in this great company was Eleutherios, born and baptized in the village of Demetsana in 1796. He later came to be known as Euthymios of Constantinople. The son of a business merchant with holdings in Moldavia, he was to settle in Constantinople, the city with which he was identified. In his brief life span of twenty years Euthymios was to plunge into the depths of degradation, then scale the heights of glory in and emotional kaleidoscope.

While still a young teenager, Eleutherios journeyed to Constantinople. Along the way he visited Mt. Athos. This stop-over was to influence him later, when he sorely needed a spiritual revival. Having been educated in the finest schools, he was captivated by the civic charm of the grand old capital, and was very much at home there until hostilities broke out between Russia and Turkey. He made his way to Bucharest where a friend at the French Embassy welcomed him. In a few short months his life was to change.

Eleutherios fell in with a group of young Turks under whose influence he replaced his spiritual inheritance with that of the sensual hedonism of tribal sheiks. Gradually he gave way to a life of debauchery, spending his time drinking, carousing and in general, wallowing in sins of the flesh. He finally reached the point where, in a drunken stupor, he disavowed Christ, and to the howling delight of his disreputable companions, embraced their Muslim faith.

Not long after this shoddy display, Eleutherios was consumed by the spectre of damnation. With absolute repentance he fell to his knees asking for the forgiveness of Christ. It was then that Mt. Athos came into his mind's eye, for as he wept in contrition, he remembered his short but sweet visit.

In the holy confines of Mt. Athos, the youthful Eleutherios was reborn. He sought God in prayerful meditation and asked forgiveness for his foolish departure from the path of righteousness. He spent several months at the Monastery of the Great Lavra in total dedication to the word of the Lord. A former patriarch of Constantinople, Gregory, who had chosen to spend his declining years at the monastery, greatly aided Eleutherios in his acceptance of the monastic life. At the Skete of St. Anne he was tonsured, being given the name of Euthymios.

He remained on the Holy Mountain long enough to become an instrument of God; many miracles were wrought by his hands. Euthymios felt compelled to return to Constantinople to support the besieged Christian faith. Once there, he was betrayed to the Turks and imprisoned for having mocked the Muslim faith in Bucharest and for his complete return to Christianity. But the requirements for sainthood had become so stringent over the centuries, decreasing with the passing years primarily because of the universality of the Christian faith, that by the time the nineteenth century arrived there was a very faint prospect of any saint arriving with it. The exception to this ever demanding rule had to be a man of rare exception, not necessarily distinction, and St. Euthymios was, as we have seen, just that exceptional man. He had risen above the human frailties that had nearly cost him his soul, but in his repentance, duplicated many times over by Christian brethren for transgression, he went that step beyond to earn the immortality that lies within the grasp of any true follower of Jesus Christ.

On 22 March 1814, at the age of twenty, this Christian stalwart was beheaded. A tiny chapel on Mt. Athos is dedicated to his memory and every year special liturgical services are chanted by his brother monks.

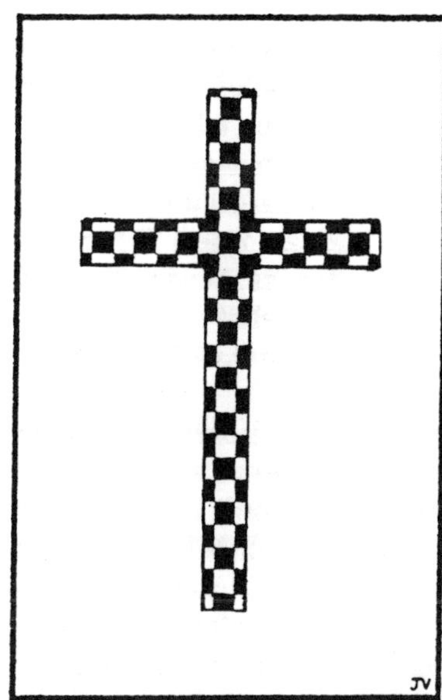

March 22

Saint Drosis

The early martyrs of Christendom were not suicidal fanatics but victims of outrageous persecution who had the Christian courage to face a relentless enemy which, after years of brutality, failed to stem the tide of the rising faith in Jesus Christ. One of the many first century martyrs was a girl named Drosis, whose life is all the more remarkable when it is considered that she saw the light of Jesus Christ through the miasma of paganism in spite of the fact that she was the daughter of Emperor Trajan.

Ranking with Nero in pagan savagery, Trajan was merciless in his unrelenting persecution of innocent Christians. In this hostile atmosphere it is a mystery of God that Drosis was able to capture the mood of the Christian message that was all about her in her father's regal quarters. She is all the more to be admired for accepting Christ with all her heart in spite of the hatred that pervaded the royal palace.

Drosis looked on with growing horror at the atrocities committed against Christian. Helpless to prevent the sickening tortures, she saw her chance to be of some help in the final atrocity of Roman law forbidding the burial of Christians who had been put to death. In a final gesture of madness, a government edict made it a capital offense to remove a Christian body for burial and since the slaughter of Christians was a daily occurrence, bodies were denied a decent burial. In defiance of Roman law, the daughter of the emperor did whatever she could to help Christians bury their dead, willing to risk her life in that effort.

In need of materials to anoint the bodies and the linens to be used as winding sheets for burial, the Christian friends of Drosis looked to her for help and she was never found wanting. She gathered reams of costly linen from the royal storehouse, swearing the storekeeper to secrecy with the help of a sizable bribe and in the darkness of night carried the linens with a trusted servant to waiting Christians. Sentinels, posted to keep all persons at a distance from the bodies, took up positions at a distance themselves. The disappearance of bodies was usually dismissed with a shrug of the shoulders, but a twenty-four watch was posted nevertheless. This did not deter Drosis who continued her help undetected even by her betrothed, a man named Adrian.

In the course of this deception, she came to know a group of fearless women known as the "Five Nuns of Antioch" who dedicated themselves to the removal of martyred Christian bodies for proper burial. As resourceful as they were courageous, these five nuns, outwitted sentinels, always managing to catch them off their guard to remove a body, often returning to repeat the process. Drosis was so moved by the nuns she not only brought them linens but joined in the removal of bodies. One night however, flushed with their success, all six grew more daring and were seized by sentinels and taken off to prison for punishment.

On learning of his daughter's arrest, Trajan ordered her immediate release, assuming she had been bewitched or suffered from a mental aberration, refusing to believe his daughter was a Christian. The five nuns, were another matter and had to be made an example. He ordered that they be tossed in molten copper.

In a troubled sleep, Trajan had a dream in which he saw five white sheep and a shepherd saying that they were no longer of his kingdom but of the kingdom of Heaven. Interpreting this to mean that the five nuns had been spirited away and that his daughter would be snatched from him, he posted guards around the clock to protect his daughter. He then ordered giant furnaces to be built just outside the city gates, daring the Christians to fling themselves into the fiery pits and perish as martyrs to join their God. He had carved on the walls of the furnace for all to see the words: "People of Galilee, you who worship the crucified one, save yourselves from persecution by casting yourselves into the furnace of your choice, thereby saving us the trouble."

When told of the grim words, Drosis, already despondent over the fate of the nuns, made up her mind that she would die for Christ with them. She slipped out past the guards, found an abandoned quarry and after baptizing herself, prayed that the Lord take her. She remained in the pit for seven days, dying on the eighth day, which was 22 March 99.

March 23

Saint Nikon and the 199 Martyrs

The cruelty of the third-century pagans in their persecution of Christians is nowhere more savagely recounted than in the story of St. Nikon and the 199 Martyrs, for here was brutality at its very worst, a bloodletting that is unmatched for sheer horror. It is one thing to suffer an agonizing death, but to witness the systematic murder of beloved friends is unspeakable suffering impossible to describe. If St. Nikon had done nothing but bear this horrible torture, he would have earned a place of serenity among the saints, but, happily, he was a monk of such stature that during his lifetime his service for the Lord placed him among the great holy ascetics.

St. Nikon was born in Neapolis, Italy, during the third century, to a pagan Greek father and a Christian mother of unknown national origin, presumably Greek, and was outstanding in his studies, with a penchant for the military, as a result of which he enlisted in the Roman army. His excellence earned him an extended leave of absence, which he chose to spend in the distant city of Byzantium. The ship he boarded was forced to put in at the island of Chios for some minor repairs and as he lingered ashore he met a holy man who engaged him in conversation about the Church and all its good works. He was so absorbed in this he failed to return to the ship when it departed, but it mattered little, for by then he had acquired a deep interest in religion and had to hear more from the holy man of the island.

Convinced that his career lay not with the military but with the Lord, Nikon entered a monastery and in due course was tonsured a monk, thereafter advancing rapidly to become a priest, in which capacity he was to serve only three years before becoming a bishop in charge of one of the largest monasteries of the time in Sicily. Under his direction the cloister progressed and membership swelled to 190 monks, all of whom were carefully selected for their proven piety and dedication. A contingent of nine monks was accepted from another island and that brought the number of monks to the fateful number of 199, none of whom dreamed what lay in store for them.

The monastery gradually became a haven for countless Christians who went to the cloister to hear the sermons by the various monks and in turn brought many who had been pagans and were converted to Christianity. While the crowds grew in number the monk membership remained at 199, all of whom applied themselves to the spiritual needs of the community. Representatives were sent from the mainland churches to observe the activity of the Nikon cloister and to learn from him the methods applied to the service of God and man.

With all this traffic of Christians, the monastery was a beehive which attracted the attention of authorities who heretofore had considered the monks an innocuous band of recluses. An agent was sent from the governor's office to see first-hand what transpired and when he noted the influence that the monks had over such vast numbers of people, he returned to the governor to report what he had found. The governor was unconvinced at first, but after listening to some of the details, decided to see for himself what these holy men were doing.

After his visit he held a council in which all agreed the influence of the monks was undermining their own power over the people, and Nikon was ordered to appear before the governor. Pagan though he was, the governor did not see the necessity for killing an entire colony and called upon Nikon to abandon his project and leave the island or face certain death. Nikon declared that he was there to stay and was given another alternative, which was to disavow Christ and revert to paganism. That idea was even more repulsive to Nikon and he was summarily dismissed.

It was then the governor selected his most hard-bitten lieutenant, who was told to take a detachment of soldiers to the monastery and do whatever he had to do. That was tantamount to signing the death warrant for each and every monk. Once again the demands were made, and when they were not met, the soldiers turned on the hapless monks while Nikon was forced to witness a carnage without parallel, until every monk had been slaughtered, whereupon Nikon was tortured unmercifully before joining his 199 brethren in death for Christ on 23 March 251.

March 23

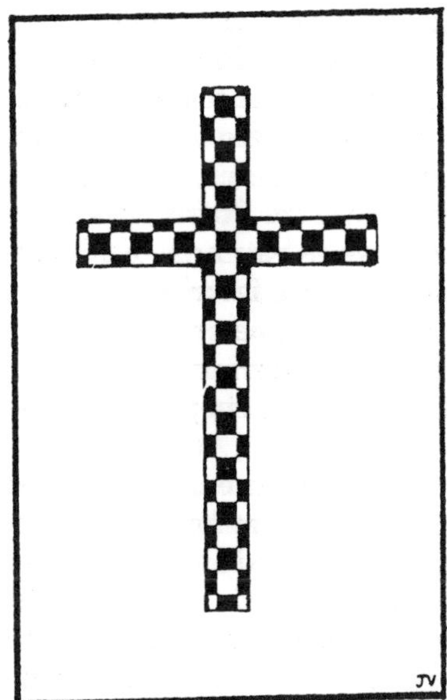

Saint Luke of Mytilene

Just prior to the collapse in 1453, the ever-shrinking Byzantine Empire managed to stave off the Muslim hordes, but in captive areas of the fourteenth century a young man named Luke chose to elect discretion as the better part of valor in order to save himself, but soon after realized his shameful mistake in time to save his soul. He not only displayed Christian courage in the end, but became an example of piety in the tradition of those who give themselves wholly to Jesus Christ.

Luke was born in Andrianople, of a Bulgarian father and Greek mother. Orphaned as a child, he passed from one family to another until, at age fourteen, he wandered aimlessly until settling in a town under Turkish domination. Forced to live mostly by his wits, he got into an argument with a young Turk whom he thrashed in a fist fight. Severely reprimanded by a Turkish official who happened to be passing by, he was placed with a Turkish family after promising to reject Christianity and become a Muslim.

Young Luke was given menial chores in the household but soon began to brood over his defection. A strong Orthodox Christian, he had really not denied Christ in his heart but it vexed him to appear to be a Muslim dressed in Turkish fashions and scorned by Christians who knew of his apostasy. Conscience stricken, he went to the Russian Embassy in Constantinople for help but was told that although Orthodox, they were diplomats of Russia on a state level and could not intervene in church matters. His Turkish masters learned of his visit to the embassy and he was harshly treated. When they threatened to turn him over to the authorities, he did not hesitate to go to the embassy again, this time with a fervent plea for help.

A sympathic member of the embassy staff managed to get him

on a boat bound for Smyrna, from where he sailed to the island of Thera, where he became seriously ill. He was felled by a strange illness to the point where he thought he would be stricken blind. The strange malady persisted and the people who had given him shelter finally called for a priest, believing that the young man was doomed. Luke confessed his sorry defection to the priest, saying that he had repented his action but that God was punishing him nevertheless. The understanding priest assured the young man that God would not punish a repentant young lad, no matter what the offense, and together they prayed for the boy's recovery.

When the malady had run its course and the boy's health was restored, the priest advised Luke to go to Mt. Athos where he could nourish his spirit through prayer. Again his departure was arranged for him and he boarded a boat heading for the the Holy Mountain. He had no difficulty in being admitted to this ancient cloister after telling his story to the monks.

Luke was made a novice under the guidance of a monk named Bassarion, with whom he became friends. Tonsured a monk, he was leading the quiet life of a devoted servant of God when he decided to leave Mt. Athos, fully satisfied he had made his peace with the Lord. When asked why he was leaving, he could only answer that there was a voice within him that was telling him to go to the island of Mytilene. When asked why Mytilene, he could only account for it by saying the same voice was directing him there.

Welcomed by every Christian, he was the guest of an Orthodox priest to whom he confessed he was perplexed by the urgency to abide in Mytilene. The answer was not long in coming. By coincidence a member of the Turkish household from which he fled was on the island and recognized him. Reported to the authorities, he was taken prisoner. It was then when he realized his atonement would be complete only when he had made it known to the authorities that he had regained his senses and had returned to the Christianity into which he was baptized.

Brought to trial on charges of having apostasized, Luke made no protest of innocence, declaring for all to hear that his only offence was against Christianity for which he had atoned. Given the choice between a return to Islam or death, he chose death as a proof of complete repentance. Hanged in the town square, his body was trussed with weights and tossed into the sea, eventually to wash ashore and buried with solemn honors. He died for Christ on 23 March 1384.

March 24

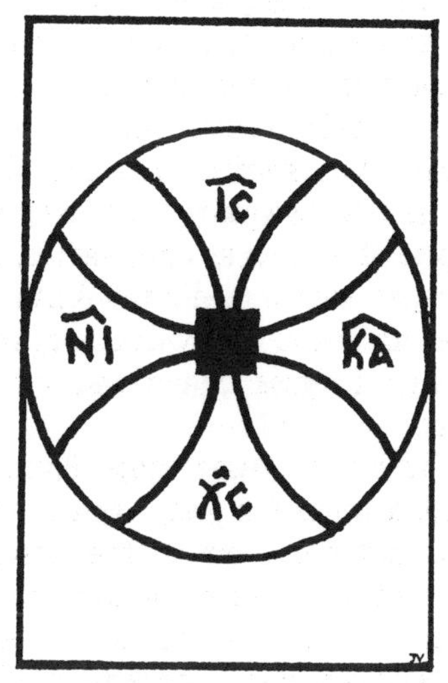

Parthenios III
Patriarch of Constantinople

If somehow Christianity had reached the American Indians by 1620 and there had landed on their shores a horde of Muslims instead of British Pilgrims, then Christian Indians to this day would be under the brutal Muslim thumb and fighting to keep Christianity alive much as the Greeks did in the nearly four centuries of Ottoman conquest. When considered in this light, one has to pause to pay tribute to a gallant Greek Christendom that bore an oppressive yoke for more years than it has taken America to become the greatest nation in the world, a nation which allows religious freedom but has its roots in Christianity, which to all intent and purpose is the religion of the country.

Nearly two hundred years had elapsed since the Turkish invasion when from 1639 to 1657 there was a succession of three patriarchs of the Greek Orthodox Church who bore the name Parthenios, all of whom were to meet brutal ends at the hands of the invaders and the last of whom so served Christ that he became a saint. The last of this trio of holy men, and the greatest, was Patriarch Parthenios III, a lamb of God so heedless of the dangers about him because of his intense devotion to the Christian Church that he is remembered as much for his courage as for his piety.

When Parthenios accepted the Ecumenical Throne in 1656 in the ancient city of Constantinople, he was well aware of the fate of his two predecessors and of the imminent danger to himself. Despite the fact that there was an understanding between the Turkish majority and the Greek minority, the hostility between the two was extremely volatile, and those hardy Greek souls who chose to remain in the land of their forbearers did so despite the fact that they were forced to walk a religious tightrope. The solid ground of Islam had no room for Greek Christians and the flimsiest strand on which he was allowed to tread was reserved for the patriarch, the leader who symbolized all that Islam despised. The menance was to Parthenios not a deterrent but a challenge to take a stand for Jesus Christ.

No more than they could conquer their souls could the Turks conquer the hearts and minds of the Greeks whose artistic skills and commercial enterprise they looked upon with envy and were forced to tolerate in the interest of the country as a whole. It was to the Greek merchants and artisans that the Turks looked and accorded a great deal of freedom of operation. This compromise of the two religions was such that a peaceful coexistence was a virtual impossibility during the ecumenical reign of Parthenios III.

A native of Mytilene, Parthenios advanced in the hierarchy with rapid strides, serving as metropolitan of the island of Chios before becoming patriarch. In a span of thirty years between these two posts, he demonstrated a great intellect as well as an intense devotion which had earned him the respect of clergy and laity alike. He was the natural choice for the patriarchate, but at the time of his ascension in 1656, feelings were running high, eventually intensifying to a degree that assured violence at any given moment.

The year in which he served was a year of constant harrassment for Parthenios, a year of unending indignities heaped upon him which he bore with Christian calm and courage. His refusal to display a public anger or file a formal protest against reactionaries who sought his downfall brought further bitterness and a plot was hatched to destroy this holy man whose only concern was for peace among all people.

Some correspondence between the patriarch and the metropolitan of Kyzikos in Asia Minor was seized by authorities and construed to be seditious, and he was charged with high treason by the Tartars of the area. Despite the fact that the sultan found no menace in this correspondence, a hue and cry was raised against the patriarch, and the sultan stood by while an angry mob stormed the Patriarchate. Parthenios was dragged out into the streets and hanged. He died for Christ 24 March 1657.

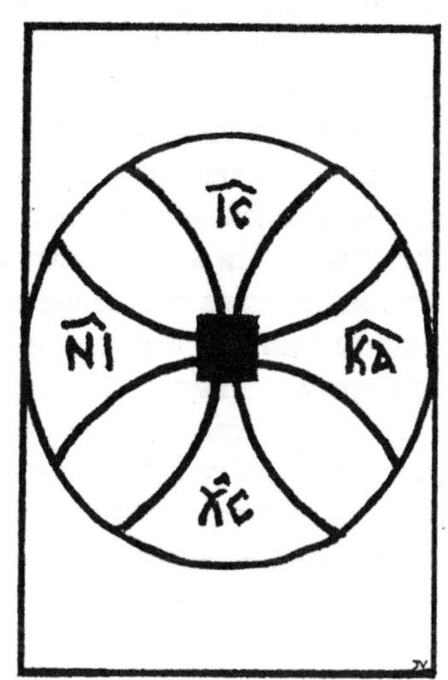

The Annunication of the Theotokos

Of all the solemn days in Orthodoxy the day of March 25 is one not only of religious significance but of political significance as well, allowing the Greek Orthodox to commemorate God's message to Mary and the independence of Greece on the same day. The expression, "For God and Country," has real meaning for the Orthodox Greek on the 25th day of March, a day on which he can celebrate two events without diminishing either one for the obvious reason that devotion and patriotism have the same emotional root—love. If Christianity could be compressed into a single word, that word would be love. The same holds true for patriotism.

Uppermost in the true Greek's mind on March 25, however, is Mary, chosen from all the women in the world to be the Mother of Jesus Christ. When the angel Gabriel brought the momentous message from God this day, the gentle Mary must have felt a solemn pride, but at the same time a disquieting apprehension at the prospect of this awesome responsibility. Assured by the Archangel, Mary's answer was a simple: "Let it be according to the will of God," and the rest is glorious history.

The world of Mary of two thousand years ago is envisioned as one in which life was simple and free of the complexities that plague the modern world, but in that age of self-sufficiency there were problems which would be insurmountable today. The mother of that day was all things to her family, and it can safely be said that when the Archangel Gabriel departed, the prospective Mother of God must have for several moments felt terribly alone. Everyone knows about the nativity and the mission of Jesus Christ, but the details of the days, months and years in between are known but to Mary and to God.

The political importance of March 25 is fully realized only when the suffering of four centuries is called to mind. In 1453 the Ottoman hordes overran all of Greece and most of the Balkans and held hostage a people whose culture dated back more than two thousand years, and who gave more to the world than it could ever receive in return, and it seems that the world just stood by while the cradle of democracy and Christianity was being defiled by a scourge that would have undone a less hardy breed. Hopelessly outnumbered, Greece endured nearly four hundred years of brutal oppression, but the spirit of its people knew not a single moment's weakness.

The fires of rebellion that the Turks thought they had snuffed out, but which had smouldered in Hellenic hearts for almost 400 years, were kindled into a conflagration on 25 March 1821, not by a bemedalled general but by a man of the cloth, Bishop Germanos of Patras, Greece, who chose the day of the Annunication knowing God would be on the side of the Greeks. The good bishop held the Cross of Jesus Christ aloft on the 25th day of March, 1821, and proclaimed freedom for all Greek Orthodox Christians. It was a motion seconded by every Greek in the country. In addition to engaging in a war for independence, the Greeks were actually waging a holy war because it was not only Greek against Turk but Christian against Muslim, and the subsequent Greek victory was a triumph of Christianity.

The Greek-American can count himself fortunate, indeed, if he speaks both Greek and English, because English is the language of America and Great Britain, the latter a traditional ally of both America and Greece. In whatever language the New Testament of the Bible is read, it has been translated from the original Greek, the language selected by the apostles of Jesus Christ as the language of the New Faith.

Let Matthew Arnold tell us about the Greek language. He said, "Herein lies the reason for giving boys more of Latin composition than of Greek, superior though the Greek literature be to the Latin; but the power of the Latin classic is in character, that of the Greek is in beauty. Now character is capable of being taught, learnt, and assimilated; beauty, hardly."

If there is a magic number it is 25—the day of Annunciation and of Greek Independence in March of every year until the end of time.

March 26

Malchos the Monastic

Had it not been for St. Jerome, a church historian and theologian of the fourth century who chose to recount the events in the life of St. Malchos, the incredible saga of the latter might have come down as another fragment of legend. Instead, we have the highly plausible story by the former who felt compelled to detail the inspirational story of his contemporary. Malchos embodied the virtues found only in men who are the complete servants of God, but of all the attributes to be found in a human being he best epitomized that kind of courageous patience found in the story of Job in the Old Testament.

Malchos did not abide in the stomach of a whale, but he was for an extended period of time swallowed up in a milieu not of his own choosing, from which he was to disgorge himself only after endless months of captivity. Born in Maronia, a scant thirty miles from the historic city of Antioch (the city in which originated the term "Christian"), he was a typical ascetic of the era. But then he came to a crossroads in his life, and the course he chose drastically altered its outcome.

Apprised of an inheritance which had been bequeathed to him, Malchos requested permission to leave the monastery to see to the proper disposition of his newly acquired wealth. The request was denied by a skeptical abbot who suspected the motives of such an undertaking, fearing the naive monk might fall prey to opportunists and perhaps be led astray. He suggested that the monk appoint an executor within the framework of the Church who would have better knowledge of such matters, leaving Malchos unencumbered by responsibilities that would interfere with his devotions.

The youthful Malchos did not share the abbot's dim view of

the young monk's ability to cope with whatever might arise; and he surreptitiously left the monastery, confident that he would return after proving himself in the outside world. He fell in with a caravan heading toward his destination, but he hever reached that destination. Less than a few hours underway, the caravan was set upon by a roving band of thieves. After plundering what was of value, the brigands took the healthy young monk as a captive, together with a girl that had been in the caravan.

Made a slave to the giant-sized Ethiopian chieftain of the robbers, young Malchos accepted his lot as punishment for having disobeyed his abbot and resigned himself to his fate, exhibiting a patience in his menial service which eventually won the respect of the brute who was his master. The months wore on, but the resolute captive showed no signs of resentment, only a calm detachment which belied the yearning within him to be once again inside the walls of his monastery.

As a reward for his patient loyalty, Malchos was offered the girl captive as his bride. The monk politely refused the offer since he had taken the vow of celibacy, but when told that this would be an affront to the chieftain who had no understanding of such things as celibacy and would tolerate no refusal of his token, the monk acceded. He went through the motions of a wedding which was illegal and never consummated. The supposed newlyweds were given a brief liberty at the edge of the camp which bordered the raging Euphrates, cutting off any chance for escape.

In the cover of darkness Malchos inflated two goatskins with which the two escapees forded the river and made for the hills. The pursuit was not long in coming, and they soon found themselves near recapture, taking refuge in a cave. They watched in terror as first one, then another of the bandits came into view, seeming to be heading directly for the cave. But at a distance the bandits were attacked by lions. The fugitives did not linger to witness the carnage but took to their heels and eventually made their way to safety.

Welcomed back to the monastery where they never tired of hearing of his exploits, Malchos arranged for the girl's acceptance in a nunnery, and thereafter the lives of both were given over to the Lord. Malchos, especially, attributed his deliverance to God; he never ceased to be grateful.

March 27

Matrona of Thessalonike

Enslavement was an accepted practice in all the societies and religions of the fourth century, but it was not so much a matter of religious principle being violated, as an overlooking of moral principle by those who could afford to buy a slave, whatever the creed of the family. Even the wealthy Jew of that period, whose people had known bondage in prior centuries and whose descendants have suffered the holocausts of the twentieth-century anti-semitism, was not above buying a slave for the family household. Such was the case with Matrona of Thessalonike who was a Christian who was bought for a wealthy Jewish woman.

Matrona is thought to have been a waif without family of her own and was, therefore, not torn from parents or siblings when led from the auction block in the slave market. It is quite possible that her lot was considerably improved when she became the maid in a household that was far more comfortable than any she might have previously known. She might even have wished for such a household, although it is quite certain that she would have preferred a Christian family since she had been reared as a Christian. But there is no indication that the difference in religion was of any consequence to either the mistress or her maid, since the difference lay more in social standing than anything else.

It was about the year 307 that Matrona served in this comparatively affluent household where her duties extended beyond the home itself to trips to the market with her mistress, as well as escorting her to the synagogue for services. While waiting at a discrete distance from the synagogue entrance, it occurred to Matrona that she could make better use of her time by attending a Christian service. Not all Christian services were public affairs in those days of pagan persecution, but Matrona found a place nearby where Christian worship was observed in secret; it was to this hidden church that she would hurry once her mistress had disappeared into the synagogue.

One account has it that the name of the mistress was Mantilla, which was sometimes confused with Matrona, thus leading to some embarrassing situations. So while in the synagogue on her Sabbath, Mantilla was contemplating a change in her maid's name to avoid any further confusion. She had decided on a name and left the synagogue early to tell Matrona of her plan, but the maid was nowhere to be found. To make matters worse, Matrona had tarried longer than usual with her Christian friends; and by the time she returned to the synagogue her impatient mistress had gone to authorities to report a missing slave and then returned home.

A state official had gone to the house for details about the missing girl when the thoroughly frightened Matrona came running in. An alarm had been sent out for the girl's apprehension; when she came panting into the house, the official assumed that the girl, finding herself on report as a runaway slave, had chosen to return with the story that she had left her post outside the synagogue and had lingered with a few friends. She was not believed when she could not name her friends—she knew they would be hunted down and their church would be found out and destroyed.

The mistress was of no help to Matrona, who pleaded for her forgiveness to no avail, not only for having abandoned her mistress, but for now offering as a defense some imaginary friends, seemingly adding insult to injury. The official suspected the truth but needed the permission of the mistress to place Matrona under arrest. Thus, Matrona was given over to the authorities by an indifferent and vindictive mistress who knew what the consequences would be if the girl insisted on holding her tongue.

Taken to prison, Matrona was forced into admitting that she had been with Christian friends in worship of the Savior, but beyond that she would say nothing. No amount of torture could force the girl either to betray her friends or to denounce the Messiah. She was systematically and cruelly being drained of life, but she held out to the end, finally succumbing for Jesus Christ on 27 March 307.

March 27

The Prophet Hanani

The Greek Orthodox Church looks upon some men not only as prophets but as saints as well. Among them was a so-called minor prophet who bore the name of Hanani. In ancient times the Bible was written in Hebrew but also in Greek since the Greek tongue was the classical language of the civilized world, thus accounting for closer scrutiny by those whose knowledge of Greek enabled them to appraise men who preceded Jesus Christ by centuries as saints who belong in the company of the martyrs of the New Testament.

According to the Scriptures, the relatively obscure Hanani made his presence known in about the year 830 B.C., at a time of turbulence among the chosen people of Israel. The country was divided into two camps on ideological grounds and had a ruler in each sector, the one to the north under King Baasha, and to the south under King Asa, who eyed each other with ever growing suspicion which was to develop into outright hostility.

Hanani surfaced at this time in biblical history and proved himself to be a prophet of God. Armed with the power of a man in touch with God, he devoted himself to preaching His word and endeavoring to restore order and unity to a race threatening self destruction. His message was conveyed to the common man but it fell on deaf ears of rival kings whose responsibilities to their people and to God were subordinate to their own selfish ambitions. If there was any hope for the salvation of this proud and delivered nation, now divided, it lay in the hands of Hanani, the one man of God capable of dealing with kings and equipped with the prophetic courage to take them to task.

On learning of the military union, between King Asa and the King of Syria, Hanani upbraided King Asa in no uncertain terms, assuring him that the power of God would smite both him and the Syrian king. He then proceeded to urge him to form a union not with the Syrians but with his own brethren and return to the observance of the Law of the Ancient Covenant. In an admonition worthy of Moses, he called for a return to the reason for his being king, which was to see to the welfare of his people. He warned the king that without God on his side, he could not hope for any victory.

Reference is made to 2 Chronicles of the Holy Bible (16.7-10) which reads: "At that time Hanani the Seer came to Asa, King of Judah, and said to him, 'Because you relied on the King of Syria, and did not rely on the Lord your God, the Army of the King of Syria has escaped you. Were not the Ethiopians and the Libyans a huge army with exceedingly many chariots and horsemen? Yet because you relied on the Lord your God he gave them into your hands. For the eyes of the Lord run to and fro throughout the whole earth, to show his might in behalf of those whose heart is blameless toward him. You have done foolishly in this; for from now on you will have wars.'"

The prophecy of continued warfare has proved correct, as indicated by the seemingly unending hostilities of the Middle East, at the center of which Israel stands alone but undivided thus far. At any rate, the words of Hanani still ring with the truth, but in his own time he was to pay dearly for saving a nation, all because of an evil king's unwarranted wrath. Instead of showing gratitude for what might have brought him back to reason, the king blindly vented his spleen against the prophet and ordered him to be thrown into prison.

This act was calculated to humiliate Hanani who did indeed suffer indignities by witless jailers who taunted him. There is no evidence that he was ever tortured, except for the mental stress brought on by abusive treatment. For all his earthly power and selfishness, King Asa was not fool enough to trifle with a man accepted as one who was an appointed spokesman of the Lord. Little did he know that in the end his reward was to be discredited and not honored. He is said to have ruled for forty-one years and died after an agonizingly prolonged illness.

Meanwhile, with nothing to gain by keeping a servant of God in prison, it was ordered Hanani be set free after a short period of degradation. He emerged from confinement all the more resolved to preach the word of God for the remainder of his years. He is venerated as a saint by the Greek Orthodox Church which commemorates him on March 27.

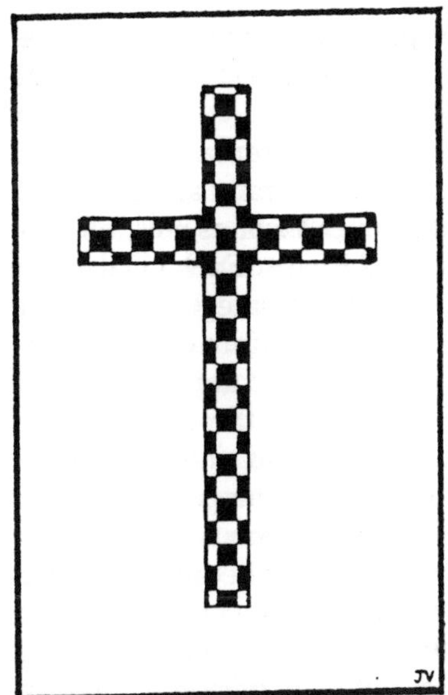

March 28

Herodion

Among the first converts to the New Faith of the Messiah was a man who was called Herodion, a kinsman of the mighty St. Paul, the greatest figure in Christianity, whose conversion alone offers convincing proof of the divinity of Jesus Christ. Herodion did not achieve the immortality of sainthood because he was a close kin of St. Paul's but because, inspired by Paul, he chose to assume a position of leadership with missionary zeal, so much so that he was a standout among the Seventy Apostles of the Savior, that hardy band of auxiliaries to the Twelve Disciples who placed their lives and their fortunes on the line for the Man of Nazareth.

Herodion is addressed by St. Paul in the 16th Chapter of Romans, Verse 10, which reads, "We salute Apelles approved in Christ, salute them who are of Aristobulos' household; salute Herodion my kinsman . . . ." From this mention of relationship through blood or national origin, it can be concluded that Herodion was from the region, at least, of St. Paul. Although not remembered as a student of the rabbinical tutor Gamaliel as Paul was, Herodion was nevertheless a devout member of the deeply religious circle which surrounded Gamaliel and whose first reaction to the word of Jesus Christ was anything but favorable. Like Paul, Herodion not only accepted the truth of the Savior, but went forth to carry His message, heedless of what he certainly knew would stir something more than antipathy from some elements.

The peripatetic preaching of Herodion matched in scope any of the other apostles who traversed the length and breadth of the Roman Empire and even beyond in their determination to bring the light of the New Faith to all whom it was possible to reach. At an historic meeting of the apostles, it was decided who was to go where in a campaign which fanned out from Jerusalem.

Herodion was assigned to the company of the eminent St. Peter in an itinerary which commenced at Antioch, a city where Christianity took firm hold and from which were to emerge many of the early Fathers of the Christian Church. From there these early crusaders ventured throughout the Near East and into Asia.

This arduous undertaking consumed not a matter of weeks or months, but years which were marked with success in all areas. But there was also a resentment in some quarters that went beyond the jeers and catcalls into physical abuse at the hands of flint-hearted pagans. When Herodion finally completed this extended phase of his mission, he was welcomed in Greece where his reputation as a seasoned and resolute campaigner for Christ preceded him. As a result he was ordained bishop of New Patras where he was to serve for ten years with distinction. The ultimate challenge lay in the capital city of Rome; after a decade of spiritual leadership, during which time Christianity burst into full bloom in the land of the ancient gods, Herodion made his way to Rome, there to join with other great figures of Christianity in the political and cultural center of the Roman Empire.

Among the Christian leaders in Rome in the days of Nero were Olymbas, Rodion, Herastos, Sosipater and Kuratos. With these men Herodion shared the perils of being a Christian in a city whose sophisticated populace, while yielding many converts to the missionaries, was a great deal less receptive and even more hostile than its rural counterpart. The well-known catacombs and subterranean hideouts were a far cry from the magnificent spires that tower over present-day Rome, but the enthusiasm of the relatively small number of Christians was as sincere and intense in the candle-lit bowels of the earth as in the grandeur of the cathedrals that were to follow.

The name of Herodion became a household word with the Christians in Rome; and, like other great religious leaders, his name came to be known to the state, as well, who placed Herodion on their most-wanted list soon after he had commenced preaching in the Eternal City. What ensued followed the pattern of persecution set not too many years before his coming, and after capture he was summarily sentenced to death. He was beheaded at the direction of Nero, giving his life for Jesus Christ on March 28, a date observed with deep solemnity by the Greek Orthodox Church.

March 29

Mark of Arethusa

In a startling departure from the script expected of a saint who has died in martyrdom, St. Mark miraculously managed to survive an ordeal of torture to transform his tormentors into compassionate human beings and go on to great glory in the name of Jesus Christ. Just when he was about to die, a remarkable reversal of the customary ending of a saintly life served to make the invincible St. Mark unique among those who have suffered and died for the Messiah.

After the proclamation of Constantine the Great granting Christianity toleration, the transition from paganism to Christianity was not accomplished immediately. Mark of Arethusa lived in a period of turmoil in the early fourth century, during which time he was of inestimable value as a young priest who shouldered the responsibility of bringing order out of religious chaos and conflict.

With the mandate from the emperor several priests came forward to replace pagans and temples with Christians and churches, but nowhere in the empire could they find a more capable promoter for the Prince of Peace than the ebullient Mark. He was a young priest with great promise when he emerged from his small parish near the city of Arethusa (in the province of Thessalonike) to undertake the spiritually rewarding, but ever hazardous, chore of physically transforming pagan temples into Christian churches. He left the tranquility of his parish on the banks of the river Strymon, later called Rendina, to assume much more awesome and demanding duties in the name of the Savior. These duties brought him both glory and grief, but eventually brought him the highest in spiritual attainment. He was well into this laudable campaign when he was appointed bishop of Arethusa, an office whose influence he would bring to many other areas in the course of his holy work.

Specially appointed to direct the changeover, Mark countered the expected resistance in some areas with compelling oratory which won enough converts to acquire a strength in numbers sufficient to offset the last-ditch defenders of paganism. Then came the actual transformation whereby temples became churches with the replacement of the sacred cross of Jesus Christ for idols. When the architecture of a temple did not allow for conformity with a church, it was simply taken down piece by piece and rebuilt to Christian standards. Those edifices that posed too many problems were made into hospitals or places of refuge for the needy.

Mark showed not only a bold administrative capacity while these proceedings were taking place, but a genuine concern for the populace as a whole. Thus he acquired a reputation for generosity, compassion and humility which stamped him as a rare human being and dedicated servant of God and man. Even those who opposed him grudgingly admitted that for all of his quiet demeanor he was not a man to be trifled with, nor one who would slacken the pace of his mission.

Years of devotion to this procedure brought Mark and his Christian community a hitherto unknown tranquility. But this peace was shattered when the Emperor Julian the Apostate succeeded to the throne in A.D. 361 and disavowed Jesus to revert to paganism. Almost overnight the advances of Christianity were stemmed. With this shabby disavowal came a regeneration of ritualistic idolatry and a subsequent renewal of the persecution of Christians.

Mark found himself the target of the rabble he had put to rout. These people had been given heart by a perfidious ruler who was not the least interested in having his people live in harmony. Instead, he encouraged the pagans to vent their spleen on Christians once again. Mark was dragged into the streets by a frenzied mob who tortured him without mercy, again and again inflicting the cruelest of punishment they could devise. Their rage subsided in the face of the durability of the holy Mark who summoned renewed strength and convinced the mob that the Lord had given him a seeming indestructibility. He went on about conversion until he died on 28 March 389.

March 29

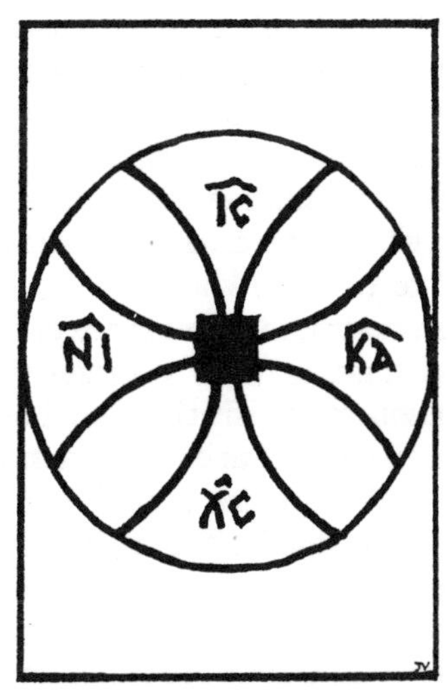

Saint Ionas

Christianity had taken root early in Persia. Its growth required much time. Hence Christianity needed men of extreme courage and dedication, such as St. Ionas. Born in Persia, Ionas was an early convert to Christianity and in an environment more conducive to cruelty and deceit than in love and peace, he mangaed to embrace Jesus Christ with a total devotion that led him to the gates of a monastery when he was a youth. Monasticism was a well guarded way of life in a country whose ruler, Shapur II, was an avowed enemy of the Savior and would crush an expression of Christianity whenever it was found out. Ionas accepted the attendant perils of his beliefs without reservation, as much at ease surrounded by menaces of Persia as he would be in a church surrounded by icons.

As it was, Ionas had to settle for a life of asceticism in an area that was bleak, barren, and forbidding. On a jagged hillside which goats or other creatures found virtually inaccessible, he and other devoted monks carved out a monastery in which they followed the rules of monasticism to the letter. It was a small miracle that they were able to fashion a shelter with the simplest of tools, but more miraculous was the fact that they were able to sustain themselves. It was the equivalent of squeezing blood out of a stone.

The closest friend of Ionas a monk named Barachisios, whose name matched the terrain in strangeness, but whose mind was attuned to the Christian religion to a degree that matched the highest of hierarchs. Together they formed a tandem for Christ which had to be formidable to survive in this region. Over a period of years they not only grew closer to God but developed contacts with the outside world in order to go to those in need of their wisdom and prayers. In remote villages they came to be known in the small circle of Christians and were called upon to help in celebration of the holidays and sacraments.

One day word came to Ionas of the plight of nine Christians imprisoned in the village of Marmaboh. To distinguish them from the felons there, in the faint hope that something could be done for them, their names were given to Ionas and bear mention. They were Zanithos, Lazaros, Maruthas, Narsis, Elias, Maris, Abibos, Symeithis and Savvas, all devout Christians. Together with his friend Barachisios, he proceeded to the overwhelmingly pagan village where they cautiously made inquiries on the pretext of being close kin of first one of the condemned and then another. With whatever meager funds they were able to gather, they sought out the chief jailer whom they knew was not beneath taking a bribe.

With cautious optimism they awaited the release of at least a few of the nine after the jailer had accepted the bribe, but their hopes were dashed when word came to them that all nine had been executed. The treacherous jailer compounded his despicable misdeed by not that he had accepted a bribe but that he had been approached on grounds of mercy by the two monks. The two monks were lured out of hiding by the announcement that next of kin were free to remove the bodies of the executed men and when they came forward they were promptly arrested.

After what passed for a trial, in the course of which both Ionas and Barachisios denounced paganism, they were condemned to die but had so incensed their captors that they were ordered to be tortured as horribly as possible. When word of the manner of torture reached the civilized world even the most calloused shuddered at the thought of reaching such a terrible end. It is inconceivable that any human being could bear to witness, let alone inflict the heinous tortures that were to precede the deaths of these innocent monks. Man's inhumanity to man has never been so viciously displayed as in the cruel torture of these two.

Ionas was lashed to a wooden plank and flogged until he was virtually skinless on the back, thereafter to be dragged out into the square to remain throughout the cold night. Similarly trussed, Barachisios was whipped and then, because they managed to survive, hot copper balls were placed under the armpits of each man and molten metal poured over their eyelids. This done the captors proceeded to mutilate the unfortunate men by cutting off fingers, then toes, then ears, and tongues. They were mere sections when tossed into a pit. They were martyred on 29 March 330, two days after the nine martyrs on March 27.

March 30

Saint John of the Ladder (Klimakos)

The symbolic ascent to heaven is customarily portrayed by the flight skyward with angelic wings; one of our saints, however, depicts the ascension by the more practical use of a ladder. This symbolic ladder is to be scaled in a series of spiritual rungs where increasingly more exertion is required in order to see the kingdom of God. The author of this approach was St. John of the Ladder who was one of the greatest writers in Christianity. "The Ladder of Perfection" is a treatise on spiritual exercises and actions which present in a brilliant and scholarly fashion and approach to the throne of Heaven.

Born in the sixth century, John spent the first sixteen years of his life in Palestine, the ancient Holy Land of his birth whose traditions he respected and whose Christian heritage he cherished. His early ambitions were realized when he went to the Monastery of St. Catherine at Mt. Sinai, the oldest Christian monastery in the world. There he became one of the most scholarly monks in Christendom. The site of St. Catherine's was conducive to prayer and meditation, for there the scene of the burning bush took place and there Moses received the word from God himself. Moreover, to this place the grieving St. Helen, mother of St. Constantine the Great, came on a pilgrimage to the Holy Land some three hundred years before.

Mt. Sinai is unique in that it has been for centuries a holy magnet for Jewish, Muslim, and Christian pilgrims. While not as large or as imposing as Mt. Athos, Mt. Sinai still boasts of its antiquity and its prominence in the Old Testament. For that reason, John felt at home in this desert retreat and was inspired by this proximity to God to advance the cause of Christianity in writings that have illumined the Church with their brilliance and clarity of thought.

John is remembered not only as the author of the masterful "Ladder of Perfection," but also as the originator of hesychasm, the divine quietness that leads one to God through constant prayer, the prayer which has come to be known as the pure or intellectual "Jesus Prayer." Regarding this John wrote: "Let the remembrance of Jesus be present with each breath, and then you will know that value of hesychia." He continued to champion this doctrine which found eager support among Christian thinkers, chief among whom was St. Gregory Palamas, whose sponsorship brought about official Church recognition of hesychasm in the fourteenth century.

For more than seventy years, John of the Ladder practiced what he preached in the confines of his desert monastery. He achieved such a reputation for piety and wisdom that men from all walks of life were drawn to his side and came from all over the east to make a pilgrimage to his retreat. From John's strong faith and fervent prayer came the power of healing through the divine intervention of Jesus. If nothing else, St. John's visitors would leave him with a serenity which they had never before experienced and with a sense of fulfillment that would last a lifetime.

At a time when Christianity was being tested to the fullest, St. John of the Ladder conveyed the divine grace that can only be achieved through Jesus Christ. He was able to advance the cause of Christianity without traversing the land, because the shining light which he received through his isolation with the Lord was carried out into the spiritual darkness by the grateful pilgrims who received his blessing.

From the name which identifies this St. John one would conclude he was a carpenter, but this man of peace spent a lifetime contemplating the love of the carpenter of Nazareth. The intensity of his devotion to the Savior is one of the sustaining factors which, transcended through everyone who calls himself a Christian, making the faith in Jesus Christ indestructible. He witnessed no burning bush but he walked with God nonetheless. One of Christendom's finest figures, he died on March 30 at the age of eighty-six. His feast day is celebrated on the fourth Sunday of Lent.

Akakios, Bishop of Melitene, Armenia

Unnamed and unnumbered Christians of the third century met death by violent and inhuman means as perhaps in no other century. Unique enough to become a saint of the Church was the courageous bishop of the early Church, Akakios, bishop of Melitene, Armenia. Of those who laid down their lives by being tortured for the sake of Jesus, Akakios was tortued but somehow not killed. This departure from the classic stories of the saints has posed a never-to-be-solved enigma.

Nothing is known of Akakios' life prior to his emergence as an eminent religious leader of his time. A man of God, a scholar, a philosopher, and a dauntless standard-bearer of Christianity, Akakios was elevated to the post of bishop of Melitene in Armenia. Church historians have credited Armenia with being the first country to establish Christianity as its national religion. In some measure this was due to leaders such as Akakios—leaders which Armenia provided and can point to with understandable pride.

Inevitably Akakios, who enjoyed wide acclaim as a spiritual leader among the Christian community, became bothersome to the pagan authorities. Emperor Decius was unalterably opposed to Christianity and condoned the atrocities committed against hapless Christians by his subordinates. By his order Akakios was arrested and put under the custody of Marcianus, the provincial governor of Cappadocia, for offenses against the state. This merely meant that Akakios was too good a Christian. When the dungeon door clanged shut behind him, Akakios knew what lay in store for him. However, he could never have anticipated the end result.

The governor was in no hurry to pass judgment, thus leaving him to the cruel devices of his jailers. Over a period of six agonizing months. Akakios was physically tortured to the point of near expiration, allowed to heal, and thereafter tortured again and again and allowed to heal. This vicious cycle of cat and mouse hardly left an area of his body without a scar. During the healing periods, however, Akakios wrote an impassioned and eloquent account of his faith in Jesus Christ. The script was a marvel of Christian devotion and was ultimately read by the emperor himself.

Called at long last before the governor, Akakios expected to hear the death sentence. To his great surprise and to the astonishment of all who heard, the governor declared that by the order of Emperor Decius he was free to return to his episcopal see at Melitene. The paradox has never been fully explained, although speculation has provided many versions. All accounts have some sound basis, but none has been proved. If nothing else, this turn of events served to mark Akakios as a unique saint in our ecclesiastical history.

The suffering of Akakios presaged the suffering his fellow Armenians in years to come, years that have left emotional scars on Armenians right down to the present generation. Outnumbered and oppressed by a relentless enemy they were the first to declare themselves a Christian nation in spite of, and perhaps because of, their miseries wrought upon them by a merciless foe. With men such as Akakios and St. Gregory the Theologian symbolizing Christian courage and durability, this tiny nation endured unspeakable genocide, suggesting that there has always been in their midst an Akakios sharing their torture. Akakios was certainly no stranger to inhumanity and it would appear that his courage and forbearance was in some way transferred to his countrymen and their descendants. Even though they are fully aware that vengeance belongs to the Lord, the cruelties of the past, not without some justification, has carried over so that the scars that were as visible on the tortured body of Akakios still sear the minds and hearts of those who have followed in agony, blinding them to exactly where revenge lies, taking it upon themselves to remind the world about the tragedy of the Armenian nation. On March 31, late in the third century, Akakios died of natural causes, still bearing the scars to remind the faithful that he lived and died for Christ.

INDEX OF SAINTS IN VOLUME ONE

ΤΩ ΘΕΩ ΔΟΞΑ